Advance Praise for
Exemplars of Assessment in Higher Education

"In a time when higher education professionals must step up their efforts to assess teaching and learning in order to improve outcomes for all students, this book provides exemplars in the field of assessment from colleges and universities who represent diverse missions and student populations. Recommended by their respective accreditor, the institutions highlighted in this book provide the reader a wealth of information about effective assessment structures and practices that can be molded to fit a variety of educational cultures and environments."—**Stephanie Droker,** *President, Accrediting Commission for Community and Junior Colleges*

"*Exemplars of Assessment in Higher Education* celebrates institutional and program success as measured by authentic assessment and student learning, providing a welcome respite from a national higher education environment that so often equates higher education's success solely with student loan metrics and graduation rates. It illustrates cooperation, partnership, and shared purpose among accreditors and the institutions and programs that they accredit. Faculty, administrators, and accreditors will find ideas and inspiration from others who have gone before on the assessment journey."—**Laura Rasar King,** *Executive Director, Council on Education for Public Health*

"*Exemplars of Assessment in Higher Education* provides a one of a kind insider's look into higher education as it relates to the undeniable importance of assessment—both of students and of an institution as a whole. *Exemplars of Assessment in Higher Education* provides the building blocks that allow the reader to embrace assessment and understand its critical role in assuring the quality of education being provided. I am delighted to endorse this publication and hopeful that it provides the reader with a go-to manual in understanding and utilizing assessment at their own institutions."—**Heather M. Stagliano,** *Director of the Council on Podiatric Medical Education, American Podiatric Medical Association*

"If I were granted one wish, it would be that all of higher education would better use assessment data to guide the ongoing enhancement of student learning. *Exemplars of Assessment in Higher Education* shows us how meaningful assessment can help to guide us as we work to ensure that our students are learning what we promise in our institutional or program mission statements. Whether you are a faculty member, an assessment professional, or an administrator, this book shows how the assessment process can provide a roadmap to institutional effectiveness and is, most certainly, a wish come true."—***Catherine Wehlburg***, *Editor-in-Chief, New Directions for Teaching and Learning*

"This collection puts a human face on assessment activity, revealing challenges and innovations as institutions try to meet accreditation requirements while improving teaching and learning. The full range of complexity of the task is on display in the chapters, each centering on the difficult task of understanding student development and acting on the results. Anyone facing challenges in their own assessment program (and who isn't?) needs to read this book."—***David A. Eubanks***, *Assistant Vice President for Assessment and Institutional Effectiveness, Furman University*

"Souza and Rose have produced a wonderful and much-needed volume that engages practitioners in bringing the oft-described assessment for accountability together with assessment for improvement in learning. By focusing on the major regional accreditors' standards for assessment of student learning and then examining how a diverse set of campuses and programs use those standards, they illustrate how their actions and policies to achieve improved student learning provide the evidence that accreditors need for summative assurance of quality standards. A truly welcome change from check-the-box routines that may satisfy the minimum report requirements but do not help students, faculty, or organizations achieve quality."—***Terrel L. Rhodes***, *Senior Scholar, AAC&U, and* ***Kate McConnell***, *Vice President, AAC&U*

"Student learning assessment is not often linked with the word 'inspiring.' This book is truly inspiring and affirming that programs and institutions are finding real value in committing to assessing and improving student learning all across the United States. It puts to shame the occasional naysayers that assessment is of no value. There is so much to learn here with so many helpful approaches that address not only how to undertake assessment but to identify steps to success. It is definitely a good read at all levels within institutions."—***Ralph Wolff***, *President of the Quality Assurance Commons and former President of the Senior College Commission of WASC*

EXEMPLARS OF ASSESSMENT IN
HIGHER EDUCATION

EXEMPLARS OF ASSESSMENT IN HIGHER EDUCATION
Diverse Approaches to Addressing Accreditation Standards

Edited by Jane Marie Souza and Tara A. Rose

Foreword by Heather F. Perfetti

Copublished with

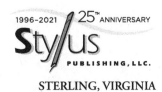

STERLING, VIRGINIA

COPYRIGHT © 2021 BY STYLUS PUBLISHING, LLC.

Published by Stylus Publishing, LLC.
22883 Quicksilver Drive
Sterling, Virginia 20166-2019

All rights reserved. No part of this book may be reprinted or reproduced in any form or by any electronic, mechanical, or other means, now known or hereafter invented, including photocopying, recording, and information storage and retrieval, without permission in writing from the publisher.

Library of Congress Cataloging-in-Publication Data
The CIP data for this title has been applied for

13-digit ISBN: 978-1-64267-248-0 (cloth)
13-digit ISBN: 978-1-64267-249-7 (paperback)
13-digit ISBN: 978-1-64267-250-3 (library networkable e-edition)
13-digit ISBN: 978-1-64267-251-0 (consumer e-edition)

Printed in the United States of America

All first editions printed on acid-free paper
that meets the American National Standards Institute
Z39-48 Standard.

> Bulk Purchases
>
> Quantity discounts are available for use in workshops and for staff development.
>
> Call 1-800-232-0223

First Edition, 2021

CONTENTS

FOREWORD   ix
Heather F. Perfetti

PREFACE   xi
Jane Marie Souza

INTRODUCTION   xiii
An Overview of Exemplars in Assessment
Tara A. Rose

PART ONE: STUDENT LEARNING AND ASSESSMENT

1. THE EVOLVING MEASURE OF LEARNING   3
   Bill Moseley and Sonya Christian

2. STUDENTS AS PARTNERS IN COCURRICULAR ASSESSMENT   14
   Jessica Greene, Burton Howell, and Michael Sacco

3. ASSESSMENT OF STUDENT LEARNING IN THE ARTS, HUMANITIES, SOCIAL SCIENCES, AND SCIENCES   26
   Jeffrey R. Lindauer and Patricia A. Coward

4. LEVERAGING TECHNOLOGY TO FACILITATE ASSESSMENT PROCESSES   39
   Scott Carnz, Mary Mara, and Amy Portwood

5. INDIGENOUS ASSESSMENT
   Cultural Relevancy in Assessment of Student Learning   51
   Stephen Wall, Lara M. Evans, and Porter Swentzell

6. ONE INSTITUTION'S JOURNEY TO ANNUAL PROGRAM ASSESSMENT   70
   Carol Traupman-Carr, Dana S. Dunn, and Debra Wetcher-Hendricks

vi CONTENTS

7   A SYSTEMATIC APPROACH TO BUILDING A CULTURE
    OF ASSESSMENT
    A Multiyear, Cohort-Based Professional Development Model   81
    Mary Kay Helling, Jana Hanson, and Kevin Sackreiter

8   INTRODUCING ASSESSMENT-TASK CHOICE IN AN
    ONLINE BACHELOR COURSE   95
    Ryan Jopp, Keryn Chalmers, Sandra Luxton, and Jay Cohen

9   EMPLOYING PEER LEARNING AND ASSESSMENT AT SCALE   110
    Brian Harlan, Shawn Moustafa, and Roxie Smith

10 MANY BIRDS WITH ONE STONE
    Developing a Multipurpose Student Assessment System   122
    David D. Dworak

PART TWO: STUDENT LEARNING AND ASSESSMENT IN THE DISCIPLINES

11 ASSESSMENT OF PUBLIC HEALTH COMPETENCIES AT
    MULTIPLE LEVELS   139
    Sondos Islam

12 ELEVATING ASSESSMENT PROCESSES THROUGH
    STAKEHOLDER ENGAGEMENT   152
    Leigh M. Onimus and Joyce A. Strawser

13 COMPETENCY-BASED STUDENT ASSESSMENT IN ONLINE AND
    IN-PERSON MASTER OF PUBLIC HEALTH PROGRAMS   166
    Kimberly Krytus, Sarah Cercone Heavey, and Gregory G. Homish

14 DESIGNING AND ASSESSING COCURRICULAR STRATEGIES
    TO PROMOTE PERSONAL AND PROFESSIONAL DEVELOPMENT   181
    *Burgunda V. Sweet, Katherine A. Kelley, Melissa S. Medina, and
    Marianne McCollum*

PART THREE: FACULTY ENGAGEMENT AND ASSESSMENT

15 GIVING LIFE TO INSTITUTIONAL STUDENT
    LEARNING OUTCOMES   197
    Dan Shapiro

16 ASSESSING FOR LEARNING
    The Scholarship of Teaching and Learning and Campus Assessment Culture   213
    Kristina A. Meinking

PART FOUR: INSTITUTIONAL EFFECTIVENESS AND ASSESSMENT

17 A STRUCTURED PROTOCOL FOR DEMONSTRATING
    INSTITUTIONAL EFFECTIVENESS   229
    Eric D. Stamps

18 TRANSFORMING FROM WITHIN
    Strategic Planning as a Tool for Institutional Reflection,
    Direction, and Transformation   240
    R. Ray D. Somera and Marlena Montague

19 BEING SAGE ABOUT INSTITUTIONAL EFFECTIVENESS   254
    Elisa Hertz

20 DO WE HAVE IT? DO WE DO IT? DOES IT WORK?
    A Three-Question Framework for Addressing Accreditation Standards and
    Ensuring Institutional Effectiveness   266
    Dawn L. Hayward, Nancy Ritze, and Rebecca Gullan

EDITOR AND CONTRIBUTOR BIOGRAPHIES   283

INDEX   299

FOREWORD

As president of the Middle States Commission on Higher Education (MSCHE), an institutional accreditor recognized by the United States Department of Education, it is an honor and privilege to reflect on this important publication that provides an inspiring collection of exemplars in the field of assessment representing diverse colleges and universities. I have worked collaboratively with Jane Marie Souza and Tara Rose for several years through the Association for the Assessment of Learning in Higher Education (AALHE), and this publication builds upon the synergy between institutions and accreditors that has been nurtured through AALHE panel presentations and publications. I want to express my sincere appreciation to Souza and Rose as well as AALHE for supporting important dialogue and conversations alongside accreditors about assessment expectations for many years. This publication reinforces the value of sharing narratives reflective of assessment. The institutional and accreditor response to Souza and Rose reaffirmed not only the continuing interest in the intersection between assessment and accreditation but also the strong desire to share an array of assessment approaches in the hopes that doing so will be useful to others. Perhaps most importantly, this collection is a celebration of assessment exemplars that are, by design, intended to improve the student learning experience. This speaks to the foundational principle for accreditors: *continuous improvement*.

How institutions approach assessment differs dramatically, which is for good and valid reasons, is highlighted in the descriptions of assessment within programs or across institutions that follow in this publication. Accreditors appreciate that assessment comes in a variety of forms, and they train evaluators, who engage in the work of accreditation through peer review, that no single approach to assessment can be applied to all programs or to every institution. While often informed through best practices, assessment must be molded to individual institutional circumstances so that results are most meaningful, authentic, and useable. Accreditors across 12 agencies recommended exemplars for this publication, an affirmative nod that contributions to educational quality through assessment are to be found through differing models across diverse institutions when applying nuanced accreditation standards. The exemplars highlight different approaches to assessment, but they also capture common, important principles. Reiterated throughout the exemplars is the importance of assessment being systematic and intentional and promoting evidence-based decision-making using sustainable practices that are not burdensome and that maximize efficiency. Finding ways to celebrate the challenges and successes of assessment can be an empowering experience across institutions, while also serving to improve communication and contribute to more positive cultures of assessment. Ensuring assessment across all levels of the institution is critical and requires support and appropriate resourcing, all of which are also important topics addressed by the authors.

The exemplars feature champions of assessment, who deserve recognition. The authors and their colleagues are expanding upon what they have learned as champions of assessment at their own institutions to inspire readers of this publication to reflect on their own contributions to strengthening their programs, services, and institutions. While you will see assessment activities that are aligned with accreditation expectations, the authors have grounded their narratives of assessment in a framework focused upon quality and improvement rather than compliance. Accreditors see that goals of assessment are best achieved when the institutional culture is one that embraces assessment for reasons other than compliance. While assessment may feel to constituents like an activity of accountability simply for accreditors, it is most appropriate to approach assessment as an activity of accountability for students. Assessment results that improve institutional effectiveness, heighten student learning, and better align resources serve to make institutions stronger for the benefit of their students, and those results also serve the institution or program well during the holistic evaluation required through accreditation.

This publication provides diverse assessment practices while reiterating the role of accreditors as partners in the development and sustenance of engaging, meaningful assessment. The timing of this publication is ideal, as it will contribute to the ever-evolving nature of assessment dialogue and inspire institutional leaders to revisit their assessment practices across the institution to ensure mission and goal attainment. Accreditors appreciate the unique role we occupy within the higher education community, one that balances quality assurance, peer review, and ongoing improvement with compliance and accountability. Through exposure to many different models for educational excellence, accreditors benefit from understanding and sharing across institutions how assessment is being leveraged to support change, innovation, and growth that serves students, constituents, and the higher education community well. That benefit has been extended to others through this timely publication.

Heather F. Perfetti, JD, EdD

PREFACE

Tara Rose and I are excited to be able to share this collection of exemplars with you. Its inception occurred as part of our activities with the Association for the Assessment of Learning in Higher Education (AALHE), who agreed to serve as copublishers along with Stylus Publishing, LLC. Tara and I have been active in AALHE many years, having both served as president and currently serving as board members. Over the years, AALHE conferences and publications proved to be excellent venues for communicating the message that accrediting agencies are partners with institutions in championing quality in higher education.

The relationship between accrediting agencies and their member institutions has long been an interest of mine. Having served as a peer reviewer for four accrediting bodies and a council member for one, I realized the value of promoting understanding of the accreditation perspective and processes. I was encouraged to see that AALHE's fall 2014 the publication, *Intersection*, included an interview that David Eubanks, then editor-in-chief, conducted with Michael Johnson, then senior vice president and chief of staff for the Southern Association of Colleges and Schools Commission on Colleges. Shortly thereafter, when I succeeded Eubanks as editor-in-chief of the publication, I continued adding interviews with accreditors as part of each edition. This work culminated in a 2018 special edition that included conversations with all the former regional accreditors as well as the Distance Education Accrediting Commission. I am very grateful to all the institution-based interviewers and the participating agencies for helping deepen the understanding of this complex relationship and underscoring our common ground of prioritizing student success.

The early interest in the written interviews inspired me to host a panel session at the 2016 annual AALHE conference in Milwaukee, Wisconsin. Michael Johnson graciously agreed to partner once again with AALHE and served on the first panel, *Conversation With Accreditors*. Joining him were Barbara Johnson, vice president for accreditation services at the Higher Learning Commission, and Terri Flateby, then associate vice president for institutional effectiveness at Georgia Southern University, representing the concerns of higher education institutions. The popularity of the *Conversation With Accreditors* panel session led to it becoming an annual event, and fellow board member Steven Hawks, director of undergraduate assessment at the University of Minnesota-Twin Cities, joined me to include audience participation via Twitter. The AALHE conference in June 2020 marked the fifth accreditor panel session.

It was just after the 2019 accreditor panel session that Tara Rose, AALHE colleague and director of assessment at Louisiana State University, approached me with an idea. She noted that during the session, participants were asking for examples of what the accreditors considered to be effective assessment practices. She wondered if it would be possible to compile some specific, institution-based examples to share with the assessment community. This thought led to a series of discussions giving rise to this publication.

Before any real work began on the text, we wanted to float the concept with an accreditor. We needed to assess the likelihood of agencies being willing to suggest institutions to contribute to our compendium of examples. We would like to acknowledge Heather Perfetti, president of the Middle States Commission on Higher Education, for serving as a sounding board for our approach to this project. She immediately saw value in the effort and encouraged us to persist. Tara and I grew genuinely excited about the prospect of being able to provide a collection of exemplars in assessment from institutions that were suggested to us by accrediting agencies. Our confidence only grew when we received an enthusiastic response for our concept from David Brightman, senior editor for higher education at Stylus Publishing, LLC. His guidance was essential in our pursuit of the project.

We would like to acknowledge the vice presidents and executive directors from the 12 accrediting bodies who suggested institutions for this publication: J. Gregory Boyer (ACPE), Stephanie Bryant (AACSB), David Chase (WASC), Stephanie Droker (ACCJC), Larry Earvin (SACSCOC), Ellie Fogarty (MSCHE), Linda Hughes-Kirchubel (AACSB), Mary Kiersma (ACPE), Laura Rasar King (CEPH), Eric Martin (HLC), Leah Matthews (DEAC), Patricia O'Brien (NECHE), Heather Perfetti (MSCHE), Mac Powell (NWCCU), Destiny Quintero (HLC), Heather Stagliano (CPME), Anthea Sweeney (HLC), and Denise Young (SACSCOC). Without their input and the insightful contributions of authors from 24 colleges and universities representing a diversity of institutional types, this book would never have come to fruition.

Irrespective of their institutional size or type, Tara and I hope readers will find value in these examples of how assessment practices might be implemented to improve educational quality. We hope to inspire experimentation with new strategies that align with both institutional mission and the standards of accrediting bodies, recognizing that we are all partners in promoting quality in higher education.

Jane Marie Souza

INTRODUCTION

An Overview of Exemplars in Assessment

Tara A. Rose

This compendium provides examples of assessment practice in 24 distinct higher education institutions (HEIs), 23 in the United States and one in Australia. The Association for the Assessment of Learning in Higher Education (AALHE) has been working with accreditors for many years, seeking to support the complex relationship between accrediting agencies and the institutions they accredit. When institutions are preparing a self-study for an accreditation interim report or reaffirmation, HEIs continue to struggle with understanding precisely what is being asked for by accreditors. Accrediting agencies provide standards and guidelines on the type of evidence that could be used to make the case for reaffirmation. However, institutions often have concerns about how peer reviewers will interpret the approach taken. In spite of the fact that the accrediting agency commissioners ultimately make the accreditation decisions, the comments of the peer reviewers may leave institutions questioning what accreditors would deem to be examples of good assessment practices.

All institutions represented in this book were suggested by their accreditor as having an effective assessment approach in one or more of the following assessment-focused areas: assessment in the disciplines, cocurricular, course/program/institutional assessment, equity and inclusion, general education, online learning, program review, scholarship of teaching and learning, student learning, or technology.

About AALHE

AALHE, founded in late 2009, is an organization of practitioners and educators interested in using effective assessment practice to document and improve student learning. As such, it serves the needs of those in higher education for whom assessment is a tool to help understand learning and to develop processes for improving it. The association's mission is to develop and support a community of educators and inform assessment practices in higher education to foster and improve student learning and institutional quality.

In January of 2020 AALHE adopted its first foundational statement to define assessment in its broadest sense. Past presidents Jane Marie Souza and Jeremy Penn led a 13-member working group charged with drafting a general definition that could serve as a foundation on which to build a more refined set of statements to include future topics such as equity in assessment, cocurricular assessment, research in assessment, and so on.

Member input was solicited, reviewed, and incorporated prior to the final draft statement being put to vote. With more than half the full membership casting votes, the following statement received 89% approval:

> Assessment is the process of collecting and analyzing information to determine if progress is being made toward a desired end. While this broad definition is applicable to a range of goals and organizational contexts, AALHE focuses on the assessment of student learning and institutional effectiveness within the context of higher education.
>
> Student learning outcomes assessment is a process in which members of the higher education community identify what students should be able to do by the end of an educational unit and determine the degree to which they meet these goals. It also requires us to consider how to use the information systematically gathered on student performance to improve the teaching/learning process.
>
> Institutional effectiveness assessment focuses on the extent to which an institution is making progress towards its mission and vision. When engaged in this process, members of the higher education community use the information collected to inform action taken for improvement.
>
> The aim of student learning assessment and institutional effectiveness assessment is the ongoing enhancement of quality. AALHE supports these efforts in quality improvement by promoting assessment not just "of learning" but more importantly "for learning." (AALHE, 2020, paras. 1–4)

Contributing Institutional and Specialized Accreditors

The accrediting agencies listed in Table I.1 are recognized as reliable authorities concerning the quality of education or training offered by the institutions of higher education or higher education programs they accredit.

How the Book is Organized

The book is organized into four parts: (a) student learning and assessment, (b) student learning assessment in the disciplines, (c) faculty engagement and

TABLE I.1
Contributing Accreditors

Agency	URL
Accreditation Council for Pharmacy Education (ACPE)	acpe-accredit.org
Accrediting Commission for Community and Junior Colleges (ACCJC)	accjc.org
Accrediting Commission for Schools Western Association of Schools and Colleges (WASC) Senior College	acswasc.org
Association to Advance Collegiate Schools of Business (AACSB)	aacsb.edu
Council on Education for Public Health (CEPH)	ceph.org
Council on Podiatric Medical Education (CPME)	cpme.org
Distance Education Accrediting Commission (DEAC)	deac.org
Higher Learning Commission (HLC)	hlcommission.org
Middle States Commission on Higher Education (MSCHE)	msche.org
New England Commission of Higher Education (NECHE)	neche.org
Northwest Commission on Colleges and Universities (NWCCU)	nwccu.org
Southern Association of Colleges and Schools Commission on Colleges (SACSCOC)	sacscoc.org

assessment, and (d) institutional effectiveness and assessment. Each part includes chapters, from a variety of accreditors, addressing standards in diverse ways.

Part One: Student Learning and Assessment

The theme for Part One is student learning and assessment and includes 10 chapters. While the primary focus for each chapter is the assessment of student learning; secondary foci include badging, cocurricular, technology, cultural relevancy, programmatic assessment, online learning, and post-graduation success.

Chapter 1: Bakersfield College
"The Evolving Measure of Learning" describes an evolution of higher education and how the college has approached the assessment of student learning

over the last 30 years. Powerful technologies now available to institutions can continue to confidently shift the learning paradigm to be more dynamic, customized, and portable, allowing for a more transparent and detailed view of learning than was previously possible.

Chapter 2: Boston College
"Students as Partners in Cocurricular Assessment" describes how the college embraces the concept of student "formation" or the notion that all campus constituents work toward advancing students' integration of their intellectual, social, and spiritual selves. This chapter provides a framework that may be adopted/adapted to other campuses interested in assessing the student growth residing in more affective or emotional domains that are perhaps considered too abstract to assess.

Chapter 3: Canisius College
"Assessment of Student Learning in the Arts, Humanities, Social Sciences, and Sciences" shares how the institution created an effective system of student learning and a culture of assessment with support from senior leadership, dedication by administration and faculty, and the development of systems to help guide the process.

Chapter 4: City University of Seattle
"Leveraging Technology to Facilitate Assessment Processes" explores a variety of technology tools to assist in the assessment of student achievement of program learning outcomes. A combination of off-the-shelf tools and proprietary solutions have allowed the university to develop a system that provides on-going, regular assessment data that is visible to university leaders for use in program revision, development, and other campus planning activities.

Chapter 5: Institute of American Indian Arts (IAIA)
"Indigenous Assessment: Cultural Relevancy in Assessment of Student Learning" discusses the need to determine the "who" and not just the "what" of assessment. For IAIA the "who" was their community: employees, students, alumnae, and their families. This chapter shares how an assessment process was designed based on Indigenous research methodologies to help guide decisions, planning, and structures.

Chapter 6: Moravian College
"One Institution's Journey to Annual Program Assessment" shares the college's efforts in moving from an academic assessment process that was

met with considerable faculty resistance to an effective process that is valued and seen as an approach to fulfill the desire for evidence of student development.

Chapter 7: South Dakota State University
"A Systematic Approach to Building a Culture of Assessment: A Multiyear, Cohort-Based Professional Development Model" describes how one institution developed and implemented a quality initiative. The initiative resulted in updated academic and cocurricular assessment plans, the implementation of an assessment management system, and the development of sustainable assessment resources, practices, and institutional support.

Chapter 8: Swinburne University of Technology
"Introducing Assessment-Task Choice in an Online Bachelor Course" summarizes the initiation, implementation, and outcomes of a choice-based assessment regime in an online course in a bachelor business program.

Chapter 9: University of the People
"Employing Peer Learning and Assessment at Scale" relates how a fully online, tuition-free institution leverages open educational resources, technology, and student graders as key components in the institution's overall instructional model.

Chapter 10: U.S. Army War College
"Many Birds With One Stone: Developing a Multipurpose Student Assessment System" shares how the college developed a systemic and documented student assessment system that provides feedback for student awareness, aids in evidence-based institutional decision-making, and supports talent management efforts of the profession.

Part Two: Student Learning and Assessment in the Disciplines

Part Two focuses on student learning assessment within schools recognized by specialized accreditors. Specific disciplines include business, pharmacy, and public health.

Chapter 11: Charles Drew University of Medicine and Science
"Assessment of Public Health Competencies at Multiple Levels" shares how the university faculty revised their curriculum and assessment activities to meet the new standards, from the Council on Education for Public Health (CEPH), the accrediting body for all public health programs.

Chapter 12: Seton Hall University
"Elevating Assessment Processes Through Stakeholder Engagement" describes how the School of Business used a strategy of engagement with external stakeholders and faculty across the university to enhance the relevance and impact of undergraduate and graduate assessment processes. The school shares approaches to engage each distinct group of stakeholders and the benefits realized from connecting these individuals.

Chapter 13: University at Buffalo–SUNY School of Public Health
"Competency-Based Student Assessment in Online and In-Person Master of Public Health Programs" explains how the School of Public Health migrated their Master of Public Health program from a content-based to competency-based curriculum in order to meet skill needs in the public health workforce. Program faculty, staff, and students joined a curriculum revision implementation team to facilitate change, identifying gaps in the curriculum and new assessment activities to strengthen competency-related content and competency attainment.

Chapter 14: University of Michigan, Ohio State University, University of Oklahoma, and Regis University
"Designing and Assessing Cocurricular Strategies to Promote Personal and Professional Development" explains that the development of competency in the affective domain is often best achieved through implementation of a thoughtfully and intentionally designed cocurriculum, and the true value of the cocurriculum lies in its ability to connect didactic and experiential learning while building students' affective competencies.

Part Three: Faculty Engagement and Assessment

Part Three addresses faculty engagement in learning assessment. The two chapters bring faculty to the forefront of assessment processes relating to general education and the scholarship of teaching and learning.

Chapter 15: California State University Monterey Bay
"Giving Life to Institutional Student Learning Outcomes" is based on three intersecting themes: leveraging accreditation, faculty engagement, and professional development. With the three themes in mind, this university shares their story of how institutional learning outcomes were created, how they are assessed, and how faculty and staff use assessment results to align and improve student learning within and across general education and the disciplines.

Chapter 16: Elon University
"Assessing for Learning: The Scholarship of Teaching and Learning (SoTL) and Campus Assessment Culture" explains ways in which their institution's programs, initiatives, and other interweavings of SoTL have created and cultivated specific faculty habits of mind. These habits of mind in turn have begun to change attitudes and approaches to assessment on campus, encouraging some faculty and departments to shift from a compliance mindset to one that sees assessment as a generative process.

Part Four: Institutional Effectiveness and Assessment

Part Four focuses on institutional effectiveness assessment and approaches to continuous improvement. These four chapters demonstrate the connectedness of student learning, strategic goals, and institutional planning.

Chapter 17: California School of Podiatric Medicine at Samuel Merritt University
"A Structured Protocol for Demonstrating Institutional Effectiveness" has created a structured protocol for curricular assessment and strategic planning that incorporates programmatic accreditation requirements, university learning outcomes, and program learning outcomes that ultimately help demonstrate institutional effectiveness. The chapter outlines the collaborative process that the school has used to develop, refine, and implement this assessment system.

Chapter 18: Guam Community College
"Transforming From Within: Strategic Planning as a Tool for Institutional Reflection, Direction, and Transformation" shares how the college used the strategic planning process as a tool to mobilize and harness human capital to invest in a collective undertaking that has led to the transformation of the institution through a "Students First, Mission Always" value system. The college shares how the grounding in island culture tapped and capitalized on cultural strengths and foundations, such as the cultural significance of the *latte stone*, an iconic symbol of the resiliency of the CHamoru people, the indigenous inhabitants of Guam.

Chapter 19: Guttman Community College
"Being SAGE About Institutional Effectiveness" describes the college's institutional effectiveness framework—Systematic Approach for Guttman Effectiveness (SAGE). SAGE uses a "bottom up" approach to integrate planning, assessment, and resource allocation in support of the college's mission and continuous improvement.

Chapter 20: Gwynedd Mercy University and Bronx Community College "Do We Have It? Do We Do It? Does It Work? A Three-Question Framework for Addressing Accreditation Standards and Ensuring Institutional Effectiveness" shares how applying a simple framework of three questions—"Do we have it?"; "Do we do it?"; "Does it work?"—can provide a powerful and meaningful approach for this otherwise complex task. This chapter describes how utilizing these three questions can help faculty and staff demonstrate compliance with standards and identify opportunities for improvement.

Carnegie Classification

We know that the art of assessment is not a one-size-fits-all activity. While we are confident that our readers can take away something from each institution's exemplar assessment practices, there are situations in which an assessment practitioner might want to consider focusing on assessment approaches that work best for certain types of institutions based on their Carnegie Classification (see Table I.2). "The Carnegie Classification® has been the leading framework for recognizing and describing institutional diversity in U.S. higher education for the past four and a half decades" (Center for Postsecondary Research, 2017, para. 8). Therefore, we provide a table of chapters sorted by Carnegie Classification.

TABLE I.2
Carnegie Classification and Chapter Alignment

Carnegie Classification Levels (2018)	*Chapter Number*
Associate's Colleges	18, 19, 20
Baccalaureate/Associate's Colleges	1, 9, 11
Baccalaureate Colleges	6
Master's Colleges	3, 4, 15, 20
Special Focus—2-Year	14
Special Focus—4-Year	10, 14, 17
Tribal Colleges	5
Doctoral Universities	2, 7, 12, 13, 14
Doctoral/Professional Universities	14, 16

Note: Data based on Basic 2018 Carnegie Classification Codes

Conclusion

There are over 4,000 higher education institutions in the nation with 3,000-plus holding accreditation status by a Council for Higher Education (CHEA) recognized institutional accreditor. For the majority of institutions, achieving accreditation is an absolute necessity. However, we view accrediting agencies as our partners in higher education, championing quality, integrity, and continuous improvement. It is our goal that the following institutional chapters, suggested by accreditors, provide assessment practitioners, administrators, faculty, and staff with real world examples of "what works" in assessment across a diverse selection of institutions.

References

Association for the Assessment of Learning in Higher Education. (2020, January). *Foundational statement #1: What is assessment in higher education?* https://www.aalhe.org/foundational-statement

Center for Postsecondary Research, Indiana University School of Education. (2017). *Carnegie classification of institutions of higher education.* https://carnegieclassifications.iu.edu/

PART ONE

STUDENT LEARNING AND ASSESSMENT

I

THE EVOLVING MEASURE OF LEARNING

Bill Moseley and Sonya Christian

Bakersfield College, one of 115 California Community Colleges, has been an active part of the evolution of assessment practice since the 1990s. Early on, this evolution was marked by the development of student learning outcomes, which were mapped to program outcomes for the purpose of an aggregated calculation of program assessment data. The introduction of institutional learning outcomes broadened the scope of assessment practice by making an explicit connection to the college's institutional values and mission. Later, technology assisted in both the scale and the depth of analysis of the assessment data. The introduction of *microcredentials*, also known as *badges*, as discrete representations of knowledge or skills provided an opportunity to better align assessment with both instruction and career objectives. Bakersfield College is integrating badges with the assessment framework at the student learning outcome level, to leverage assessment practice as the criteria for the awarding of badges. This integration provides a means of recording and communicating discrete academic achievement. These badges empower and extend the value of assessment data by communicating it in meaningful ways to students, other institutions, and future employers.

The Context for Change

Bakersfield College serves over 40,000 students in the central and south San Joaquin Valley. Founded in 1913 with 13 students, the college is a Hispanic-Serving Institution, with 70.6% of students belonging to this ethnic group. While many students reside in the City of Bakersfield, a significant number live in the rural areas and smaller towns throughout Kern County. The college maintains a physical presence in several of these outlying areas and supplements offerings with a comprehensive distance education program.

This chapter addresses the evolution of student learning and assessment over the last 30 years, from 1990 to 2020 and beyond, in 3 eras. The first, from 1990 to 2010, was characterized by the development of assessment strategies in higher education. During the second era, from 2010 to 2018, there was advancement of new tools and technologies to support the development and execution of assessment. The third era begins in 2018, and continues to the present day and beyond. This era is characterized by a synthesis of innovative ideas about knowledge and assessment with new technologies that enable these ideas to reach full potential.

Development of Assessment Strategies 1990–2010

Early advances in assessment were driven by the recognition that, in order to evaluate the effectiveness of educational programs, some quantification of learning beyond grades and units was necessary. From the early 1900s to the 1970s, the focus had been on scalable, standardized assessment of learning through objective examinations given to graduating college students.

> But as we saw at the end of the 1970s, objective testing was not the way faculty members wanted student learning to be assessed. They were more comfortable with open-ended, holistic, problem-based assessments, which were more in tune with what they thought they were teaching. (Shavelson, 2007, p. 30)

Faculty members believed that assessment practice needed to be more tightly coupled with their teaching. Driven by parallel growth in action research methodology, the assessment movement grew out of the academy's desire to direct their own assessment work in ways that were relevant to, and connected with, teaching and learning. In 2006, the Secretary of Education's higher education commission recommended that higher education should "measure and report meaningful student learning outcomes" (Shavelson, 2007, p. 30).

The college's assessment committee was formed in 2010 and led by the Academic Senate. Programs were required to use *student learning outcomes* (SLOs) in the course outline of record to guide instruction and assessment. These SLOs were mapped to higher level *program learning outcomes* (PLOs), which represent the key learning outcomes at the program level. In practice, however, the measurement of student performance on SLOs was often situated as an "add-on" to the core instruction and learning assessment in the class, leading faculty and students to feel that the SLO assessment was not connected in an authentic way. Faculty began to recognize a need for a tighter integration of SLO assessment with the core teaching and learning assessment practices employed at the course level.

Advancement of Tools and Technologies to Support Assessment 2010–2018

In the period between 2010 and 2018, growth and change in the universe of assessment was driven and characterized by the introduction of technology. Technology had two impacts on assessment. First, it facilitated the scaling of assessment work by providing internet-connected platforms for managing the large amounts of data generated by assessment, and in some cases, the delivery of the assessments themselves. The second impact provided a mechanism for more advanced analysis of the data at an institutional level. Assessment data could now be analyzed, disaggregated, and deeply understood in ways that were not easy or even possible before. The byproduct of these enhanced capabilities was integration of assessment with accreditation standards, which represented the last stage in the assumption of ownership by the academy. This ownership was driven by the desire to maintain a self-regulated system of learning, in contrast to other systems of education that are regulated and assessed by government agencies.

The work of Guided Pathways (Bailey et al., 2015) was the dominant framework for a college-wide redesign effort that resulted in the faculty-led refinement of programs of study, starting with the end in mind. Using PLOs as the overall target, faculty looked critically at the alignment of curriculum and SLOs. Clarifying both the learning and the path to program completion created a coherent curricular pathway for students and a fundamental shift in how faculty viewed the student journey through courses toward program completion. Given this shift, the traditional cafeteria-style course catalog was no longer an adequate tool for communication to students. In partnership with the California Community Colleges Chancellor's Office (CCCCO), the college developed Program Pathways Mapper (Bakersfield College, n.d.), an online visualization tool that starts with the program learning outcomes and the careers available, along with salary information. The visualization tool is currently being used by 30 community colleges in California and is being scaled up to the California State University (CSU) System.

Bakersfield College has seen gains in student achievement as a result of its detailed curricular mapping to baccalaureate completion at CSU Bakersfield (CSUB). During the past 5 years, the number of transfer students from Bakersfield College to CSUB who complete a bachelor's degree has increased by 19%. Of Bakersfield College students who transfer to CSUB, 47.7% complete their program in 2 years, compared to 42.4% of all students transferring to CSUB and an even smaller CSU system-wide rate of just 32.6%.

The guided pathways movement has positively influenced governance structures. Bakersfield College intentionally designed the committee structure to ensure continuous, systemic evaluation and improvement of the quality and currency of all instructional programs. The Program Review Committee, working in conjunction with the Accreditation and Institutional Quality Committee, the Assessment Committee, the Curriculum Committee, and individual departments, provides a robust integrated framework for quality assurance. The tight integration resulted in a deeper understanding of how all the different parts play a role in the ultimate goal of improving student learning and student achievement. The system now ensures regular and systematic review of all courses and programs, alignment of content and teaching strategies with current best practices, and ensures that all learning outcomes are relevant and appropriate. Finally, this integrated system ensures that the four *institutional learning outcomes* (ILOs)—think critically, communicate effectively, demonstrate competency, and engage productively—are assessed broadly and regularly. By confirming clear alignment of all course-level SLOs to the college's ILOs, Bakersfield College is able to assess and monitor student attainment of ILOs. Further, transfer rates and job placement data provide concrete evidence of student attainment and practical application of ILOs.

Although the college's ILOs do not use the specific language of the accreditation standard, Figure 1.1 shows the alignment.

Bakersfield College's assessment committee is the primary agent responsible for ensuring the definition and assessment of all outcomes at the course, program (including a baccalaureate degree), and institutional levels. The assessment committee works with the curriculum committee to ensure that all course outlines of record have appropriate SLOs. The assessment committee works with the program review committee to ensure that PLOs are assessed as part of the program review process. The intentional design of the formal governance structure at Bakersfield College ensures dialogue among the faculty about creating, updating, and assessing learning outcomes at all levels.

Innovation of Badging and Assessment 2018–2020 and Beyond

In the early 21st century, the technology sector began experimenting with microcredentials, or badges. Digital badges were born in the world of video games, where these digital achievements were originally mapped to specific

Figure 1.1. ILO to accreditation language mapping.

Bakersfield College ILO	Communication Competency	Information Competency	Quantitative Competency	Analytic Inquiry	Ethical Reasoning	Engage Diverse Perspectives
I. Pursue knowledge and evaluate its consequences	✓	✓	✓	✓		✓
Think critically, abstractly, logically, and algorithmically to evaluate and solve problems		✓	✓	✓		
Integrate new information to formulate principles and theories and display openness to different opinions		✓		✓		✓
Share the desire for intellectual creativity and acquisition of knowledge	✓					✓
II. Communicate clearly and effectively in both written and oral forms.	✓				✓	✓
III. Demonstrate knowledge and abilities in a chosen area of study	✓	✓	✓	✓	✓	✓
Demonstrate an understanding of resources and procedures of a field and the ability to use them	✓	✓	✓	✓	✓	
Demonstrate the ability to use current technology to acquire, organize, and analyze information appropriately		✓		✓	✓	
Possess a core of knowledge and skills in a chosen field	✓	✓	✓	✓	✓	✓
IV. Appreciate civil responsibilities	✓	✓		✓	✓	✓
Reflect upon the cultural and ethical dimensions of life				✓	✓	✓
Contribute to society as an actively engaged citizen	✓	✓			✓	✓

tasks and accomplishments in games. In this context, badges were used as a game mechanic, to influence and motivate movement toward specific tasks and goals desired by the game's creator, especially at times where the game itself might lack the tools or structure to move a player in that direction (McDaniel, 2016). As this mechanic became popular and the idea of *gamification* spread to education and the workplace, badges began to appear elsewhere. Mozilla and other organizations developed standards for open badges, allowing badges to be compatible with one another, regardless of their source.

The platform of microcredentials, when used to record and convey student skills that are captured in student learning outcomes and measured by authentic assessment techniques, presents a unique opportunity for the evolution of credit for learning. The alignment of platforms, ideas, and current assessment practice with powerful and usable technologies has set the stage at Bakersfield College to develop a higher resolution picture of each student's learning—one that can travel with them throughout their educational career, and into the workplace.

The Carnegie Unit as the Problem

In 1906, the Carnegie Foundation created the *Carnegie unit* as a means of defining both a "high school" and a "college," with the goal of ensuring student qualifications for college entrance and also developing a standard for the funding of pensions for college faculty, who at the time did not have retirement plans funded by their institutions. Even at the time of its creation, the Board of Trustees for the Carnegie Foundation expressed multiple concerns with the possible negative implications of the move to equate a unit measurement of learning with hours spent in a classroom. A report by Tomkins and Gaumnitz (1964), written several decades after the launch of this idea, said:

> The Carnegie Unit, unique to the American system of secondary education, is being reexamined. Is it outmoded? Do the far-reaching changes occurring in the objectives of secondary education, in the number and types of pupils attending, in the high school–college relationships—to name only a few—call for new methods and instruments of pupil evaluation and accounting? (p. 1)

Sixty-five years have passed since this report was published, and more than a century since the inception of the Carnegie unit, and yet it is still the predominant model for the representation of learning in higher education.

In *Degrees That Matter,* Jankowski and Marshall (2017) remind us that "Seat time and credit accrual are only proxy measures for student learning; they say nothing about what students have learned while sitting in their seats or in the process of accruing their credits" (p. 56). The assessment movement, which gained momentum in the 1970s, holds some hope in terms of measuring student performance in the class context, but has yet to make that data a part of the individual student record, or transcript. As such, students may never be aware of the outcomes they have mastered in the course of learning that never appear on the transcripts: a missed opportunity to provide specific feedback to students on the critical points of learning at the course level. In fact, many institutions still struggle to disaggregate their assessment data by individual student demographics because they do not have data recorded at the individual student level, but rather aggregated at the course level. The current system of communicating what the student has learned (skills and abilities) from the institution is still the transcript. A *transcript* typically contains three types of information: (a) the name of the courses taken, which may or may not give an accurate depiction of the subject matter, (b) the number of credits, or Carnegie units the course was worth, and (c) the grade received for each class. An employer may or may not look at this transcript in the hiring process. If they do not, then they just know that a student studied a subject, like "Psychology," for either 2 years (AA/AS) or 4 years (BA/BS). Based on that broad stroke, assumptions are made about what a student is qualified to do in the workplace. Learning is happening in college, but it is inadequately captured and communicated to the people who need it.

Bakersfield College has embarked on a highly innovative project that captures learning by mapping SLOs to badges within a course and then represents these badges within the Pathways Program Mapper tool that shows the path to degree completion. The next stage of this project is to develop a learning record for each student that becomes a portable portfolio of his or her learning. This instructional alignment of courses sequenced with an eye to program completion is part of the more general alignment discussed by Jankowski and Marshall (2017). This sort of authentic assessment encourages more situated learning opportunities and pedagogical best practice.

The Goal of the Assessment

The real value of badges as bite-sized representations of knowledge and skill is that they represent a higher-resolution picture of learning than is available through current systems. This fact is important because a job market is emerging where more nuanced descriptions of positions and careers are being used to guide searches and where discrete skills are being gathered as part of the large body of workforce data. For education to be relevant in this changing world of work, the measure of learning must match the granularity of the skills available in job postings. If a job posting asks specifically for "basic use of R for statistical analysis," then a transcript showing "Basic Quantitative Methods—3 Units" might not be useful because it lacks descriptive specificity. However, if the course is broken into discrete critical outcomes, and those are matched with badges to represent individual mastery of each one, then the employer can more easily determine whether the student has the exact skills needed to do the job. Education has a strong start with the creation of student learning outcomes in institutional assessment work. If those outcomes are paired with digital badges and awarded to students as they complete the assessments, then these two systems can be aligned, bridging the current measure of learning with a future that is infinitely more useful to students.

The data generated by the pairing of badges to SLOs are arguably even more useful for program review and assessment for the purpose of planning, because the richness of the data generated from assessing every SLO for every student in every class will surpass anything currently gathered. With this level of granularity in its data, an institution will be able to shape and hone programs, supporting student needs with a level of personalization that rivals Amazon.com. At the same time, these credentials will be fully owned by the student and fully authenticated to the institution. Badges will travel with students as they complete degrees from different institutions, apply for jobs, and even continue learning postemployment. Students will be the keepers of their own data and can easily include them in a résumé, a job application, or as part of their online presence.

Activities to Support the Achievement of the Goal

Bakersfield College has undertaken the creation of academic badges for students as well as professional development badges for employees.

Case Study: Bakersfield College Academic Badging

At this time, academic badging development is focused on Bakersfield College's fully online career and technical education programs where open educational resources are simultaneously being developed. Faculty follow a series of procedures for the development of badges.

1. Student learning outcomes are reviewed to ensure that they represent a discrete, measurable skill or knowledge set that is critical to the course.
2. Each of these outcomes is then mapped to its own badge, with the assessment for that skill embedded in the badge.
3. Badges are created for each course, with the SLO-level badges mapped to them.
4. Finally, a badge is created for each program, with course-level badges mapped to that badge, completing the hierarchy.

Using the Pathways Program Mapper tool, students and employers will be able to view and traverse this hierarchy, enabling them to see not just the discrete skills a student has obtained, but even the exact method used for assessing that skill (see Figure 1.2).

Case Study: Bakersfield College Professional Development Badging

Badging for professional development has taken on a similar path at Bakersfield College. As seminars and professional development activities are created, instructors are asked to think through the targeted outcomes for the workshop or session, and these outcomes are operationalized in the form of badges with their own embedded assessments. As with academic badges,

Figure 1.2. Commercial music program badging schema.

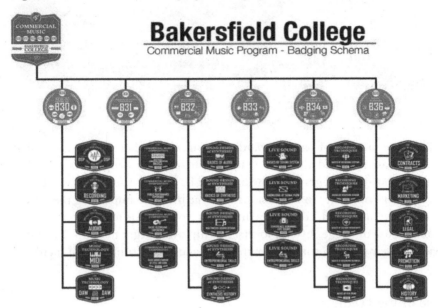

these badges represent a discrete skill or set of knowledge and contain information on how the outcome was assessed, who granted the badge, and the date of issuance. As is the case with academic badges, the recipient will own and manage their professional development badges and can include them in email signatures, résumés, or collect them in an electronic portfolio. Anyone who sees the badge will be easily able to ascertain the validity of the badge by viewing its metadata (Figure 1.3).

Assessments Used to Determine Progress

The work related to badging is just the first step in exploring a sweeping cultural shift in the way learning is viewed, captured, and communicated at Bakersfield College. As other institutions explore microcredentialing as a measure of skills or knowledge, there will come a tipping point where these silos of knowledge begin to connect. Through these connections, the field can share and refine ideas, identify the merit of those ideas, and scale those strategies.

Specifically, the success of badging efforts at Bakersfield College will be measured in three distinct ways. The first assessment of the badging efforts

Figure 1.3. Sample of Bakersfield College professional development badges.

will be the number of badges awarded to students and employees, as well as their use as measured through analytics provided by Badgr.com, the platform for hosting and granting the badges. The second assessment will be the engagement of faculty in discussions with the intent of improving the system and scaling up. The third assessment of this work will be related to the adoption and use of badges by employers. As employers begin to adopt the use of badges, their value to students, employees, and the institution will increase.

Use of the Findings

Badges are ubiquitous in game design and in gamification work around motivation. Their effectiveness in communicating discrete knowledge and specific achievements, as well as their value as a motivational tool, are well documented. Although their use in higher education is limited currently, Bakersfield College will present and publish its results widely.

Clearly, the work of assessment has also reached an age of maturity where its value is beyond question. The availability of the technological tools to measure individual student performance efficiently and transparently on assessment measures has reached a point where this level of detail in assessment work is becoming a reality. By extending the value of assessment using microcredentialing, higher education can give students more control over their own personal learning data, and more effectively communicate with the rest of the world what students have learned.

Conclusion and Future Plans

This chapter describes an evolution in how higher education in general, and Bakersfield College in particular, have approached the assessment of student learning over the decades from 1990 to 2020. Powerful technologies, now available to institutions, can continue to shift the learning paradigm to be more dynamic, customized, and portable than was ever before possible. The resolution of the picture depicting student learning is increasing, allowing a more transparent and detailed view of learning than has been previously possible. The gradual changes of the first 20 years show signs of acceleration at a greater rate—even more so over the last 3 years—suggesting an exponential trajectory for these changes. It is truly an exciting time to be in the world of higher education. It is truly an exciting time to be at Bakersfield College.

References

Bailey, T. R., Jaggars, S. S., & Jenkins, D. (2015). *Redesigning America's community colleges: A clearer path to student success.* Harvard University Press.

Bakersfield College. (n.d.). *Academics.* https://programmap.bakersfieldcollege.edu

Jankowski, N., & Marshall, D. (2017). *Degrees that matter: Moving higher education to a learning systems paradigm.* Stylus.

McDaniel, R. (2016). What we can learn about digital badges from video games. In D. Ifenthaler, N. Bellin, & D.-K. Mah (Eds.), *Foundation of digital badges and microcredentials: Demonstrating and recognizing knowledge and competencies* (pp. 325–342). https://doi.org/10.1007/978-3-319-15425-1_18.

Shavelson, R. J. (2007). Assessing student learning responsibly: From history to an audacious proposal. *Change: The Magazine of Higher Learning, 39*(1), 26–33. https://doi.org/10.3200/CHNG.39.1.26-33

Tomkins, E., & Gaumnitz, W. (1964, January 1). *The Carnegie unit: Its origin, status, and trends.* U.S. Department of Health, Education, and Welfare. https://doi.org/10.1177/019263656404828801

2

STUDENTS AS PARTNERS IN COCURRICULAR ASSESSMENT

Jessica Greene, Burton Howell, and Michael Sacco

Foundational to a Boston College education is the concept of *formation*, the notion that all campus constituents work toward advancing students' integration of their intellectual, social, and spiritual selves. Boston College directs significant attention to formative education in order to enhance students' own lives while promoting justice and the well-being of the common good. As such, formation vocabulary is embedded in Boston College's mission, vision, strategic plan, guidebooks, admissions tour narratives, and syllabi. Boston College's status as a leader in formative education is likewise communicated to campus constituents.

Goal of the Assessment

A response to the fair question "How do you know formation is working at Boston College?" is challenging to generate, in part due to the melded academic and affective growth formation intends to prompt, yet may not reveal itself until post Boston College. This challenge is familiar to Jesuit higher education; for example, Rev. Peter-Hans Kolvenbach, former superior general of the Jesuits, offered commentary on the role of Jesuit universities via his 2000 address and noted the need for assessment of student formation:

> Today's predominant ideology reduces the human world to a global jungle whose primordial law is the survival of the fittest. Students who

> subscribe to this view want to be equipped with well-honed professional and technical skills in order to compete in the market and secure one of the relatively scarce fulfilling and lucrative jobs available. This is the success which many students (and parents!) expect. All American universities, ours included, are under tremendous pressure to opt entirely for success in this sense. But what our students want—and deserve—includes but transcends this "worldly success" based on marketable skills. The real measure of our Jesuit universities lies in who our students become. (Kolvenbach, 2000, p. 8)

This understanding, "the real measure of our Jesuit universities lies in who our students become," reinforces assessment's relationship with, and relevance to, the study of student formation. Thus, the goal of this project was to develop and test formation-related learning outcomes with Halftime, a longstanding and signature cocurricular program at Boston College. A weekend-long, off-campus overnight retreat, Halftime invites undergraduates to reflect on how an academic major and future career fit in with the development and pursuit of the student's authentic self. It is an opportunity to have conversations with near-peer students, faculty, and staff about recognizing one's gifts and talents for one's own joy, while fulfilling a need in the world.

Strategy to Support Achievement of the Goal

To achieve a sound plan for the assessment of student formation, three guiding questions were developed:

1. What is formation and what are the conditions or attributes that make a cocurricular program/experience formative?
2. What learning outcomes are associated with formation?
3. An existing assumption is that, since formation reflects personal affective growth, it is too complex to assess/measure—what types of data collection could be implemented that do tap into formation?

Student formation at Boston College:

> proposes certain intellectual, social, moral, and spiritual standards to its students as worth acquiring and living by, equips them with the knowledge and skills to understand and critically interpret the world in light of these values, and respects [a student's] freedom to discern how these standards can be embodied in the decisions they make about their own lives. (Boston College, 2007, p. 2)

This description of student formation is grounded in Boston College's Catholic heritage, stemming from both the Jesuits' own formation process, which promotes the integration of intellectual, social, and spiritual values, and the Boston College mission. In fact, as described by Borrego (2006), "the mission of an institution greatly influences the type of programs and activities that count as learning" (p. 12). As such, a multitude of cocurricular programming at Boston College supports students' progress through their undergraduate education, recognizing that as "they embark on a developmental journey, [students] leave behind old ways of understanding, believing, and relating to the people around them, and move toward new forms of identity and more critically aware forms of knowing, choosing, and living authentically" (Boston College, 2007, p. 2). In fact, as described by Kuh et al. (2002), formation is akin to the complexities surrounding student development and "the unfolding of human potential toward increasingly complicated and refined levels of functioning. As a set of outcomes, student development encompasses a host of desirable skills, knowledge, beliefs, and attitudes students are supposed to cultivate in college" (p. 101). Formative programs foster this development, which aims to interconnect the intellectual, social, and spiritual dimensions of a student "in order to facilitate the full human flourishing of all our students" at Boston College (Boston College, 2007, p. 2).

What then constitutes a "formative program"? The response to this question is difficult when one considers its scope. As reinforced by Keeling,

> [this is] a significant challenge facing university campuses [i.e.,] how to develop the "whole student" whose entire curricular and cocurricular experience align with the achievement of the campus mission and learning outcomes. To accomplish this task, we truly need to consider the entire campus as a learning environment with curricular/cocurricular experiences equally vital for student success. (Keeling, 2006, para. 1, as cited in Platt & Sayegh, 2015)

While there is value in being able to articulate what formation is as a means of supporting Boston College's mission, there is also a practical aspect in terms of articulating how formation impacts student learning. That is, while the concept of student formation may be grounded in discernment principles within a Jesuit, Catholic ethos, its purpose translates well into current higher education research on high-impact practices. While these practices may take many forms, they share several features such as promoting "active engagement, requiring students to spend considerable time on task, . . . involve collaboration, and [asking] students to take responsibility for their learning" (Vaz, 2019, para. 4), elements that are comparable to those within the student formation domain.

For example, as described by Kuh (2008, pp. 14–17), key characteristics of high-impact practices are what result in their effectiveness. As the cultivation of Halftime's learning outcomes began to take shape, so did the mapping of each characteristic of high-impact practices to themes that align to characteristics embedded in Boston College's formative programs, as presented in Table 2.1.

This process of cross-walking characteristics of high-impact practices to elements rooted in Boston College's formative programs, such as Halftime, contributed to the development of a description of formation and a set of related conditions (Table 2.2), which in turn supported the process of articulating learning outcomes.

TABLE 2.1
Example of Shared Characteristics of High-Impact and Formative Practices

High-Impact Practices	Key Characteristics	Formative Programs
. . . typically demand that students devote considerable time and effort to purposeful tasks; most require daily decisions that deepen students' investment in the activity as well as their commitment to their academic program and the college . . .	Considerable time →	Extended retreats, year-long service placements, etc. require considerable time commitments
	Considerable effort →	Physical effort involved (service trips) and emotional effort (embedding oneself in the unfamiliar)
	Decision-making →	Extensive reflection and discernment opportunities—all of which involve decision-making
	Deep investment →	Openness to being vulnerable and authentic demands deep investment

TABLE 2.2
Describing Student Formation

Element	Explanation
Description:	Student formation is the process of supporting students' integration of their intellectual, social, and spiritual selves so that they can be best prepared to live a life of meaning and purpose.
Conditions:	While not an exhaustive set, a cocurricular program (or experience) is considered to be formative if it meets the following primary conditions. • Intentionality—the program needs to intentionally aim to be formative • Reflection—the program needs to offer opportunities for guided reflection • Integration—the program should aim to "hit" the three areas of intellectual, social, and spiritual growth • Discernment—the program needs to offer opportunities for critical thinking and decision-making

Assessments Used to Determine Progress Toward Goal

This process of operationalizing formation, and recognizing its alignment with high-impact practices, led to two Halftime learning outcomes:
Upon participating in Halftime, students will be able to . . .

1. identify one way Halftime has impacted their own vocational discernment process, and
2. identify one reflective habit that they have integrated into their lives.

The next challenge was how best to collect data in exploration of these learning outcomes. For example, the initial preference was to use some means of direct evidence—student learning that is typically considered tangible or visible and is evaluated by a subject matter expert (e.g., faculty). This inclination, however, introduced the dilemma of concretizing what student formation "success" looks like. When one considers success in the context of higher education, "some might argue [its] only reason is [the] transfer of learning" (Halpern & Hakel, 2003, p. 38). As expressed by the iceberg illusion (Figure 2.1), however, this "transfer of learning" is tricky to demonstrate within the context of student formation, because the desired growth is less about a score on a midterm exam and more about the expansion of one's heart and perspective.

Figure 2.1. The iceberg illusion.

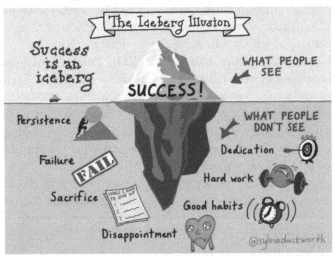

Source: Duckworth, S. (n.d.). *The iceberg illusion* [Online image]. Sylvia Duckworth Drawings. https://sylviaduckworth.shop/product/the-iceberg-illusion/. Reproduced with permission.

This challenge is reinforced when one considers that the introduction of learning outcomes in higher education was initially focused on academic affairs and educational disciplines (Adelman, 2015; AAC&U & NLC, 2007). More recently, there has been a shift from classroom-specific to more holistic student learning and development, a view championed by the American Association of Colleges and University's Liberal Education and America's Promise (LEAP) initiative. From that organization's guidance the assessment of attitudes and values outcomes, which include "affective outcomes, personal/professional/social values, [and] ethical principles" (Driscoll & Wood, 2007, p. 53) has emerged. This context subsequently led to the selection of National Survey of Student Engagement (NSSE) and College Senior Survey (CSS) items/results, that is, indirect evidence, to serve as the assessment data source.

Directed by researchers at Indiana University's Center for Postsecondary Research, NSSE annually collects information about undergraduates' participation in programs and activities related to student learning and personal development. The CSS is led by the Higher Education Research Institute, and its purpose is to track seniors' cognitive and affective growth during college by measuring such areas as the impact of service-learning, leadership development opportunities, faculty advising, instructional practices, satisfaction with campus facilities, and plans for the future. Items from the NSSE and CSS survey administrations at Boston College were mapped to Halftime's learning outcomes. Question selection was based on input from program administrators and resulted in a pool of items that blended subject matter expert input with a reasonable degree of face validity.

Using Propensity Score Matching (PSM), comparison groups were constructed in order to evaluate the formative impact of Halftime on program participants. Based on demographic variables, PSM assigns individuals who did not participate in a program the probability or likelihood of participating, thereby creating a comparison group that is similar to the participant group. This process resulted in equal-sized groups of Halftime participants and nonparticipants (Table 2.3).

Three tools were used to analyze the survey items and the differences on the item outcomes between the participant group and the nonparticipant group: chi-square tests (for items with categorical outcomes), t-tests (for items with roughly continuous outcomes), and linear regression to assess the value-added dimension of Halftime.

Learning Outcome: Halftime and Vocational Discernment

Several items demonstrated that participants in Halftime were meeting learning outcome number one (Figure 2.2). Perhaps most substantive was the difference between Halftime participants and nonparticipants on the item "making connections between your intellectual and spiritual life" with 84% of Halftime participants responding positively to this item, compared to 64% of nonparticipants.

Figure 2.2. To what extent has your experience at BC contributed to your development of each of the following?

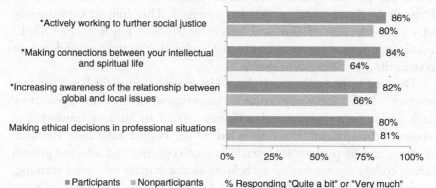

Note. * indicates p<.05, Jesuit Consortium items within National Survey of Student Engagement.

TABLE 2.3
Sample: Halftime Participants and Nonparticipants

	NSSE		CSS	
Halftime Program	Participants	Nonparticipants	Participants	Nonparticipants
	120	120	116	116

Additionally, there was a statistically significant difference between Halftime participants and nonparticipants on the importance of working for social change (p=.022), with Halftime participants responding that it was more important to work for social change than nonparticipants (Figure 2.3).

Learning Outcome: Halftime and the Integration of Reflective Habits

Survey respondents were asked to rate themselves on a series of traits compared with the average person their age (Figure 2.4). As with the first learning outcome, there was a statistically significant difference (p=.017) between Halftime participants and nonparticipants on their self-rating of self-understanding, a characteristic thought to affiliate with reflection.

Use of the Findings

Boston College's commitment to student formation is evidenced in its excellent cocurricular programming; however, the assessment of these programs has been challenging in that their collective, ambitious goal is to create experiences which catalyze "powerful learning [that] transforms how students view

Figure 2.3. When thinking about your career path after college, how important is working for social change?

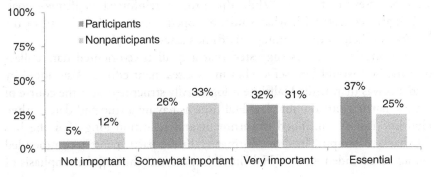

Figure 2.4. Rate yourself on self-understanding as compared with the average person your age.

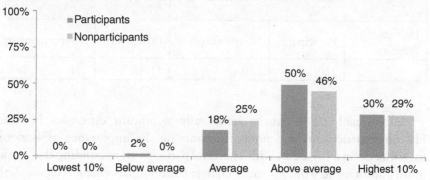

themselves and the world" (Fried, 2006, p. 5). The use of existing survey data to assess Halftime has served as a solid springboard for exploration, yet it has highlighted that reliance on indirect evidence is inadequate to fully understand student formation outcomes. The recognized benefits of using existing survey results, in terms of eliminating the need to collect new data as well as the solid psychometric properties they offer, were not outweighed by their lack of explicitly tapping into dimensions of student formation.

Thus, the use of these findings resulted not in program changes per se, but in changes to the assessment plan; rich discussion among program staff ensued, leading to the incorporation of students into the assessment process—not as data subjects, but as learning outcomes partners. In fact, "asking students to consider the best way to show that they have met the learning outcomes is often a very effective strategy" (Driscoll & Wood, 2007, p. 83).

Subsequently, several focus groups of recent Halftime participants convened, and brainstorming sessions centered on how Halftime meets its intended learning outcomes (a pseudo-curriculum mapping exercise) along with identifying methods, beyond self-report survey data, that might best serve as assessment tools. While this process reinforced Halftime's goals as being in concert with what students hoped they would derive from the program, it helped to recalibrate Halftime's assessment plan.

Specifically, students suggested that a qualitative-oriented data collection method would best serve Halftime's assessment efforts. Also noted by students was that, while Halftime is logistically structured over the course of 2 days, participants do not view Halftime as having a true end date; rather, Halftime fosters continued discernment and reflection long after the bus ride back to campus. In short, former Halftime participants recommended taking an extended view of Halftime's impact and shifting the emphasis of the current learning outcomes from the "knowledge" category of Bloom's taxonomy to the "application" category. Students' reminder to program staff was that the true gift of Halftime is its lasting impact on personal behavior that reveals itself in small ways over a long period of time.

Revisiting Vocational Discernment as a Learning Outcome

While Halftime's discernment-related learning outcome does highlight the goal of enabling students to connect Halftime to sound decision-making, focus group participants noted that this connection extends far beyond a resolution of knowing what comes post Boston College. It was an invitation to accept, and even celebrate, the uncertainty inherent in the journey. One student remarked, for example, that she had always felt inadequate or "behind her peers" when it came to knowing what she wanted to pursue after college. Halftime has been essential to her understanding that vocational discernment is very much a nonlinear process. Halftime has offered the "permission and roadmap" the student needed both to recognize her joys and talents, and be comfortable with some degree of ambiguity, thereby reinforcing Halftime's impact may be more appropriately measured over time.

Revisiting Reflection as a Learning Outcome

Focus group students reported that, post-Halftime, they noticed a difference in how they expressed themselves in "everyday life." In the Halftime setting, participants were encouraged to openly share with others. As a result of these honest exchanges, with undergraduate peers who were also strangers, students described gains in self-confidence and a desire to bring this same level of authenticity and vulnerability to their friend groups on campus.

> When I got back from Halftime, I realized that I had shared things about my life with people I hardly knew. I liked the way that being authentic made me feel and decided to try and talk to my roommates about some of the same issues and feelings I shared on Halftime. As a result, my buddies, in turn, opened up to me about aspects of themselves that I never knew. I would have never thought that my going on a retreat would end up making me closer to my roommates, but it did. (Student Participant)

Conclusion

Student formation at Boston College is fundamental to the undergraduate experience, and programs such as Halftime help to ensure the institution's integrity as a formative education leader. The measurement of formation, however, much like with any affective attribute, is a tall order. While the initial assessment cycle's use of survey data offered some insights, incorporating former Halftime student participants as partners in the assessment process was eye-opening to program staff. This revelation was true both in terms of validating what is working as intended, as well as highlighting how formation, and its facets such as discernment and reflection, are expressed to students during and after Halftime. Moving forward, student assessment partners will continue to serve as key contributors to the assessment of formation.

References

Adelman, C. (2015, February). *To imagine a verb: The language and syntax of learning outcome statements* (Occasional Paper No. 24). University of Illinois and Indiana University, National Institute for Learning Outcomes Assessment.

Association of American Colleges & Universities (AAC&U) & National Leadership Council (NLC). (2007). *College learning for the new global century: A report from the National Leadership Council for Liberal Education & America's Promise.* Association of American Colleges & Universities.

Borrego, S. E. (2006). Mapping the learning environment. In R. Keeling (Ed.), *Learning reconsidered 2* (pp. 11–16). American College Personnel Association.

Boston College. (2007). *The journey into adulthood: Understanding student formation.* https://www.Boston College.edu/content/dam/files/offices/mission/pdf1/umm1.pdf

Driscoll, A., & Wood, S. (2007). *Developing outcomes-based assessment for learner-centered education: A faculty introduction.* Stylus.

Duckworth, S. (n.d.). *The iceberg illusion* [Online image]. Sylvia Duckworth Drawings. https://sylviaduckworth.shop/product/the-iceberg-illusion/

Fried, J. (2006). Rethinking learning. In R. Keeling (Ed.), *Learning reconsidered 2* (pp. 3–9). American College Personnel Association.

Halpern, D. F., & Hakel, M. D. (2003). Applying the science of learning to the university and beyond: Teaching for long-term retention and transfer. *Change: The Magazine of Higher Learning, 35*(4), 36–41. https://search.proquest.com/scholarly-journals/applying-science-learning-university-beyond/docview/208050621/se-2?accountid=13567

Keeling, R. P. (Ed.). (2006). *Learning reconsidered 2: Implementing a campus-wide focus on the student experience.* ACPA, ACUHO-1, ACUI, NACA, NACADA, NASPA, and NIRSA.

Kolvenbach, P.-H. (2000, October 6). *The service of faith and the promotion of justice in American Jesuit higher education* [Conference address]. Commitment to Justice in Jesuit Higher Education Conference, Santa Clara University. https://onlineministries.creighton.edu/CollaborativeMinistry/Kolvenbach/Kolvenbach-SantaClara.pdf

Kuh, G. D. (2008). *High-impact educational practices: What they are, who has access to them, and why they matter.* Association of American Colleges and Universities.

Kuh, G. D., Gonyea, R. M., & Rodriguez, D. P. (2002). The scholarly assessment of student development. In T. W. Banta (Ed.), *Building a scholarship of assessment* (pp. 100–128). Jossey-Bass.

Platt, S., & Sayegh, S. (2015, October). *Student learning outcomes alignment through academic and student affairs partnerships.* University of Illinois and Indiana University, National Institute for Learning Outcomes Assessment.

Vaz, R. F. (2019, June 4). High-impact practices work. *Inside Higher Ed.* https://www.insidehighered.com/views/2019/06/04/why-colleges-should-involve-more-students-high-impact-practices-opinion

3

ASSESSMENT OF STUDENT LEARNING IN THE ARTS, HUMANITIES, SOCIAL SCIENCES, AND SCIENCES

Jeffrey R. Lindauer and Patricia A. Coward

Creating an effective and sustainable student learning assessment system and developing a culture of assessment requires administrative support, direct oversight, faculty development and buy-in, and constant refinement of processes and policies. This chapter explains the steps taken by a small, private, liberal arts-focused institution to create a student learning assessment system in a college of arts and sciences. The college concentrated on improving the student learning assessment system after an accreditation report identified deficiencies in documentation of student learning. Initially, efforts focused on educating faculty in assessment concepts and identifying early adopters who could help develop colleagues' knowledge and competency in assessment. Simultaneously, the college created a unit-wide assessment committee in charge of reviewing annual major assessment reports and providing faculty feedback on the validity and reliability of their assessment plans. The college assessment coordinator then aggregated program assessment information to communicate assessment system progress to unit administration and other stakeholders. The process evolved over several years, and the assessment of student learning is now firmly embedded in the culture of the College of Arts and Sciences.

Goals of Our Assessment

During one of Canisius College's regular accreditation self-study cycles, the 2005 evaluation team representing the Middle States Commission on Higher Education (MSCHE) noted one requirement related to then Standard 14: Assessment of Student Learning.

> Although there is evidence in the self-study and in the interviews and documents that some units of the College have articulated their expectations, there are significant gaps that need to be filled in order to comply fully with the requirements in *Characteristics of Excellence*. Although constructing such a plan and getting all units to articulate learning expectations are formidable tasks, these must be accomplished in order to comply with the Standard. (MSCHE, 2005, p. 20)

Canisius College is a comprehensive university located in Buffalo, New York, offering undergraduate, graduate, and professional programs to approximately 3,000 students. As one of 27 Catholic and Jesuit colleges in the United States, Canisius provides students with a transformative education rooted in a 450-year-old academic tradition of excellence, leadership, and service to others. The Jesuit values of *cura personalis* (care for the whole person), the pursuit of excellence, a commitment to social justice, and developing students who are "men and women for and with others" are central to the college's mission. Students are prepared for purposeful careers—and lives—through exceptional programs and liberal arts foundation that instill lifelong habits of reflection and critical thinking. Canisius strives to educate the whole person—intellectually, ethically, and spiritually—providing an experience that is highly personalized and collaborative.

The undergraduate majors in the College of Arts and Sciences, the Wehle School of Business, and the School of Education and Human Services offer students a wide range of professional and disciplinary programs that represent both traditional and emerging areas of study. The faculty in all of these schools are dedicated to academic excellence and providing their students with outstanding preparation for careers or for graduate study.

In response to our 2005 accreditation review, the College of Arts and Sciences intentionally developed structures to ensure both the assessment of student learning and the creation of a culture of assessment within the college. The definition of a *culture of assessment* has been explored by a number of assessment scholars, concluding that when an institution commits itself to assessment of student learning, it often leads to meaningful change and improvement (Fuller & Skidmore, 2014; Fuller et al., 2016; Suskie,

2009; Weiner, 2009). Presently, all College of Arts and Sciences programs, including the core curriculum (general education) are actively engaged in the assessment of student learning and have focused processes that have led to improvement in a number of areas. This chapter outlines the process faculty, staff, and administration took to achieve the goals of developing a system to assess program-level student learning; creating a culture of assessment among faculty, staff, and administrators; and ensuring quality in the assessments.

Activities/Strategies to Support Achievement of the Goals

The administrative structures of Canisius College are similar to other small, private, liberal arts-focused institutions. The Academic Affairs unit has three distinct schools, each with its own mission and discrete assessment practices, some determined by their accrediting bodies. Early on, the college administration determined that because of the disparate characteristics and needs of the schools, the administration of student learning assessment would be decentralized, with each of the three schools overseeing and planning its own assessment processes.

The 2005 MSCHE review team's conclusions regarding assessment revealed that, although assessment of student learning at Canisius College was happening in some areas, it was underdeveloped and poorly understood by most faculty and administrators. While the School of Education and Human Services had a well-developed assessment process in education due to its specialized accreditor (National Council for Accreditation of Teacher Education), the Wehle School of Business and the College of Arts and Sciences were deficient or developing. Most notably, systematic assessment of student learning was not occurring at any level in the College of Arts and Sciences at that time. As a result, the administration took several steps to begin changing the college's culture, with an emphasis on assessment of student learning. The institution hired two new personnel: a director of the Center for Teaching Excellence and an associate dean in the College of Arts and Sciences. Beginning in 2006 these individuals worked together to begin a program of education and planning for the assessment of student learning, specifically in the College of Arts and Sciences.

The first challenge was to convince faculty that assessment of student learning was both worthwhile and necessary in order to comply with the MSCHE standards. Most faculty had been working more or less autonomously, assuming that student grades would suffice as indicators of student learning. Therefore, early initiatives consisted of educating faculty in the language of assessment. We presented best practices in assessment to various groups of faculty—summative assessment, direct and indirect evidence, learning goals and objectives, rubrics, methods and measures of student learning, and so on (Allen, 2004; Banta et al., 2009; Suskie, 2009; Walvoord, 2004). We found that the most resistance came from the humanities faculty, which was no surprise because the humanities tend to be more subjective than the sciences or social sciences (Rohrbacher, 2017). Therefore, much focus was aimed at helping faculty in programs such as English, history, philosophy, and religious studies and theology understand how they could approach the practice of assessment in ways that both honored their disciplines and offered useful information that would lead to improvement of student learning.

While there was a college-level administrator responsible for planning and implementation, best practice indicates that assessment of student learning is most effectively accomplished as a faculty-driven activity (Banta, et al., 2009). However, faculty who were unfamiliar with much of the assessment of student learning work that occurred in the late 1990s and early 2000s had a steep learning curve. The College of Arts and Sciences immediately formed an Outcomes Assessment Advisory Committee consisting of six faculty members and an administrator/staff member. The committee was, and continues to be, composed of two tenured faculty members each from humanities, social sciences, and natural sciences. This new committee consulted on all aspects of assessment planning by reviewing all forms, frameworks, and policies. As faculty members, this group guided and helped shape the way programs throughout the college would approach the assessment of student learning.

The process, from initial steps to implementation of actual assessments, took 12 to 18 months. The Outcomes Assessment Advisory Committee asked programs to create *learning goals and objectives* (LGOs) with support and training from the Center for Teaching Excellence and the associate dean. Once the LGOs were established, programs were asked to map their goals to their curricula and to develop assessment plans with a timeline that would result in LGOs being assessed on a 4-year cycle. With LGOs, curriculum mapping, and assessment plans in place, programs submitted annual reports on their assessment activities (see Table 3.1). These reports followed a template that required programs to complete descriptors in each of the following categories (Instone, 2012):

- year assessment was conducted,
- population—assuring that students were at or near the completion of their programs,
- method—type of instrument used to assess,

- measure—how the instrument was evaluated,
- results—number of students who met, exceeded, or did not meet expectations,
- analysis of results—making sense of the results and identifying factors that contributed,
- actions—any changes in curriculum, pedagogy, methods/measures, and/or LGOs,
- link to previous assessments: compare results to any previous assessments of the LGOs, and
- communication—how/when results were shared and who was involved with actions.

The committee was charged with reviewing the annual assessment reports and offering any feedback/advice using the following criteria (Instone, 2012):

- Student learning objectives are appropriately significant and realistic in number (typically three to five goals and three to five objectives for each goal).
- Methods and measures are logical and adequately measure student achievement of the objectives and the methods and measures are in alignment with one another and with the goals and objectives.
- Selection of students and artifacts meet Outcomes Assessment Advisory Committee guidelines and are clearly described.
- Reported results identify the level of expected performance; indicate the number of students exceeding, meeting, and not meeting the objectives; and verify that the analysis and interpretation are thorough, logical, and derived from the results. Sample artifacts and scored measures are submitted representing each of the three evaluative levels.
- There is a description of actions to be taken based on the findings. If no actions are being taken this should be noted with corresponding rationale.
- Specific references are made to previous assessment outcomes for the objective and places current results in context (Closing the Loop).
- It is clear that faculty are involved at all points in the process of sharing and discussing results, and in plans to improve student learning.
- The timetable is reasonable. Every objective should be assessed at least once every 4 years.
- The timeline includes an indication of when objectives will be reassessed.

TABLE 3.1
Feedback Rubric

Department Name Assessment report review and feedback rubric 20xx–20xx College of Arts and Sciences (CAS)	
From the Outcomes Assessment Advisory Committee: It is our goal to help programs develop assessment processes that are useful, reasonably accurate and truthful, carefully planned and organized, systematic and sustained. The review rubric and our feedback are based on best practices for student learning assessment and accreditation requirements. It is our hope that aspects of student learning can be captured in the annual assessment reports and the knowledge gained from the information collected used to improve that learning.	
Learning objective/s assessed: Estimated number of graduating students in 20xx–20xx: General Comments:	
Learning Objectives	
Learning objective is expressed in clear, specific terminology and indicates what a student should know, do, or value (active verb and measurable)	*Suggestions for Consideration:*
	Additional information or clarification requested:
Program response:	
Assessment Type	
Summative assessment: work completed at or near the end of the program. Rationale provided if alternative to summative assessment used	*Suggestions for Consideration:*
	Additional information or clarification requested:
Program response:	
Participants and Student Artifacts	
Selection of students and artifacts meets CAS guidelines and is clearly described	*Suggestions for Consideration:*
	Additional information or clarification requested:
Scored artifacts uploaded	
Program response:	

Method	
Method is aligned with the learning objective (e.g., test, assignment instructions, paper prompt)	*Suggestions for Consideration:*
	Additional information or clarification requested:
Method uploaded	
Program response:	
Measure	
Measure is aligned with the learning objective and method (e.g., rubric, test blueprint, relevant questions, and scoring)	*Suggestions for Consideration:*
	Additional information or clarification requested:
Subjective artifacts are evaluated with more than one rater/scorer: Objective artifacts use a reasonable number of items	*Suggestions for Consideration:*
	Additional information or clarification requested:
Measure uploaded	
Program response:	
Results, Analysis, and Interpretation	
Specifies level of achievement associated with each level of expectation (e.g., score of 90 or better exceeds, 75–89 meets, 0–74 is below)	*Suggestions for Consideration:*
	Additional information or clarification requested:
Results: The number of students not meeting, meeting, and exceeding expectations reported	*Suggestions for Consideration:*
	Additional information or clarification requested:
Clear attempt made to make sense of the information collected. The analysis and interpretation are thorough, logical, and derived from the results	*Suggestions for Consideration:*
	Additional information or clarification requested:
Program response:	

Actions to Maintain/Improve Student Learning	
Describes specific actions to be taken based on the findings. If no actions are being taken this is noted with corresponding rationale (note: discussion is a prelude to an action—not the action itself)	*Suggestions for Consideration:*
	Additional information or clarification requested:
Program response:	
Closing the Loop (Continuous Improvement)	
Specific reference to previous assessment outcomes for the objective and places current results in context	*Suggestions for Consideration:*
	Additional information or clarification requested:
Program response:	
Program Involvement in Assessment Review	
Assessment findings and report discussed with program members for input prior to submission	*Suggestions for Consideration:*
	Additional information or clarification requested:
Program response:	

In the first years, the reported processes were often weak, as faculty were learning what worked and what did not work in their assessment practice. Over time, a number of programs improved assessment practices and began to buy in to assessment, especially when they learned something useful that could impact their curricula. In one case, a program discovered through curriculum mapping that some of their objectives were not being introduced or reinforced anywhere in their required coursework. For them, the fix was easy—they revised some courses to address the objectives. Each time that the assessment process resulted in curricular improvements or in more effective or efficient assessment practices, the associate dean would share the story with department chairs and program directors, documenting and acknowledging the positive effects of the process.

An indication of the emerging culture of assessment was evident when faculty on the committee were training themselves in assessment practices, with guidance from the Center for Teaching Excellence and the associate dean. As faculty on the committee practiced their oversight of assessment processes, they were learning (and critically analyzing) best practices and developing a language of assessment, ultimately bringing their expertise back to their colleagues. In fact, several of these faculty then became the assessment coordinators for their programs.

The following process has been adopted for assessment review. The Outcomes Assessment Advisory Committee's procedures facilitate consistency, timely feedback, and opportunities for programs to address questions prior to final evaluation. Program assessment reports are submitted soon after the spring semester ends and the committee reviews those reports during the summer. The administrative committee member organizes teams of three faculty members (one member representing each of the subdisciplines) with each committee member serving on two review teams. Each team reviews five–seven reports, so each committee member reviews 10–14 reports in total. Upon completing the review, committee members discuss relevant feedback or request clarification to include in a rubric designed by the committee to comment on the quality of the elements listed in Table 3.1.

Committee member feedback is available to the program by the end of each summer, and program faculty are asked to respond to any areas of concern emerging from the program assessment review. During the fall semester, the committee finalizes the report of the programs reviewed during the current cycle and forwards the results to the dean of College of Arts and Sciences.

The Outcomes Assessment Advisory Committee review process has facilitated the culture of assessment in the College of Arts and Sciences. From the beginning, the teams understood the expectation to provide feedback on the quality of the process, rather than on the specific assessment results. Thus, programs that had few students meeting an objective were encouraged to address the deficiency rather than being criticized for finding the gap. Common committee feedback included issues such as the need for stronger rubrics for subjective work or assuring that the population reflected a summative assessment. This feedback loop has contributed to improving assessment processes in all programs over the period of a decade. In large part due to consistent and regular feedback, the assessment of student learning is now firmly embedded in the culture of the College of Arts and Sciences. Initial voices of resistance have quieted, and faculty members routinely refer to assessment when creating new programs and courses.

Assessments Used to Determine Progress Toward Goal

In the early stages of designing and implementing the assessment process, the College of Arts and Sciences emphasized quality control and documentation of any progress made toward the achievement of a culture of assessment.

TABLE 3.2
College of Arts and Sciences Assessment Dashboard

	Year	08–09	09–10	10–11	11–12	12–13	13–14	14–15	15–16	16–17	17–18	18–19
Program A	New Program											M
Program B		M	M	M	M	M	M	M	E	E	M	D
Program C		M	D	M	M	E	E	M	D	M	M	D
Program D		M	M	M	M	E	M	M	E	E	M	M
Program E		M	M	M	M	E	sm	sm	sm	E	sm	sm
D	Some info collected/incomplete or missing info/developing processes											
M	Info submitted/complete/meets guidelines											
E	Exemplary report/assessment practices/use of assessment to understand learning											
sm	Small major: average 0–6 graduating students/year, with data gathered and aggregated over several years											

The dean's summary reports model the documentation process. Those reports record progress and the feedback given to the programs to help improve their processes. The summary reports chronicle the programs evaluated, a rating of each program's progress as determined by the reviewing teams, what was assessed (i.e., content or writing), a summary of how the results were used, and the progress programs were making toward acceptable or even exemplary assessment processes and improvements in student learning. The reports document this progress with a dashboard to provide a visual summary (see Table 3.2). Each reviewing team determines the levels of achievement for each program at the conclusion of the review process.

In this table, Program A is a new program, so there has thus far been just one round of assessment, and the program meets the Outcomes Assessment Advisory Committee guidelines for effective assessment practice. Program B demonstrates that it is possible to have a mix of accomplishments over time. Because different objectives were being assessed in different years, it is possible that the assessments in 2015–2016 and 2016–2017 were exemplary because they designed an effective rubric and method that worked well and offered constructive results for those objectives. However, the process in 2018–2019 may have been deemed "developing" because they were based on a more complicated objective, and the design of an effective method of assessment was still developing. This feedback offers the program an opportunity to revisit the methods and design better assessments for that particular set of objectives.

This "dashboard" offers a visual impression of how programs progress in their assessment processes: what they did well and where they could benefit from improvement. It offers the dean the ability to see, at a glance, where the college programs were with respect to the quality of their assessments and where an investment of resources might improve those processes.

Use of the Findings

At the end of each 4-year assessment cycle, programs review annual assessment reports and complete a 4-year assessment summary that the College of Arts and Sciences administration reviews. Program faculty reflect on several things, including:

- appropriateness of the learning goals and objectives,
- whether or not all learning goals and objectives are aligned with specific learning opportunities in the curriculum,
- the adequacy of student learning evidence (direct and indirect measures),

- actions taken to improve student learning,
- examples of direct evidence that the actions taken led to improvement in student learning, and
- what was learned through the assessment process about the program's approach to, and success with, improving student learning.

These 4-year reviews provide data that has informed curricular changes including the content treated in individual courses, the sequencing of information within and between courses, and the addition of courses to address skills or knowledge gaps.

The 4-year assessment summary report is also helpful in communicating student learning to various stakeholders. For example, the college's Academic Program Board reviews programs once every 3 years. This board consists of 23 faculty, staff, and administrators with representation from all parts of academic affairs (i.e., registrar, deans, Faculty Senate, etc.) and is overseen by the vice president for academic affairs. The Academic Program Board oversees the assessment of student learning for each academic program and ensures that programs have valid and reliable assessment processes that yield meaningful data. The board is responsible for maintaining and enhancing the quality of academic programs, ultimately influencing institutional planning. It works directly with the college's Strategic Planning Committee and Budget Committee. For example, a program that has poor student learning outcomes over the 4-year period may be able to build a case that poor student performance is due to the lack of full-time faculty expertise in a specific area. The student learning information along with other data (i.e., full-time faculty to student ratio, profession staffing recommendations, etc.) may convince the Academic Program Board to recommend the college Budget Committee add a faculty line.

Conclusion

Creating an effective system of student learning assessment and developing a culture of assessment are long-term processes that require support from senior leadership, dedication by administration and faculty, and procedures developed and maintained to guide the process. Since 2005, the College of Arts and Sciences has been on a journey of continuous improvement in the assessment of student learning. The latest MSCHE reaccreditation visit/report in 2015 affirmed the college's efforts.

The College of Arts and Sciences administration, faculty, and the Outcomes Assessment Advisory Committee continue to refine the assessment process to meet the needs of multiple stakeholders. Significant lessons we learned from our experience include: (a) there needs to be a person responsible for the assessment of student learning in each school, (b) assessment of student learning needs constant attention, and (c) the process must be faculty driven.

Faculty may initially see the assessment of student learning as burdensome and another responsibility that takes them away from their teaching, scholarship, and service. However, it is possible to get them to accept and embrace the process. Ultimately faculty may even convince their colleagues that assessment of student learning can help their programs become stronger and more effective, while fulfilling the expectations of our accreditors.

References

Allen, M. J. (2004). *Assessing academic programs in higher education.* Anker Publishing.

Banta, T. W., Jones, E. A., & Black, K. E. (2009). *Designing effective assessment: Principles and profiles of good practice.* Jossey-Bass.

Fuller, M. B., & Skidmore, S. T. (2014). An exploration of factors influencing institutional cultures of assessment. *International Journal of Educational Research, 65,* 9–21. https://doi.org/10.1016/ijer.2014.01.001

Fuller, M. B., Skidmore, S. T., Bustamante, R. M., & Holzweiss, P. C. (2016). Empirically exploring higher education cultures of assessment. *The Review of Higher Education, 39*(3), 395–429. https://doi.org/10.1353/rhe.2016.0022

Instone, D. (2012). *Orientation to assessment of student learning in majors/programs in CAS: Getting started.* Canisius College: College of Arts and Sciences.

Middle States Commission on Higher Education. (2005). *Report to the faculty, administration, trustees, students of Canisius College, Buffalo, NY* [Unpublished report]. Canisius College.

Rohrbacher, C. (2017). Humanities professors' conceptions of assessment: A case study. *The Journal of General Education, 66*(1), 17–41. https://www.muse.jhu.edu/article/703254

Suskie, L. (2009). *Assessing student learning: A common sense guide* (2nd ed.). Jossey-Bass.

Walvoord, B. E. (2004). *Assessment clear and simple: A practical guide for institutions, departments, and general education.* Jossey-Bass.

Weiner, W. (2009). Establishing a culture of assessment. *Academe, 95*(4), 28–32. www.jstor.org/stable/40253350

4

LEVERAGING TECHNOLOGY TO FACILITATE ASSESSMENT PROCESSES

Scott Carnz, Mary Mara, and Amy Portwood

Colleges and universities experience a greater need than ever to show the efficacy of their programs and their teaching due to increased accountability for institutions to show student attainment of learning outcomes. Yet, there remains a lack of agreement on best approaches to assess student achievement of learning outcomes (Council for Higher Education Accreditation, 2019). Like many institutions, City University of Seattle (CityU) has grappled with the best approach to assessing student achievement and has explored a number of learning outcome assessment management systems.

In seeking software solutions to assist in the collection, distribution, visualization, and analysis of student achievement data, university leadership at CityU evaluated a variety of off-the-shelf options. Most solutions provided the ability to facilitate full assessments of student learning from the course level to the program and institution levels. However, all of the software came at significant cost and required a great deal of work to implement. Most of the solutions were also designed with traditional institutions in mind and with a focus on undergraduate programs.

CityU is a relatively small, tuition-driven institution that serves a mainly adult student population. The institution does not admit first-time, full-time freshmen. Undergraduate students, who comprise roughly 43% of the fall 2019 headcount, are primarily degree completers. The majority of the remaining students are studying in graduate or doctoral programs.

Given these demographics, none of the off-the-shelf solutions were viable for the university. They were either too expensive given the resources of a small, tuition-driven university, or they were not the right fit for our mix of students and programs. Instead, the university sought solutions that drew on its existing systems, which would be more cost effective and less labor-intensive to set up and manage.

Mapping and Assessing Learning Outcomes Within Programs

Before any platform could be utilized to assess learning outcomes, an important step was ensuring accurate mapping of program learning outcomes to individual courses and specific assignments within courses. As with the assessment management tools on the market, the curriculum management tools that existed were also very expensive and demanded a significant time frame to work with a third-party vendor to convert all curricular materials to an off-the-shelf management system. Therefore, instead of purchasing an existing tool, CityU opted to build a proprietary curriculum development system (CDS) utilizing the SharePoint platform. While there was cost in terms of staff time to develop the system, the level of customization it allowed and the time frame in which it could be implemented outweighed those costs and still meant a more affordable solution for the institution. With this system, programs developed program design guides (PDGs) that facilitated the mapping necessary to identify assignments within individual courses, from which assessment data needed to be pulled. This approach worked well with the university's centralized curriculum model in which courses are built as master shells, with the majority of the courses built and provided to instructors. The instructors then augment the contents to fit their particular approach to their courses.

CityU utilizes Blackboard as its learning management system. When the university initially adopted it, the first inclination was to utilize the Outcomes and Assessment tool that is native to the Blackboard platform. The tool allows users to identify the assignments within individual courses that assess student achievement of program learning outcomes and to pull those assessment results into an aggregated format. However, as with many of the off-the-shelf options that have been considered, the standardized reporting options that the Outcomes and Assessment tool provided were not robust enough for the level of assessment that the university sought to achieve. The main deficiency of the product was that the reporting tools are not detailed enough to allow filtering by student demographics or other characteristics that were of interest to CityU. In addition, feedback from peer institutions that were using the Outcomes and Assessment tool indicated that it was time consuming to build out and difficult to maintain over time.

As an alternative, the university turned to Blackboard's secondary rubric tool. Through this tool, faculty would grade all individual student assignments on a primary rubric, and then complete a secondary rubric on which they aggregated the individual student results to determine the degree to which the group of students as a whole had achieved the particular outcome, or component of the outcome being assessed. To facilitate the program-wide assessment, the university's IT team wrote scripts that would extract the secondary rubric assessment data from Blackboard tables and export them into .csv files.

With the data in a form that could be sorted and parsed, they could also be cross-referenced and sorted against data in the student information system and other university systems for analysis purposes. CityU utilizes PeopleSoft as a student information system and maintains a proprietary customer relationship management (CRM) system. A variety of data were and are extracted from both for use in assessment analysis.

One of the pitfalls of implementing a proprietary system is the risk of not being able to see the project completely through to the end. Such was the case with the CityU CDS. The final stage of design for the CDS was never completed. This final stage would have allowed the outcome alignments to be built into the system, rather than stored separately as they are on individual Word docs. Also, while each program director was to have their PDGs approved via curriculum councils, over time this practice was lost, so the accuracy of what was mapped and what was actually being collected was increasingly lost. Program directors made changes and stored them on their personal computers, and when they left the university their work was lost.

When secondary rubrics were implemented there was a big push by eLearning to work with program directors to update PDGs before implementing the secondary rubrics so that accuracy could be restored.

Ensuring Data Integrity

Integrating the university's various systems—student information system, learning management system, CRM, and a small host of other proprietary systems—came with a number of challenges, the first of which centered on the reliability of the available data.

Data-driven decision-making has become an essential component of policy setting, program planning and assessment, and the design of educational experiences throughout higher education (Rhodes, 2017), as well as at CityU. However, not all institutions have robust data systems, nor the culture in which the expectation is to rely on data consistently as a basis for university- or college-wide decision-making. Establishing and maintaining such data systems can be a particular challenge for smaller, private institutions like CityU.

The university had at its disposal a wide variety of data sets and ways to access them via the variety of systems previously listed. However, there was a problem: The data could be inconsistent. Depending on who was pulling the data, from where and when the data was drawn, and what permissions a particular user had, the data would be different. This situation caused a good deal of frustration, many heated discussions, and led to a general distrust of the data that were available. For an institution aiming to rely on data as a basis for its assessment and decision-making processes, this was a huge obstacle. What the university needed was what CityU's director of information technology called a *single point of truth*.

To solve the issue and provide university leaders with a single, reliable source of data that all stakeholders could agree on, in 2014 the university's IT team joined forces with the campus data team to begin a project to standardize the reporting of university information internally by creating a data warehouse. The idea behind the project was to create standard data structures with well-defined data definitions and formats. Data in the warehouse are sourced from PeopleSoft, Blackboard, and the CRM. IT created a set of institutional-level reports that contained numbers of students, enrollments, credits, and revenue by academic year and term that could be filtered by segment of the student population, school, and degree program. In addition to these original data areas, there are now course and program outcome assessment data, end-of-course evaluation data, data about inquiry and application activity, library usage data, and more. The data are stored in an MS SQL server database and are extracted on a daily basis using SQL scripts. In addition to being used for assessment purposes, business and data analysts on campus have used data warehouse data to create dashboards and reports for personnel in enrollment and advising, academic deans, program directors, and the business office.

The intended outcome of the data warehouse was to use the centralized data repository and stable definitions to create dashboards and reports to improve data-driven decision-making. The goal of the project may sound simple, but it required concerted effort by multiple departments to bring it to fruition. In particular, there was a substantial emphasis on data validation, especially since the data were being drawn from several disparate systems.

The validation process was iterative and conducted cross-departmentally and cross-functionally by several stakeholders from the core management reporting (CMR) team. The process began with user interviews to understand how various reports were being utilized and pain points experienced. These interviews were also meant to identify vital reports/data points for decision-making and to develop clarity surrounding how problems or goals were being solved with data at both the operational and strategic levels. The CMR team then worked to identify specific data sources that would be required and useful in the data warehouse (e.g., tables in People Soft). Once the identified fields were rendered into the data warehouse via an SQL server, the validation process began in earnest. All major operational data points were validated using established queries. Individual records were data mined when discrepancies were identified. Typically, the causes of those discrepancies were either data entry error, lack of clarity surrounding business process and how data were captured in the warehouse, or differentiated business processes across different departments or CityU segments (e.g., Canada, international partners, international students in the United States, and U.S. domestic students).

It is important to note that CityU's vigorous validation process resulted in substantially increased confidence in, and transparency regarding, data across all entities. A data analytics team was created to establish best practices for sharing reports and analysis across business units, as well as a Data Governance Committee to determine and manage data roles, understand and meet institutional data/reporting requirements, and streamline our data capture to meet the needs of all stakeholders. CityU is committed to ongoing validation as an institutional imperative. This goal is especially important as the data warehouse and our reporting capabilities expand and are enhanced by even more nuanced and strategic data capture, furthering our commitment to making data-driven strategic and operational decisions.

Finding Common Definitions

Critical to this effort was the establishment of some common terms and definitions for key data points. One example of establishing a common definition was clearly articulating what the campus meant by *graduation rate*. Because of CityU's unique population and the university's focus on students fulfilling their academic goals, whatever they may be, more traditional calculations of graduation rates were not meaningful for quality assessment purposes. Seeking a measure that was both useful for the institution and consistent with other measures in higher education, CityU settled on the use of the calculation for completion suggested by the *Chronicle of Higher Education's* College Completion project (O'Leary, 2021). In short, the calculation includes a broader population of students beyond those counted in IPEDS and shows the number of completions per 100 students. This was a measure that was both meaningful for the university and could be applied to the entire student population across all degree and certificate levels.

Visualizing the Data

Once data could be reliably counted on to be accurate, the team then set out to find ways to make that data visible and usable to the staff and leadership teams. It was important that in addition to having reliable data, department and university leaders had easy means to parse and interact with the data in order to make sense of them. The IT and data teams decided on Power BI as the tool to accomplish this goal. While there are several options for data visualization tools, Power BI proved to integrate well with the university's existing systems. Furthermore, being concerned with the expenditure of student tuition dollars, it was important that it was also a more affordable option.

Since 2017, the teams have worked to build a series of dashboards in Power BI that make visible the key data campus leaders must continuously

Figure 4.1. Core theme I dashboard.

Core Theme 1. Deliver High-Quality Relevant Education				
Objective	Indicator		Measure	Target
Objective 1A CityU supports the achievement of student learning outcomes	1A1. Program learning outcomes (PLOs)	1A1a. Student attainment of program learning outcomes	PLOs Achieved CLICK FOR MORE DETAILED ANALY... 84%	**Achieved** Percentage of program learning outcomes (PLOs) at standard or exceeds standards 80%
	1A2. CityU learning goals (CULGs)	1A2a. Student attainment of CityU learning goals by academic program	CULGs Achieved CLICK FOR MORE DETAILED ANALY... 87%	**Achieved** Percent of CityU learning goals (GULGs) at standard or exceeds standard 80%

Core Theme 1. Deliver High-Quality Relevant Education				
Objective	Indicator		Measure	Target
Objective 1B CityU champions effective and innovative teaching	1B1. Instructional quality	1B1a. End of course evaluations by school and delivery mode	EOCE Average Response Sco... CLICK FOR MORE DETAILED ANALYSIS 4.22	**Achieved** Increase average response score 4.0 5-point Likert scale
		1B1b. Student ratings of instructional quality a reported on student surveys	SSS Average Response Sco... CLICK FOR MORE DETAILED ANALYSIS 3.14	**Achieved** Increase average response score 3.0 4-point Likert scale

monitor to be effective and to keep their eyes on the prize: our students' success. One excellent example can be found in the dashboards that were built to monitor achievement of the university mission's core themes. A dashboard for each theme aggregates the data for the indicators of the theme's objectives and provides a determination as to whether or not the targets have been met. Figure 4.1 shows an example of the Core Theme I dashboard and two of its objectives. This visualization provides a quick, at-a-glance means to determine ongoing mission fulfillment.

One of the advantages of a data visualization tool like Power BI is that it provides the ability to drill down into the specific data set for further analysis (Figure 4.2). The subpages of the dashboard allow users to analyze the data by rubric type, year, school, and program. Users can also look at specific rubric rows representing distinct learning goals. This example shows student achievement of institutional learning goals and the options available to analyze the data in a variety of ways.

To use this as a basis for continual improvement we can, for example, look specifically at the learning goal related to college transfers. While this outcome exceeds standard in some areas, it is one of the lower-performing outcomes. We can then look at results within specific years to see if there is a trend up or down in the data. If the trend is downward, leaders can look within specific schools and programs to determine where adjustments might be warranted to reverse the trend. By finding the lower scoring programs in

Figure 4.2. Core theme dashboard details.

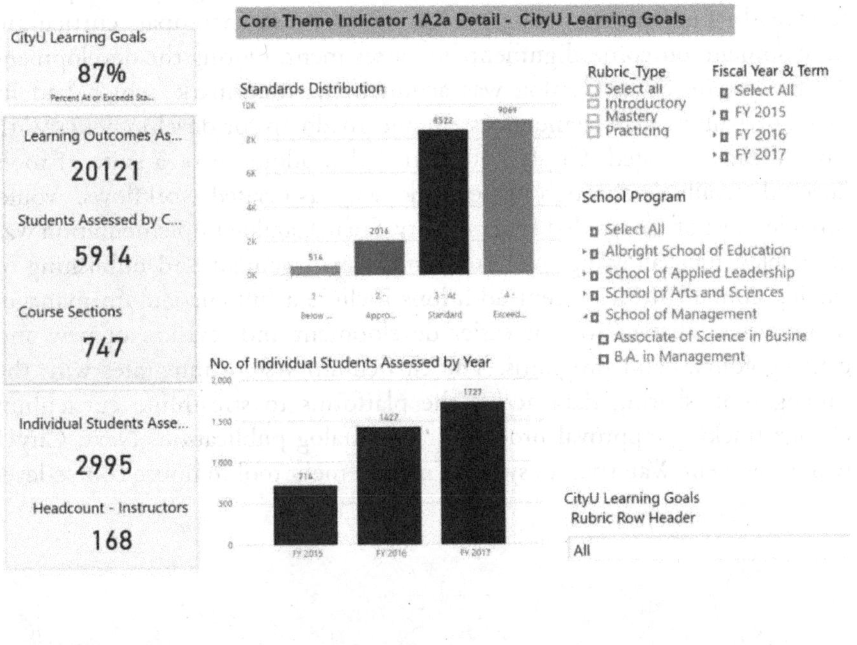

this area, it is possible to identify programs in need of improvement. Drilling down further, leaders can review the individual courses from which those assessments are drawn and work with the director to make whatever corrections (instructional, curricular, delivery mode, etc.) might be needed to drive greater student achievement of that outcome.

Assessing the Process

Any good assessment program contains a component in which the assessment process itself is assessed for efficacy and usefulness. After several years of use, campus leadership has evaluated the current processes and identified a number of refinements that will better ensure a focus on continuous improvement.

A New Curriculum Management System

Over the course of the nearly 10 years that the university's proprietary curriculum development system has been in use, the demands placed on it have become more sophisticated and it has become increasingly difficult to maintain. It has also become difficult to get the system to interact with other systems on campus, which has hampered some efforts to streamline processes across departments. Campus leadership conducted a cost-benefit analysis and determined that working with a third-party vendor to establish a new system was the most prudent and cost-effective move going forward. CityU has been working with Watermark to implement its curriculum management system.

The university initially contracted with SmartCatalog as a beta-partner to extend its university catalog publishing system to encompass curriculum development, outcome alignment, and assessment. During the development of the system, SmartCatalog was acquired by Watermark, which had its own curriculum management system and roadmap for development. With time already invested, CityU determined that adoption of a suite of tools currently available through Watermark, with associated workflows, would provide most of the needed functionality. SmartCatalog implementation was completed first, allowing for more nimble management and publishing of catalog content. More recent additions include a full curriculum management system that allows for easier development and revision of new and existing courses and programs. The curriculum system integrates with the catalog tool, sharing data across the platforms to streamline curriculum change tracking, approval processes, and catalog publication. Next, CityU will implement Watermark's syllabus management tool to house course-level details such as assignments and academic policies, and ExLibris' Leganto tool to manage course resource adoptions.

Revising Outcome Assessment Data Collection

Migration to the new curriculum management system prompted a review of the university's program outcome assessment practices. After several years of collecting secondary rubric data, a review of the longitudinal data identified a few consistent issues. The main advantage of the use of secondary rubrics was that faculty could assess individual students and provide developmental feedback without impacting course grades, particularly at the introductory and practice levels. However, there were a number of challenges with this approach.

The first and most significant challenge was the faculty completion rate of secondary rubrics. Our institution largely utilizes scholar-practitioner faculty who work in their field in addition to teaching in their discipline. Therefore, one of the most common complaints the university heard from faculty regards the burden of grading. Asking faculty to grade individual student assignments and then asking them to aggregate those results and assess overall student achievement of learning outcomes at the introductory, practice, and mastery levels was a burden many felt was too great. Others would simply forget to take the additional step to complete the secondary rubric after completing the grading rubric.

Another challenge of this approach was that many of the program outcomes being assessed were complex, with multiple sublevel outcomes. These complex outcomes were being assessed with high-level rubrics that were not sufficiently validated across instructors. This fact meant that the resulting data were questionable and difficult to use in driving action. Further, alignment between complex program outcomes and course assignments sometimes resulted in an assessment that only addressed one of four elements in an outcome. Again, this meant the data were questionable.

Given these issues, academic leadership decided to forgo secondary rubrics and instead rely on data from the primary grading rubrics. This decision in turn prompted a review of the individual program learning outcomes. Many of CityU's programs are professionally focused and in the past have had specific program outcomes that would change fairly frequently as industries changed rapidly. As existing programs reviews are completed, program outcomes will be revised such that they are written at an appropriately broad level to avoid the need for frequent revisions.

CityU's program outcome data will be drawn from learning outcomes structured with rubric criteria that roll up to determine overall achievement of program outcomes, capturing single concepts relevant to the program outcome. Learning outcomes will be embedded in primary grading rubrics. The intent is to increase the value/validity of the data by having more consistent data available. Assessment drawn from primary grading rubrics results in larger data pools, as there is no reliance on faculty remembering to complete a secondary rubric. By nature of completing their course grading, faculty are providing data for outcome assessment. Having more data available means bigger Ns, which mean more reliable data.

Another advantage to making this switch is that students will receive feedback on their achievement of outcomes. Some programs will apply this information toward the student grade, while others will only use it as feedback. The same process will be used for all general education or specialized accreditation outcomes.

Despite the move to the use of primary rubrics, the university still does not plan to adopt the native Blackboard Outcomes and Assessment tool. Each assignment that serves as an assessment point will be tagged in Blackboard as *CityU Learning Goal*, which will allow the scripts written by the IT team to extract the data from Blackboard tables and then align them to the outcome maps for each program for inclusion in the data warehouse. This approach provides greater flexibility in reporting, is easier for end-users who may be responsible for outcome alignment, and is less time-intensive to implement.

Improving Data Visualization

The next iteration of data visualization that the university is working on is the development of program health cards within the Power BI landscape. These health cards aggregate a variety of data into a single dashboard that deans, program directors, and program managers can use to monitor the on going status of their programs. program health cards will include operational data about student flow: new start, persistence, drop, and completion rates. They will also provide some financial data related to the management of teaching costs. Most importantly, the dashboards will provide an ongoing view of student achievement, including data on end-of-course evaluation scores, grade distribution, general education outcomes assessment (for undergraduate programs), and program outcomes assessment drawn from the rubrics in the learning management system. The data team completed a first draft with programmatic operational data as a proof-of-concept. Figure 4.3 shows an early draft of health cards for four programs in the School of Health and Social Sciences. The figure indicates that there are items up from the previous year, items that are flat year-over-year, and items that are down. The items with scores grant zero "points" if an item is down from previous year, five points if it is flat year-over-year, and 10 if it is up from the previous year.

Figure 4.3. Health card.

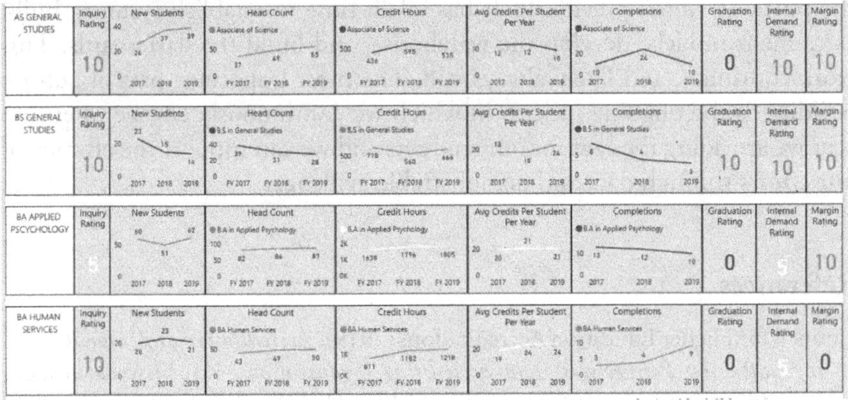

As with the Core Theme dashboards, each of these data sets will have the ability to drill down to the course and faculty levels, with the aim of providing directors the ability to manage continuous improvement in real time without having to wait for annual program reviews. Power BI allows filtering of data across multiple fields including school, student demographics, location, instructor, program, academic year, or term, and so on, allowing for more refined and nuanced analysis of outcome and other data.

The health cards will generate and inform academic program assessment reports and guide the university in continuous improvement efforts. The ability to parse data in Power BI by student demographic data will also guide CityU in efforts to close equity gaps in student achievement.

Conclusion

It takes commitment from senior leadership to focus resources on leveraging technological solutions that establish usable and meaningful data systems. It takes flexibility and a willingness to evolve with technology to keep systems fresh and relevant. It takes further focus to establish a culture that uses the data regularly and is comfortable relying on them as a means to base decisions. Efforts must provide a framework for staff on how to interpret and understand the data, how to use them in evaluation and assessment of operational effectiveness, and how to use them to help determine best solutions to institutional issues. Done well, this strategy supports the institution's focus on student success and a true reflective practice to improve in this area.

CityU is still maturing and evolving in its use of technology and data for the purposes noted previously. It has taken time to establish systems, build assessment models, develop the warehouse, and build the dashboards. This work continues, and likely always will. The most important part of culture building is the ongoing process in which we continuously engage to ensure that we are doing the best for our students and we can support the efficacy of our efforts through data and demonstrable evidence.

References

Council for Higher Education Accreditation. (2019). *Accreditation and student learning outcomes: Perspectives from accrediting organizations.* https://www.chea.org/sites/default/files/pdf/Accreditation%20and%20Student%20Learning%20Outcomes%20-%20Final.pdf

O'Leary, Brian. (2021, January 14). Student outcomes [data]. *Chronicle of Higher Education.* https://web.archive.org/web/20161103084115/http://collegecompletion.chronicle.com/about/

Rhodes, T. (2017). *The VALUE of learning: Meaningful assessment on the rise.* Association of American Colleges & Universities. https://www.aacu.org/liberaleducation/2017/winter/rhodes

5

INDIGENOUS ASSESSMENT

Cultural Relevancy in Assessment of Student Learning

Stephen Wall, Lara M. Evans, and Porter Swentzell

At the 2019 Higher Learning Commission (HLC) conference there was a session titled "Streamlining Assessment." The presenters used an interactive technique to get the 100 or so audience members on their feet. Once the audience was standing, the presenters asked that everyone whose institution had problems with assessment, whose assessment process was not working or had created problems, to please sit down. Everyone sat down except for Stephen Wall, a professor at a small tribal college focused on arts and culture.[1] If other colleagues had been in this session, rather than strategically dispersed to other sessions, they also would have remained standing. How did this happen? And can the assessment model of that tribal college, the Institute of American Indian Arts (IAIA), help other institutions turn assessment into a practice that is not just useful, but beneficial? This chapter presents the institution's assessment model.

Lara M. Evans, art historian from IAIA, recalls that the institution's team spent a substantial amount of time discussing what was wrong with various assessment approaches before discarding common approaches and starting to develop their own. She says,

> It's easy to be negative and pick something apart. Creating a new solution is much more difficult; and feels terribly risky when the stakes are as high as accreditation for a college. We had to start with complicated questions, not just "what is assessment?" but *"who* is assessment for?" When the answer is that assessment is for our own community, inclusive of all of our employees, students and their families, alumnae and their families, the subsequent questions that arise shift dramatically.

Asking that question made it clear IAIA was a community doing research on itself and using that research to guide decisions, planning, and structures. Indigenous research methodologies have been used by the institution's faculty and students for decades. Designing an assessment process based in Indigenous research methodologies was a clear path forward.

Indigenous Methodologies

In her book *Decolonizing Methodologies*, Linda Tuhiwai Smith (1999) criticized research that is not done for the community, but is conducted for the benefit of people and institutions outside of the community with all of the assumptions and biases that the outside researchers bring to the research. As the title implies, Smith's book became a call for Indigenous researchers and communities to decolonize research processes and move away from methods that did not serve the needs of the researched community. Her book unleashed an avalanche of researchers, academicians, and writers who began to adopt and speak to a variety of research methods that are based in processes and values found in Indigenous communities. Smith clearly gave permission to Indigenous researchers and writers to challenge Western definitions and standards for "objective research." While all of those researchers and writers contributed a great deal to the understanding of Indigenous research methodologies, the reality is that each community must decide for itself what research methods will be compatible with community values and culture and will provide the data that fulfill the community needs. This fact leads to three specific concepts: (a) the research meets the needs of the community, (b) community cultural values are built into the research, and (c) the community is an integral part of the research process, not just as informants or sources of data. The IAIA team embarked on developing an assessment model grounded in specific cultural values and practices from at-risk, minority communities that share strategic viewpoints yet have extremely diverse traditions. These factors helped the team develop its own method, but there are paths for any institution to follow, no "indigenousness" required. A wide range of resources describing community-based participatory research can serve as theoretical grounding for any institution seeking to change assessment to fit their institution, rather than change the institution in order to make assessment happen (see, e.g., Etmanski et al., 2014; Glenwick & Jason, 2016; Long & Beckman 2016).

The IAIA Indigenous assessment committee determined that as an Indigenous art school with limited academic programs, its assessment process needed to be comparable to a research project using Indigenous research methodologies. While the institution specifically identifies the approach's Indigenous theoretical basis, community-based participatory action research has many commonalities and may be familiar to more readers. First and foremost, the college needed to "own" the project, meaning that it needed to design a process that met its needs and not the needs or expectations of an outside agency or institution. Second, the college needed to ensure that values foundational to IAIA culture were included in the assessment process. Third, IAIA needed a process that would be understood and accepted by the faculty, not just as sources of data or results of the assessment, but through their active support and participation. Lastly, the college wanted to find a way to assess student learning in a way that could help students *now*, not in 4 years.

Goal of Assessment

Assessment of program outcomes and student learning outcomes has become a major tool for the betterment of higher education. Accrediting institutions feel the pressure from the federal government to ensure the quality of higher education and pass those demands down to their member colleges and universities. To address this assurance of quality, the Higher Learning Commission, as well as other accrediting agencies, has relied upon assessment as a tool for institutional self-study and self-improvement (Lederman, 2019). The measurement of student learning has been the focus of institutional research, and because of this situation assessment has turned into one of the most contentious aspects of higher education.

Anyone who has worked as faculty or staff in the academic wing of a college or university knows how fraught the assessment process can be. The pressure of assessment puts people on edge, brings out resistance, and creates confusion. Accreditors encourage institutions to develop assessment processes designed to meet their needs and to reflect their institutional culture. However, standardized terminology and, to a degree, standardized processes familiar to accrediting agencies, are easier to adopt. Even though the standardized processes may not provide any benefits beyond accreditation, the dangers of punitive action by the accrediting body is avoided at all costs, even if that results in a working environment filled with acrimony, insecurity, and dysfunction. Assessment can do more.

Although there is no uniform or universal method of approaching assessment, a standard framework has emerged for assessment of student learning outcomes. For example, Northern Virginia Community College (n.d.) is guided by the following framework, identified in *Assessment Loop*, a section of the Office of Academic Assessment webpage:

1. Identify outcomes and map curriculum
2. Align methods and collect evidence
3. Analyze evidence
4. Share results
5. Identify and implement change
6. Assess impact of changes

For most colleges and universities, the first couple of steps are relatively easy to do, although getting it done was probably like pulling teeth. Closing the loop is the process of interpreting the results and identifying interventions that will address the identified strengths, weaknesses, or needs. Closing the loop is the heart of assessment because through that process interventions for improvement are designed and implemented. Thus, closing the loop is the culmination and integration of all of the steps. This process seems straightforward and relatively easy, but teaching and learning are inherently emotional and creative processes, vulnerable to self-doubt, blame, and ever-changing procedures, logistics, and variable resources, and assessing that process is challenging. Recommending actions, taking action, and measuring the effects of the action is actually a very long process, one that stretches out for years. Imagine each academic department must begin two assessment projects each year. The 2nd year adds two more projects, on top of measuring the effectiveness of changes implemented the previous year. By year 3, it is possible a department has six ongoing assessment projects. Data from multiple years may be necessary for each project, and if further changes are necessitated by findings, then the project must analyzed in subsequent years. In the 4th year, the department's assessment labor has ballooned to eight separate projects. Innovation in teaching and curricular design halts because the process of assessment becomes so time consuming. And yet, faculty make plans around curriculum design and institute changes without having formal assessment processes in place. If a campus has a process that works well, assessment can be designed to fit existing practices by setting up a method for the tracking of decisions and their impact. Sometimes, efforts to practice assessment harm relationships between faculty, staff, and administrators to such a degree that previously customary methods of consensus decision-making can no longer take place.

Subjectivity, Objectivity, and Measurability

Initially IAIA thought the main challenge for assessment was that outcomes were not measurable. A great deal of effort was spent writing and rewriting outcomes, searching for ways to make the outcomes measurable or working to design rubrics that would provide the foundation for assessment. This process went on for a number of years and the inability to reach the necessary consensus became a threat to accreditation.

For IAIA, the issues surrounding appropriate outcomes were based in the subjective nature of art. Designing outcomes that were measurable seemed to be a large part of the problem. In addition, faculty were intimidated by the feeling that they were doing this not for the college, but for the accrediting body. Faculty assumed they had to conduct assessment in established modes presented to them by the academic assessment literature. The institution felt vulnerable on two fronts. First, for a minority-serving institution with largely minority-identifying faculty and staff, the safest path is to take a conventional approach, trying to minimize prejudice by not calling attention to our differences. The second vulnerability is the comparatively low value assigned to artistic pursuits, irrespective of the fact that the arts are a primary economic activity for Native communities often lacking in employment and industrial production.

Through the development of the scientific method and the subsequent establishment of science as the means to accurately describe physical phenomena and develop industrial technology, quantitative data and quantitative processes became privileged and authoritative processes. Part of that privilege has been that only through mathematics can data be seen as objective and free from the influence of feeling and emotions. Over the millennia, starting with the Greeks, it has been the goal of philosophers and scientists to achieve a description of the world that is "true" and not influenced by human sensory reactions, emotions, or feelings. Such a description would provide an "objective" view of the world, which would be the reality or essence of the phenomena being observed. The search for objectivity became the standard for all research and inquiry. Indeed, researchers must show how their methodologies and analyses lead to an objective result, one free from prejudices and bias. Implicit in that search is the assumption that qualitative data are subjective and therefore unreliable.

Within the context of course and program assessment, the privilege enjoyed by quantitative data has produced assessment practices that are almost wholly quantitative-based. The validity for any process that was mathematically based was presumed. Thus, the focus of assessment has been to turn all kinds of information into numerical values, leading to statements such as the following from San Diego Mesa College (2019): "A well-developed rubric allows you to give a numerical score for qualitative assessments which make the reporting, analysis, and evaluation components much easier" (p. 38).

Easier does not necessarily mean useful. Are the actions an institution takes in response to the numerical data "numerical actions"? No, the numbers are used qualitatively to make decisions, craft policies, or develop social activities. For the small sample sizes produced at a college with only 500 FTE, every detail of how the numerical data are collected becomes crucial. The findings can be skewed by the slightest circumstance and can easily be misinterpreted. Decisions made based on these numerical data may not always be the right decisions.

Fear and the Resistance to Assessment

It must be noted that discomfort with the assessment process is not just based in the issue of measurable outcomes. Resistance to assessment can often be rooted in fear. There is a misconception that assessment of student learning or program efficacy is a reflection on the teaching abilities of faculty or the organizational ability of program staff. This fear is neither unreasonable, nor unwarranted. In a 2017 conference, a college administrator talked about the need for confidentiality in assessment because "jobs were on the line." Obviously, this administrator did not see assessment as focused on student learning, but on faculty competence. For the faculty or staff member in such an environment, assessment is a threatening process, clouded by confusing and capricious processes. No faculty or staff wants to participate in a process that may well result in their dismissal. More than a decade of postrecession budget cuts and reductions in tenured and full-time faculty positions compound that sense of precariousness. Thus, faculty and staff buy-in is a problem that limits acceptance of assessment and participation in assessment activities. In fact, buy-in under these conditions is a ridiculous expectation. No wonder so many institutions fail at this stage. IAIA's faculty diversity is unusual in higher education and creates an acute awareness of the needs of faculty of color; 60% are tribally enrolled, and many were first-generation college students. Imposter syndrome is common amongst the faculty, perhaps even the norm. Even the White faculty and staff on the campus experience some degree of imposter syndrome, because it was either embedded within their graduate education or arises from willingly working in an environment where they are a cultural minority. They may not feel they "belong" because of the profound cultural differences. Respect for one another is absolutely crucial and has to be clearly modeled to students.

The Indigenous Assessment Model

IAIA joined the Higher Learning Commission's Assessment Academy in 2015 and sent a team to attend gatherings in Chicago to learn about assessment through trainings, interactions with teams from other educational institutions, and dedicated work sessions. This setting proved key to the analytical work that led to the realization that the college needed a completely different approach to assessment. Participating in the Assessment Academy was especially helpful in providing a wide range of professionals who served as sounding boards, helping refine descriptions of ideas as they evolved. The committee's reflection on assessment at IAIA identified the following assessment issues:

- The variety of methods applied across the institution resulted in inconsistency.
- We did not have faculty buy-in.
- Existing models did not seem to fit our campus.
- We could not figure out how to "close the loop" because everyone was confused and annoyed with the process.
- Fear and even shame were common feelings for everyone involved.

The first four items in this list are ones shared consistently in discussions with other institutions at the Assessment Academy. That last one, fear, was not something the IAIA team heard other teams discuss. As IAIA reflected on these issues, members knew they would have to address each of them in unconventional ways. Efforts to secure faculty buy-in were discussed by some in the assessment field in terms very close to bullying, with bribery the only competing option. Even the term *buy-in* sets up a relationship where assessment is a commercial product.

Because assessment is about student learning, the college decided to bring samples of student work to the first Assessment Academy gathering in Chicago. A conference projector was repurposed and the first morning was spent simply looking at student work, mostly 2-dimensional art produced in multiple classes. The discussion centered on these questions: What does this example show that the student has learned? What skills does this work demonstrate? The team included the library director, dean of academics (also a studio art faculty), the director of institutional research, and two nonstudio arts faculty. Using Indigenous research methodologies, the team assumed all members of a community are qualified to participate in the research. Discussing student learning in ways that nonspecialists could see present in the student work was illuminating for everyone and reinforced the belief that Indigenous assessment could work.

The IAIA team was an oddity at the session. While most other schools worked on linear processes, rubrics, organizational maps, or information flow charts, this team simply looked at student-produced art and talked. However, that simple process was the key to coming up with an Indigenous assessment model. In the afternoon session, the team discussed what occurred in the morning, reflecting on the steps taken and the values of IAIA that were important to include.

The second session resulted in a diagram showing; a spiral drawing with six identified activities and four values (Figure 5.1). The diagram eventually became the model. The six activities included: (a) gathering the community, (b) finding the learning, (c) looking and talking with no rubric, (d) honoring, (e) improving together, and (f) repeating the cycle. The four values guiding the model were respect, community, dialogue, and honor.

The team decided to test the model the following week. It began the arrangements during the Chicago session. Members chose a group exhibition in the student gallery on campus. *The Monster Show*, coinciding with Halloween, was an extracurricular activity open to all, including students' children. No submissions were turned away. Artworks on the theme were submitted and students in the museum studies courses did the exhibit

Figure 5.1. Indigenous assessment model.

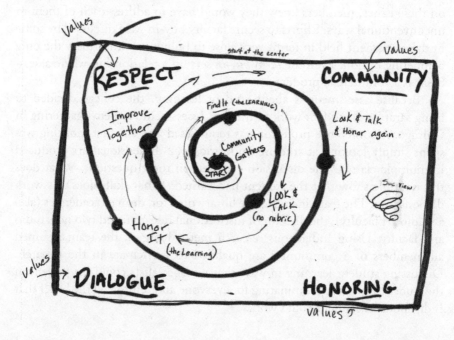

design, installation, labels, and lighting. The Looking and Talking step, a nonrubric-based group discussion with a multidisciplinary team, discussed all aspects of the exhibition, from the student learning embodied by the individual artworks, to the quality of the exhibition design and installation, to the collaborative work required for students to plan and execute the exhibition and reception. The team also obtained data about the number of students who submitted work, their majors, and class standing. It was learned that participation was evenly distributed amongst all majors, not just studio art majors. However, few juniors participated, and even fewer seniors. These first three steps of the process worked extremely well and resulted in immediate actions for the next two steps: Honoring and Improve Together. Student-organized exhibitions had been taking place intermittently in nongallery spaces on campus, usually in a lobby area, with no budget. With the enthusiastic support of the staff member responsible for the gallery, the annual schedule of exhibitions was modified to reserve space for an extracurricular student-organized exhibition each year, with a budget and full institutional support. The group thought it would be beneficial to have more participation from the juniors and seniors and theorized that committing professional space and resources to this type of exhibition would make participation more attractive to advanced students. A periodic review of submission data shows this approach to be working. The learning experience and social function of this extracurricular activity has broad reach and impact on the campus community, something that was undervalued before trying this assessment method.

Three more Indigenous assessment projects took place in the next 4 months. Development of the meta-assessment process took longer, with the reporting form development taking the next two years. The form development occurred through the process of using a draft and modifying it in response to each assessment project, sometimes even during an assessment activity. The meta-assessment report format has been stable for more than a year, but the group anticipates some edits may be needed in the coming year as the community adapts to the pandemic. Tracking COVID-19-specific assessment impacts is likely to be important for institutional memory and perhaps even historical records of this time of intensive adaptation to a worldwide disaster.

A frequent belief the team encountered is the assumption that the model only applies to one level of assessment, such as course, department, program, or degree level. The first effort used an extracurricular project, which demonstrated its usefulness for noncurricular assessment. Later projects demonstrated effectiveness for use at the course level, program level, department level, and for campus-wide assessment, such as looking at examples of student writing from courses in every degree program. The team developed a planning rubric that guides the formation and execution of an assessment project in a way that maximizes respect and reduces the personal risks that often impede genuine assessment. Within the 1st year, all full-time faculty had experienced the process, as had dozens of staff members and adjuncts. The board of trustees is interested in trying it for their own assessment. Complicated campus decisions might now start out with a conventional committee structure, but as soon as it becomes clear that an issue will have broad, long-term impacts, participants turn to the values and practices built into the Indigenous assessment model. When movement on an issue is stymied, Indigenous assessment gathers people and evidence together in a collaborative exploration that develops consensus on next steps in a faster time frame than expected.

Each project resulted in some immediate changes that were easily implemented. There were areas for improvement uncovered that would not have been discovered if the assessment processes stayed narrowly focused according to course and program-level assessment. For example, the college was able to develop consensus that improving student writing is not the responsibility of just English faculty, but all faculty. The Looking and Talking stage resulted in deep conversations about pedagogy that had not been taking place, especially cross-departmentally.

Activities to Support Achievement of the Goal

The Indigenous assessment model uses a two-step model: assessment and meta-assessment. Because this model is such a departure from most practices, the college included a third category that is not a single step, but rather a category of activity that is tracked at each step, often referred to as "closing the loop" within the assessment community.

Step 1: Assessment

The initial step in the process involves careful preparation, conducting the assessment, honoring the work, and identifying areas for improvement.

Gathering the Community

The community includes the person who has the responsibility to see that the assessment is completed, the assessment leader. The assessment leader then invites faculty, staff, and students to participate in an assessment group. Experience has shown that an assessment group can be successful with as few as four participants or as many as 20. The group should always include faculty who provided student work for the assessment project and others from their department. The group can also include faculty from other departments, interested staff, and students. The leader of the assessment group establishes a time for the gathering and secures a recording device to record the conversation. The leader then requests examples of student work and provides the work to the assessment group.

Find the Learning
It is the responsibility of the assessment leader to ensure that all of the community members have access to the samples of student work. This step will be done in a manner consistent with the capacity of the institution to distribute information: electronic, physical, or other. The assessment leader removes personally identifiable information from the student work samples, if possible. It is the responsibility of the community members to review the student work and come to the gathering prepared to discuss what the samples show in terms of student learning, although in some cases, artwork can be viewed as part of the meeting.

Looking and Talking (No Rubric)
Dialogue is the essence of the Indigenous assessment model. The assessment leader introduces the community and describes the purpose and process of that assessment gathering. The assessment leader also reminds the community that the session is being recorded and reviews the values that will guide the assessment process. Once those preliminaries are completed, the assessment leader asks the community to describe what they see as examples of student learning. The dialogue is only somewhat structured in that there is no discussion of the nature of the assignments, course, or program outcomes prior to the dialogue. Additionally, the faculty who assigned the sample student work should not talk about purpose or goals of the assignment for at least the first 20 minutes. The assessment process is trying to identify what knowledge and skills students had to have to produce the work in question, which may not be the same as the instructor's goal for that assignment. After 20 minutes, the assigning faculty may talk about the nature of the assignment since by that time obvious instances of student learning will have been identified. This first gathering usually lasts for a period of 90 minutes. The assessment leader then arranges to have a transcript created from the recording of the session.

During the team's time at the HLC Assessment Academy there was intense pressure to adopt a rubric for the purpose of analyzing student learning. However, as was stated previously, the purpose of a rubric is to transform qualitative data into quantitative data. That goal was not the group's purpose. Anyone using the rubric would narrowly consider only the "learning" represented on the rubric and would fail to recognize learning outside of those parameters. This team wanted to understand what students know and how they can make use of it. Questions about attribution of knowledge arose during the development of this method, that is, a concern that reviewers were not discerning the difference between knowledge students may have possessed before a particular course, or even before arriving at our campus. Ultimately, the team came to the conclusion that all students come to the institution with prior knowledge; the college respects that knowledge. IAIA provides a special opportunity to apply that previous knowledge in a diverse intercultural setting, while also learning new skills and gaining experience communicating with new audiences. Courses that have outcomes based in content have quantitative measures built in through the grading process, so the majority of discussions are not about the content of the course (e.g., historical events, literary concepts). In the IAIA experience, the dialogue turns to more ephemeral aspects of student learning such as risk, confidence, expression, narrative, or identity. The community discusses student learning in a broad context, not just looking at a course or program, but pedagogy and connections to other institutional practices or structural features that affect student learning.

As the dialogue unfolds, issues are identified and interventions are proposed. Observations about student learning give rise to discussions about how this learning is facilitated or endangered. This process in turn leads to what can be done to improve the student learning and how connections to other parts of IAIA enhance or detract from it. We explore barriers and search for easier access.

Honoring
It is very important that the student work be honored. The role of teachers is to help the students gain experiences that will guide future decisions and efforts. Faculty reflection on student work needs to acknowledge the student effort, whether that acknowledgment occurs in the classroom, in assessment sessions, on social media, in exhibitions, or publications. Honoring is sometimes a means of *closing the loop*. A commitment of funding or resources has been used as a means of honoring student learning. For example, a student-organized thematic exhibition was recognized as an important learning opportunity, with high levels of student participation by all majors, not just studio art majors. The assessment group committed to adding such a group show to the annual calendar for the Balzer Contemporary Edge Gallery on campus, with budgetary support for the exhibition and collaboration with a museum studies course for the exhibition design and installation. Participation of many faculty from different departments, plus the gallery director, organically led the institution to commit to supporting a similar

exhibition every year. Without that assessment process, it is likely the exhibition would have been an ephemeral, one-off type of event. An opportunity to support student learning would have been lost.

Improving Together
Improving together may be considered as taking place after completion of the assessment report, when interventions are identified. However, many ideas arise during the first assessment group meeting and are immediately put into use by faculty or staff on an individual basis. Improving together means that interventions are implemented with the knowledge of the assessment community and with other entities and people at IAIA. Together work is done to ensure the success of a change, or the continued practice of something identified as particularly effective.

Step 2: Meta-Assessment
The meta-assessment group mirrors the initial assessment group. The difference is that the meta-assessment group focuses on reviewing the transcript, the recordings of the initial assessment group, rather than looking at the examples of student work. The *gathering community* in the meta-assessment group is made of some members of the initial assessment group and new members from the community. An even split between new and previously participating members is desirable. *Finding the learning* can be discovered by reading the transcript of the initial assessment group meeting. During this step the members of the meta-assessment group read the transcript looking for topics around learning that stand out to them. They *look and talk* about their individual perceptions. Through this dialogue, the issues identified in the initial assessment are expanded upon and other issues rise in discussion. The student work is *honored*, not only by the dialogue about student learning, but through discussions about what can be done to spotlight or share the work with the IAIA community and beyond. *Improving together* is the goal of actions taken as a result of the meta-assessment discussion. As of March 2020, IAIA had engaged in 22 different Indigenous assessment projects, including reviews of departments, extracurricular activities, the library, internships programs, and administrative units. All of these assessment projects yielded analyses and strategies that were acted upon.

Closing the Loop
In the parlance of higher education assessment, the term *closing the loop* refers to using the assessment's analytical tools to create interventions to resolve any shortcomings and strengthen positive aspects uncovered by the assessment. A typical quantitative process involves developing a plan of action,

implementing the plan, and then reassessing after a period of time to determine if the intervention was successful. As one colleague stated, current assessment practices "seem to be used to justify experimental interventions," meaning that no clear path to resolving the identified issues is apparent and interventions are experimental. The impact of interventions and their efficacy is largely unknown when instituted.

The Indigenous assessment model has a different approach to closing the loop. As the data are discussed in both the initial and meta-assessments, so too are alternative strategies for achieving the desired goals. Agreement within the community is needed to establish interventions, but this is an organic process. Discussions include pros and cons of each strategy and the potential impacts of implementation. Perhaps unique to this Indigenous assessment model, it can also identify practices that are working particularly well and that should *not* be changed.

Documentation of closing the loop is found in the assessment project report. The report includes the name of the assessment group, name of the leader, topic of the assessment, and timing of recommended follow-up. The report then asks the following 11 questions:

1. How are you defining your community?
2. What are you looking at (student work, services, survey results, focus group discussion, etc.)?
3. Please summarize the discussion that took place and attach the transcription. What were the general themes? Did any specific issues come up?
4. Did you ask for any further information as a result of your discussion? Why? Please share. For instance, did you request demographic information about students? Grades?
5. How have you honored the student work?
6. Was the community involved in analysis of the results (meta-assessment) different from the community that participated in the discussion?
7. Identify next steps.
8. What has already happened as a result of this assessment project?
9. What things are you going to change as a result of this assessment project? Have you created a new spiral? Did you look and talk again?
10. What are the strengths in this assessment project?
11. In a set period of time, to be determined, a second report discusses what things were changed and how that worked out. Maybe a year?

The assessment project report identifies the issues and interventions that have been discussed and agreed upon by the community. The discussions are archived and provide a long-term guide for the implementation of the interventions and a detailed record of how and why existing features were maintained unchanged and others changed.

The Role of Quantitative Data

The Indigenous assessment model at IAIA is a qualitative process but does not reject the use of quantitative data. Quantitative data are used selectively and are interpreted and framed as a group effort. In most institutions, institutional research (IR) generally provide the data that IR feels are important. In the Indigenous assessment process, participants discuss what statistics are deemed important to understand conditions and fully flesh out the story of that assessment project. This process can be done at the initial assessment group meeting or at the meta-assessment group meeting. These discussions ensure that the quantitative data are appropriate for supporting that specific assessment. Once the data have been identified, the assessment leader includes that information in the Assessment Project Report.

Values to Support Achievement of the Goal

The Indigenous assessment model at IAIA is a values-based model (see Table 5.1). While the following four values are at the core of the assessment model, they are not the only values that are reinforced and validated through this process. These values are included in many of IAIA's statements of values but are not specifically found together in any IAIA documents. The first value is *respect* for the students' work and the work of the faculty and staff at IAIA. Second, all assessment is for the betterment of the *community* and should be inclusive and accountable to the IAIA community. Third, the college's truth (objectivity) is achieved by *dialogue*, both in the discussion of the student learning and identification of possible interventions. Lastly, the institution should *honor* the student work, from the knowledge they bring with them from their community, to the knowledge they form at IAIA.

As a values-based assessment process, IAIA instills meaning beyond fulfilling requirements from an outside agency. By anchoring the process in values rather than in an administrative requirement, IAIA has created a process that reinforces the college's basic values while providing for enhanced student learning and a stronger IAIA community.

Results of Implementing an Indigenous Assessment Model

The results of the Indigenous assessment model at IAIA go far beyond simply assessing course or programs. The serendipitous results of the process have greatly improved the IAIA community. It is hard to categorize these ancillary

TABLE 5.1
IAIA Values-Based Model

Respect	Assessment may be critical, but the criticism is provided thoughtfully and with respect. Participants in assessment listen to and respect each other's perspectives and varied opinions about the project. Every member of our community belongs in, and has the respect of, our community (Evans, 2017).
Community	Indigenous assessment involves the IAIA community. Any member of the community may participate in assessment. They do not need to have a direct relationship to the student learning, and they do not need to be an expert in any particular discipline in order to participate. We can also invite outside members into the community to get to know us and contribute.
Dialogue	Indigenous assessment is dialogue-based. Participants share their unique perspectives and engage in dialogue about the project being assessed.
Honoring	Indigenous assessment honors the work that has been done by the students, and by the faculty and staff who have designed courses, created learning experiences, and provided support services. We honor learning wherever and however it takes place.

benefits because they are so interrelated. First, because the assessment process includes participants from different departments, as well as staff and students, departmental barriers are broken down, reducing the silo affect and enhancing the sense of community. This inclusionary approach allows insight into departmental pedagogy and priorities. No longer do faculty say that they don't understand what another department is doing.

Secondly, because the Indigenous assessment process is based in dialogue and focused on student learning, the college has largely been able to reduce the fear that is endemic in many assessment programs. Faculty are not afraid to submit examples of student work and are not afraid to participate in the assessment process. That level of faculty participation also provides the foundation for candor and in-depth discussions of pedagogy, classroom management, and curriculum. Because the fear factor has been reduced, participants are more open to interventions and new ideas. The identified interventions are not the result of an overseeing committee; but are the result of negotiation that the participants themselves conducted. Assessment is resulting in a stronger IAIA academic community. Faculty, staff, and students are more aware of what is going on in other departments' courses and better able to identify challenges that are common across the board and others that are discipline- or program-specific. Complicated campus decisions might now start out with a conventional committee structure, but as soon as it becomes clear that an issue will have broad, long-term impacts, participants turn to the values and practices built into the Indigenous assessment model. When movement on an issue is stymied, Indigenous assessment gathers people and evidence together in a collaborative exploration that develops consensus on next steps and speeding implementation.

Each project has resulted in some immediate changes that were easily implemented. The college uncovered areas for improvement that would not have been discovered if the assessment processes stayed narrowly focused according to course and program-level assessment. As noted, the community was able to develop consensus that improving student writing is not the responsibility of just English faculty, but all faculty, and that helping students become more comfortable and confident in their writing involves the entire college community, not just instructional staff. The Looking and Talking stage resulted in deep conversations about pedagogy that had not been taking place, especially cross-departmentally.

Finally, this process has created a common assessment experience. By having a common understanding of assessment and common language and shared assessment experiences, with values agreed upon, the college no longer has the confusion, dread, and distrust that often accompanies opaque assessment processes in many other institutions.

Conclusion

The Indigenous assessment model at IAIA was born out of frustration, fear, and the inability to close the loop. IAIA was suffering from the same challenges that most colleges and universities have faced in their assessment programs. Looking at Indigenous research methodologies and seeing itself as a community, IAIA began the process of establishing a methodology that met the needs of the IAIA community. The result is a process the institution calls Indigenous assessment, a qualitative approach to assessment that relies on the values of community, dialogue, respect, and honoring, to assess student learning and programs. The three-tiered process includes an assessment community made of faculty, students, and staff who volunteer to review and discuss examples of student learning or program activities and a meta-assessment group that reviews the transcript of the first meeting and makes recommendations based on issues, strengths, and pedagogy discussed in the first meeting. Then the assessment leader writes the assessment report.

The adoption of this model has provided IAIA with a tool that is easy to use, reveals important information, and does so in a way that addresses the fears and concerns that had dogged previous assessment approaches. The various assessment projects IAIA has completed have led to meaningful changes and deeper insights into classes, departments, and programs. As a values-based assessment process, it has reaffirmed IAIA's core cultural values. The Indigenous assessment model has become a way to find out what students are learning and how they learn it. It also allows identification of actions with immediate benefit to students. Looking at student work without a rubric provides the opportunity to perceive issues that may have been missed completely if reviewers had relied upon categorical placement. For example, one early assessment project resulted in the observation that students were interpreting fairly open-ended activity instructions very narrowly. They were not taking artistic risks or exploring their artistic boundaries. The 30 or so participants in the assessment were able to immediately work discussions of risk-taking into the classes they teach and the extracurricular activities they organize, including asking artists-in-residence to speak about their own experiences taking artistic risks. When new initiatives develop out of an Indigenous assessment process, the planning and execution stages progress quicker than before, involving people from many areas of the college in this dialogic process and quickly marshaling support and coordination between units.

Assessment at IAIA is now an enjoyable experience. It is possible to get more from assessment than just accreditation. The college developed a method consistent with its community's values. Indigenous assessment also helps the community perceive and respond to students' ever-changing circumstances quickly and effectively, in a way that respects agency for students and employees of the college. Since developing and implementing the model, circumstances have changed radically. Adopting a community-based participatory research model for assessment may prove to be a necessary tool for institutions to adapt to the changes necessary for safety in this pandemic, while also attending to maintaining a functional community under circumstances much more isolating than usual.

Note

1   The Institute of American Indian Arts (IAIA), located in Santa Fe, New Mexico, is a 4-year college with six undergraduate BFA programs (Studio Art, Creative Writing, Museum Studies, Performing Arts, Cinematic Arts) and one BA program (Indigenous Liberal Studies). IAIA also offers an MFA in Creative Writing.

IAIA has 25 full-time faculty, a full-time equivalent figure of 507, and a head count (all status including dual credit) of 807. The studio arts program supports concentrations in painting, sculpture, photography, ceramics, jewelry, and is the degree program with the highest enrollment, approximately 1/3 of majors. The student population is very diverse. For fall 2019, there were 93 tribes represented from 34 states. IAIA also had 65 Hispanic students, 68 White students, 3 Asian-American students, 3 nonresident aliens, and 1 African American; 41 students identified as two or more races.

IAIA is accredited by the Higher Learning Commission (HLC) and by the National Association of Schools of Art and Design (NASAD).

References

Etmanski, C., Hall, B., & Dawson, T. (Eds.). (2014). *Learning and teaching community based research: Linking pedagogy to practice*. University of Toronto Press Scholarly Publishing.

Evans, L. (2017). *Indigenous assessment at IAIA* [Unpublished manuscript]. Institute of American Indian Art.

Glenwick, D., & Jason, L. (Eds.). (2016). *Handbook of methodological approaches to community-based research: Qualitative, quantitative, and mixed methods*. Oxford University Press.

Lederman, D. (2019, April 17). Harsh take on assessment . . . from assessment pros. *Inside Higher Education*. www.insidehighered.com/news/2019/04/17/advocates-student-learning-assessment-say-its-time-different-approach

Long, J. F., & Beckman, M. (Eds.). (2016). *Community-based research: Teaching for community impact*. Stylus.

Northern Virginia Community College. (n.d.). *Assessment loop*. Office of Academic Assessment. https://www.nvcc.edu/oiess/academic-assessment/loop.html

San Diego Mesa College. (2019). *Guide to outcomes and assessment*. Committee on Outcomes and Assessment. https://www.sdmesa.edu/outcomes-assessment-guide/OAGUIDE_V07_online.pdf

Smith, L. T. (1999). *Decolonizing methodologies*. Zed Books Limited.

6

ONE INSTITUTION'S JOURNEY TO ANNUAL PROGRAM ASSESSMENT

Carol Traupman-Carr, Dana S. Dunn, and Debra Wetcher-Hendricks

Moravian College is a small, private college in Bethlehem, Pennsylvania, an area rich in higher education. Our institution is a member of the New American Colleges and Universities consortium and, while we identify as a liberal arts college with the addition of preprofessional programs and graduate programs, we are increasingly looking like a master's comprehensive institution. We are the sixth oldest college in the nation, tracing our roots back to 1742, when the Moravian Female Seminary was founded. Moravian College is accredited by a number of professional agencies recognized by the United States Department of Education and has been accredited by the Middle States Commission on Higher Education since 1922.

Establishing a Process for Annual Assessment

A key element of an institution's accreditation is its ability to perform and use an annual assessment of academic programs that is systematic and run by the members of the faculty. The annual assessment provides the foundation for periodic program review, using external reviewers, as well as providing the foundation for the institution's application for renewal of its accreditation.

Although there is no single way to perform ongoing annual program assessment, we can make some recommendations that should suit a variety of institutions. Moravian College has gone through several iterations of annual program assessments since first instituting this practice across all departments and programs in 2003. Admittedly, when annual assessment was instituted that year, it was directly related to accreditation mandates, and even though the assessment plans were created by the college faculty, the move into performing regular programmatic assessments was not well received. Despite assurances to the contrary, some faculty members confused assessment with evaluation (a common problem on many campuses) and assumed that assessment results would be used for promotion and tenure decisions (another somewhat typical reaction). Each department created its own assessment plans, and the College Assessment Committee (CAC) reviewed the plans to ensure they included a feedback loop using the results. Departments created or revised student learning outcomes (many of which were tied to disciplinary standards) and submitted them to the CAC for feedback. Yet, 5 years later, we still faced struggles in meeting accreditation requirements for the assessment of academic programs, with some departments or programs seemingly "stuck" at the start of the process and uncertain how to move forward. What our institution faced was a complicated problem that had turned out to be a complex problem instead (Kamensky, 2011). Rather than being "predictable and linear," with "a clear beginning, middle, and end," "with a clear relationship between the parts" (characteristics of a complicated problem), we had created a complex situation, with the assessment process, including collection and use of results, being unpredictable, even in terms of something as simple as when we might expect to see a department's report.

A new committee, the Committee on the Assessment of Student Learning (CASL), was formed and populated with both assessment prophets and assessment atheists (or at least agnostics). Their collective work led to a revised process, better faculty involvement, more widespread assessment, and a process that formed the basis of our ongoing and ultimately more successful efforts. The revised process continued to allow departments to establish their own learning outcomes and determine what method they wished to use for the resulting assessment, but a standard timeline and reporting form were used across the board. These two changes seemed to help move everyone forward—if not at the same pace, then at least in the same direction.

More recently, we have found fairly consistent participation from the faculty across all departments and programs. A major factor in the increased level of participation is an understanding that assessment results are reviewed by the administration and are not just *busy work*. The curriculum committee requests information about how assessment results have impacted curricular changes and subsequent student learning and requires a detailed assessment plan to accompany all new program and program revision proposals. Due to the changes, a sense that assessment "matters" beyond accreditation reporting requirements is apparent.

Goal of the Assessment

Assessment has multiple goals at both the program and institutional levels, including the following:

- Help departments and programs understand whether their program is helping students meet the intended learning outcomes
- Help departments and programs determine where their curricula are not helping students achieve the intended learning outcomes, and therefore provide data for program improvement
- Assist the institution in meeting accreditation requirements of performing periodic, regular, systematic, and sustainable assessment of educational programs
- Assist the institution in providing evidence of assessment
- Assess the validity of the departmental/program learning outcomes

Routine academic program review is a means for external experts to validate departmental efforts for an institution's administration while also affording the members of departments an opportunity to tout their strengths (Dunn et al., 2011). Program review is often approached as a periodic task to be performed in a fairly comprehensive manner once every 5–7 years. For comparison, the Pennsylvania Department of Education requires all programs to be reviewed at least once every 10 years. However, that does not mean that assessment ceases between those years. In fact, annual assessment has a number of benefits for the department or program. Participating in smaller annual assessments can make the work preparing for the larger review much easier, and it can help inform midpoint adjustments, important in today's quickly changing and dynamic world of higher education.

Activities and Strategies to Support Achievement of the Goal

A key strategy is the agreement by the institution to allow departments and programs to employ a method of assessment that they deem appropriate for their program. The one-size-fits-all approach to program assessment did not appear to work well as we began to implement programmatic assessment, although there is a single procedure for all departments to submit their assessment results.

This basic process underwent substantial revision during the 2016–2017 academic year, when the college changed the oversight of assessment activities. Before that time, in an attempt to appease faculty who considered assessment activities bothersome and overwhelming, departments were given great latitude regarding what to assess, procedures for the assessments, or how to organize their assessment reports. Consequently, the quality and styles of assessment reports submitted by departments at the college varied greatly.

Our current process is based upon clearly stated guidelines regarding how to focus departments' annual assessments and how to write assessment reports. This process relies upon clearly stated student learning outcomes (SLOs) that each department has previously established, but may change when deemed necessary. In 2016, each department mapped its courses to its SLOs, essentially connecting each course to at least one SLO. This practice led to two important outcomes. First, it forced departments to consider the relevance of its courses. Departments that could not map a particular course to an SLO were encouraged to reconsider the necessity of that course in its curriculum. Second, it provided a matrix for each department to reference when determining the courses on which it should focus when assessing particular SLOs in the future. Copies of these matrices were made available to all college faculty and administrators through postings on our learning management system, Canvas.

Each year since this initial exercise, departments and programs have conducted annual assessment according to the following steps.

Step 1: Focused SLO Assessment

Early in the fall semester, members of each department cooperatively select one of the department's established SLOs on which to focus the year's assessment activities. Department chairs or assessment representatives report this decision to the director of academic assessment. Ideally, departments develop a rotation of SLO assessment if they haven't done so already. If a department, for example, has identified five SLOs, assessing them follows a regular pattern, with each SLO receiving attention every 5 years. Exceptions, of course, occur for a variety of reasons, including the immediate need to assess a particular element of the program and the potential unavailability of data pertaining to a particular SLO.

At the same time, departments should review the previous year's assessment results and follow-up plan, since at later stages in this process, they are asked to review and report an update on this information. If, in the previous assessment report, the department indicated that they would implement changes to a course or curriculum due to the assessment findings, then this is the time to start reviewing the impact of those changes.

Step 2: Determining the Assessment

Members of each department determine an appropriate and feasible way to perform the assessment and gather data. They first consider all courses mapped to the chosen SLO and taught in the fall or spring semester of the current year, as their assessment must address each of these classes. Assuming the department has assessed the chosen SLO in the past, the same process of obtaining and analyzing data as used previously provides the advantages of consistency and the ability to perform time-series analyses. However, departments may change their approaches to measurement if they have reasonable justifications for this change. Many opportunities exist for department chairs and assessment representatives to explore measurement of SLOs, including workshops and individual meetings with the director of academic assessment. In these contexts, as well as in general conversations about assessment (e.g., at faculty meetings, occasional assessment workshops), faculty are reminded that they may use qualitative, quantitative, or a combination of the two measures, depending upon the issue addressed by the chosen SLO and the nature of the data. Faculty also receive prompting to avoid limiting their assessment to summarizing student performance on graded assignments, since other measures may provide valuable insight (e.g., evaluation of class participation, journals, engagement in application of material, progress on drafts of written assignments, and similar exercises). On the other hand, it is not necessary for assessment to create extra work for faculty. When possible, existing coursework such as exams, quizzes, papers, and presentations can include assessment measures or rely on rubrics that serve as assessment tools. Common approaches to this sort of *multipurposing* involve designating student responses to a particular exam question or journal response as an assessment measure.

In addition, department faculty members should consider approaches to "closing the loop" when deciding upon their assessment measures. Although assessment often identifies areas of success, it also serves to identify areas in need of improvement. Faculty will need to reflect later upon whether efforts to make improvements have actually done so. Therefore, they should design the assessment measure to allow for reevaluation of the SLO after implementing any andragogic changes deemed appropriate based upon initial assessment results. Faculty should also discuss whether the previously implemented assessment is still appropriate and whether to prepare to deploy it again or to use another mechanism.

Step 3: Gathering Data

Using the measurement approach determined most appropriate, members of each department teaching the courses relevant to the chosen SLO coordinate collection of indicators from students in their classes. Generally, these faculty members organize this information and the department chair or assessment representative collects it at the end of each semester. Depending on the SLO chosen, the actual assessment might occur at any point in the term, but it is shared at the end of the term, as per the established timeline. Faculty are reminded not to forget to use an assessment for the previous year's SLO as well, in order to be able to get new data on student achievement and compare it to previous data.

Step 4: Reflection

In addition to addressing the SLO chosen as the focus for a particular year, each department must revisit the SLO addressed in the previous year. In particular, department members together reflect upon the extent to which they made the changes deemed necessary by the previous year's assessment. They also evaluate the effects of these changes upon student performance. This step constitutes the familiar and important "closing the loop" element of assessment. Sometimes, it can take several years before the impact of a curricular or course change can actually be measured. Therefore, faculty should not give up too quickly if the results fail to produce the desired results immediately. This case is particularly true of changes happening across multiple courses, rather than in a single course. Of course, this repeat assessment should be aligned to the actual course offerings. If changes are made to a course that is only offered every other year, then the assessment of that change should be scheduled to match that timeline.

Step 5: Annual Assessment Report

Each department submits an annual assessment report to the director of academic assessment by the end of May. The format of these reports has varied in recent years, sometimes involving the completion of a Google Form and sometimes involving narrative description. Regardless of the format, reports must contain the same information each year. The majority of the report provides information about the current year's assessment, including the following:

- Identification and, if necessary, a description of the chosen SLO
- Identification of the classes from which data for assessing the chosen SLO were obtained

- An explanation and justification of the measurement technique
- A summary of data collected, including samples of student work, assignment guidelines, and other relevant documents as necessary
- A description of department faculty's perceptions regarding what the data indicate about the extent to which students fulfilled the SLO
- Conclusions about the results of the assessment, particularly addressing plans for modifying andragogy or course content during the following academic year to improve student performance on the SLO
- A discussion of "close the loop" revisions to a course or curriculum describing steps taken to acknowledge any shortcomings in student learning identified in the previous year's assessment and faculty members' perceptions of their success in implementing changes

Step 6: Feedback Reports

The director of academic assessment provides written responses to department members after receiving their annual assessment reports. These responses allow department members to ensure that their assessment results were understood correctly and provide suggestions for future assessment activities. Most importantly, however, receiving these responses provides those who prepared them with acknowledgment of their work. Many report authors have commented about their appreciation for these responses, which indicate that someone has actually *read* what they wrote! This small action, therefore, helps to create a positive dynamic among those intimately involved in the academic assessment process and reinforces the claim that assessment is not busy work.

By midsummer, the director of academic assessment posts on Canvas the assessment reports submitted by each department. All faculty members and administrators are then able to access these reports.

Although we require a standard format for submitting the assessment results, we allow a great deal of flexibility for departments and programs in terms of how they wish to conduct their assessment. This strategy, as shown in Table 6.1, acknowledges that faculty know best how to assess their learning and permits faculty to determine a discipline-specific approach.

The idea of closing the loop has been reinforced repeatedly in the past 15 years through our assessment process. The idea, visually represented Figure 6.1, must be well known by now to anyone involved in assessment. Our assessment committee wanted to use language that would resonate with faculty, whose primary focus is on teaching and *learning*.

TABLE 6.1
Discipline-Specific Examples

Discipline	Assessment Approach
Mathematics	Quiz or test results, with the quiz or test clearly mapped to a specific program learning outcome.
Global Relations	Focus group among graduating seniors, at which they "interview" students related to the program learning outcomes; one faculty member acts as moderator, one as recorder, so that there are two "sets of ears" in the room.
Music	Senior recital, with program notes (an explanation, in the musical program, of the music to be performed, providing historical and background information for the audience) written by the student, which help to show not only progress and proficiency in performance studies, but also how the student is able to apply learning from the academic music history courses in this very practical situation. Faculty score (no pun intended) the performance and program notes and review all seniors' performances as part of their annual assessment submission.
Neuroscience	ePortfolios beginning sophomore year; they will be able to place samples of their academic, research, and service components into this portfolio and then add to it in their junior year during the Introduction to Neuroscience Methodology course. A final culmination of their work and the skills they have developed during their time in the Neuroscience Program will then be incorporated into the portfolio as they engage in their Neuroscience Seminar course. These portfolios are then reviewed by neuroscience faculty at the end of each year to gauge progress toward the learning goals.
Psychology	For graduating seniors, a series of online assessments aimed at measuring their recognition of psychology as a science while also determining which, if any, myths about the field are still perceived as valid.

Assessments Used to Determine Progress Toward Goal

Simplicity also matters. This quality may seem to be in conflict with the idea of creating a complicated process, but it is not. Assessment of student learning can be complicated. We do not always know initially if the specific

Figure 6.1. The assessment process.

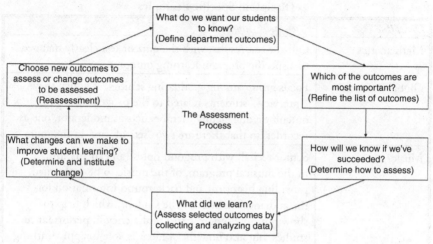

methodology we chose is the right one for assessing a particular learning goal. We do not always know what the results will show. We do not always know exactly what to do with those responses. However, by making the procedure simple and straightforward, with clear expectations for the timing and for the content of reports, we remove elements that can cause confusion and allow faculty to focus on the very important core point: assessing student learning. It would be difficult for faculty to engage in a complex process and could result in individual faculty choosing not to participate, or at least electing not to participate fully. This reality was evident as we moved from a somewhat cumbersome and accreditation-motivated process filled with assessment lingo to a faculty-owned, -organized, and -promoted process (a complicated, but straightforward one) which is primarily about program improvement.

Use of the Findings

In reaching the assessment process used today, we learned the importance of faculty leadership, an important factor in developing faculty buy-in. We are now in a position in which an assessment committee is no longer needed to forge relationships with individual departments to promote participation in the process or to urge (sometimes cajole) faculty to take part. However, faculty involvement remains an important element of a successful program assessment process. Faculty must feel a sense of ownership of the process as well, and not simply feel as though it is being imposed upon them.

The action of "closing the loop" helps to enforce this sense of ownership. Faculty tend to recognize the value of assessment activity when they are asked to consider the ways that they have adapted their course content and andragogy as a result of previous assessment work. In one case, faculty teaching an interdisciplinary course in our Peace & Justice Studies minor realized, through their annual assessment, that students felt uncertain about applying course concepts in their final projects. The faculty members responded by redesigning the project into a "team project," with very specific steps intended to scaffold the students' progress. In an example from Moravian College's physics department, a particular year's annual assessment made faculty aware of students' struggles to become comfortable with the thought processes characteristic of the discipline. After adding activities to the course curriculum, such as reflective inquiry and individual meetings with the professor, faculty identified a noticeable increase in students' self-reliance as well as in their camaraderie.

Other faculty members have submitted samples of student work to provide evidence of increased quality that reflects changes made in response to information gained through assessment. The changes made in response to assessment results, however, do not pertain only to particular classes. Assessment results have also led department faculty to restructure elements of their overall programs' structures. The Modern Languages and Literatures Department's recent curriculum revision exemplifies this sort of modification. Members of the department recognized that they had difficulty measuring the writing progress of their majors as they progressed through their courses. Therefore, the department faculty chose to eliminate the writing intensive course required for the major and, instead, adopt a writing-enriched curriculum approach. In the writing-enriched curriculum model, each course required for the major addresses writing skills to a limited extent within the context of that course. Demands of student writing increase as course levels increase, providing students with a form of scaffolding and allowing faculty to systematically measure students' progress. An important point to note regarding these and other examples is that the faculty maintain control over these changes and, therefore, can take pride in their positive results. Allowing for the departments to develop an assessment tool or mechanism that their members consider appropriate for their program is important while following an overall process that is similar despite departmental differences. Perhaps most importantly, faculty must believe that the assessment results are theirs first and foremost, and will not be used by the institution without their knowledge, particularly for budgetary decisions or for other forms of prioritization.

Conclusion

Perhaps the most important element of a successful process is the faculty knowing that assessment results are put to good use for actual institutional and program improvement and not just to meet accreditation requirements. The process described in this chapter with the specific steps involving reflection and feedback has helped Moravian College faculty recognize the value of assessment in meeting their departmental, and sometimes individual, needs. This support can have only positive impacts upon the educational experiences of our students. Just as we hope our students will learn and grow through our educational offerings, we as an institution can learn and grow through our process of annual program assessment.

References

Dunn, D. S., McCarthy, M. A., Baker, S. C., & Halonen, J. S. (2011). *Using quality benchmarks for assessing and developing undergraduate programs.* Jossey-Bass.

Kamensky, J. M. (2011). *Managing the complicated vs. the complex.* The Business of Government. http://www.businessofgovernment.org/sites/default/files/JohnKamensky.pdf

7

A SYSTEMATIC APPROACH TO BUILDING A CULTURE OF ASSESSMENT

A Multiyear, Cohort-Based Professional Development Model

Mary Kay Helling, Jana Hanson, and Kevin Sackreiter

South Dakota State University (SDSU) is located in Brookings, South Dakota, and is one of six institutions of higher education of the South Dakota System of Higher Education. SDSU is a land-grant institution with fall 2019 enrollment of 11,518. The university offers 82 majors, 35 specializations, 94 minors, 36 masters' degrees, 15 PhD programs and two professional doctorates. The university offers courses and programs at off-campus locations in the state.

Even though SDSU had a strong history and foundation of assessment, limitations and barriers existed which prompted the institution to focus on assessing student learning for its quality improvement project. One limitation of the early work on assessment was that the focus was limited to the academic programs and did not include other entities/units/activities at the university. Some cocurricular units had assessment plans, but not all, and results were of limited use and not widely shared to inform improvement. The institution did not have a central repository for assessment plans, data, and reports. While many academic programs had assessment plans, they varied in quality and in the degree to which results were used to inform needed changes to support greater student learning.

SDSU Quality Initiative

As part of SDSU's commitment to student learning, success, and development, as well as its ongoing accreditation through the Higher Learning Commission (HLC), the university selected the assessment of student learning as its quality initiative (QI) project. The QI (years 5–9 of the 10-year reaccreditation process) is an important component of the institutional improvement process in the Open Pathway reaccreditation process through the HLC.

Due to the focus on assessing student learning, SDSU participated in the HLC Assessment Academy in June 2014, which served to kick off the 4-year QI project at SDSU. The SDSU team used the HLC Assessment Academy to identify and then design the 4-year project. Participating in the formal HLC Assessment Academy provided numerous benefits in support of a more systematic approach to assessment planning. The HLC Assessment Academy provided a multiyear sequence of events including forums, a web-based library of academy projects, and access to two assigned mentors who provided ongoing input and feedback on progress during the 4 years of participation. The HLC Assessment Academy also provided credibility and structure to the process with specific deadlines for progress reports.

It was a particularly opportune time for SDSU to participate in the HLC Assessment Academy for multiple reasons: the fact that current university assessment practices had been in place for over 2 decades, the new availability of sophisticated assessment techniques and strategies, the decoupling of the assessment and testing functions through the establishment of the Office of Institutional Research and Assessment, and the hiring of a new director of institutional assessment.

A steering committee was established and functioned throughout the life of the quality initiative. Members included one to two representatives from each college; the SDSU Student Success Center; Honors College; Graduate School; Continuing and Distance Education; dean's and department heads; Office of Institutional Research and Assessment; Division of Student Affairs; Students' Association; Office of Diversity, Inclusion, Equity and Access; and the Office of Academic Affairs. An executive team was also named, which served as the university assessment committee during the 4-year quality initiative. These groups provided invaluable input throughout the project. Strong support from the president, provost, and vice president for student affairs helped to ensure wide interest and participation in the SDSU Assessment Academy. Based on the current status of assessing student learning at SDSU, the overall goals for the institution's participation in the HLC Assessment Academy included the following:

1. Renew and strengthen the university-wide commitment to assessment and inquiry about student learning.
2. Identify a centralized software/management system for assessment programs, data, and reports.
3. Extend the focus on assessing student learning to include cocurricular units and activities.
4. Provide up-to-date and comprehensive information and resources on assessment for the university community.
5. Design a training program to increase expertise in assessing student learning.

In response to these goals, the 1st year of the project was dedicated to gathering information and planning. More specifically, teams gathered data about the current status and culture of assessment at SDSU; identified potential software solutions to centralize assessment plans and data; defined cocurricular activities and student learning outcomes and measures; built a more robust and centralized student learning assessment resource base; and designed the SDSU Assessment Academy. These tasks were accomplished by five workgroups with members from academic and student affairs.

Current Assessment Practices (Workgroup 1)

Workgroup 1 administered surveys to learn more about current assessment practices as well as the culture of assessment/inquiry related to student learning. Surveys were distributed during the 2015–2016 academic year. Two different surveys (with two to three versions for different target populations) were used, including one that focused on the current status of assessment plans, data, and reports. The second survey was designed to examine the current assessment culture at the institution.

For the survey on current assessment practices, two different versions were used; one designed for academic department heads, and the other for student affairs/cocurricular leaders. The survey questions were organized into five sections, including: (a) department/program identification, (b) general information about accreditation status (if applicable), overall purpose of assessment and perceived level of administrative support, (c) current assessment practices, (d) storage of assessment data, and (e) use of assessment data. Representatives for all academic departments and programs responded to the survey with 100% participation. Respondents reported on 24 out of a possible 32 cocurricular units or programs across the university. This response did not account for all cocurricular activities/programs on campus, but was an initial attempt to tap into the current status of the assessment of student learning in the cocurricular realm.

Findings revealed the intent/purpose of the program assessment plans (establish program efficacy and/or determine if student learning outcomes are met); person(s) responsible for program assessment (e.g., department heads/assistant department heads/program coordinators at 50.7%, faculty members at 24%, committee of faculty at 16%, and some combination of the previous at 16%); the number and current level of awareness/understanding by faculty or staff of program student learning outcomes; common assessment strategies to measure student learning; degree of use of curriculum maps; where assessment data and reports are currently stored; and how assessment data/reports are used.

Findings from the survey of current assessment practices generated the following conclusions:

- Most assessment plans (undergraduate, graduate, and cocurricular) need to be updated/revised to some degree, including review or creation of curriculum maps and student learning outcomes.
- Assessment plans need to be developed and approved for new programs.
- In general, faculty and staff need to be more involved in the preparation of student learning outcomes, curriculum mapping, and development of program-level assessment plans.
- A secure/confidential location for storing assessment data needs to be identified.
- In general, assessment findings and how these findings are used to inform change need to be shared more widely, particularly with students, alumni, and other stakeholders (e.g., donors, business partners, and educational partners).

The second set of surveys focused on assessment culture at SDSU. This survey included different versions for administrators, faculty, and student affairs staff. The surveys were developed by Matthew Fuller at Sam Houston State University. The surveys were designed and validated to offer insights into how faculty and staff perceive their institution's culture of assessment. In addition to collecting open-ended data on faculty and student affairs staff members' perceptions, the survey measures six constructs: (a) perceptions, (b) use of data, (c) sharing, (d) compliance or fear motivators, (e) normative purposes for assessment, and (f) leadership. A full description of the literature review and development efforts undergirding the surveying effort can be found in Fuller and Skidmore (2014) and Fuller et al. (2016).

The Faculty Survey of Assessment Culture was administered in the spring 2016 semester to anyone teaching a credit-generating course. A total of 553 SDSU faculty were invited to participate and 142 completed the survey (26% response rate).

SDSU also participated in the Student Affairs Survey of Assessment Culture to further examine perceptions about institutional cultures of assessment. That instrument parallels the faculty survey and allows for useful comparisons between faculty and student affairs staff members' perceptions. The instrument measures the same six constructs as the faculty survey, but is administered to anyone considered to be midmanagers or higher within SDSU's division of student affairs. A total of 96 student affairs professionals were invited to participate in the survey and 32 completed the survey (33% response rate).

Results were initially used to inform the development of the curriculum for the SDSU Assessment Academy (2015–2019). The purpose of the SDSU Assessment Academy was to increase faculty and staff knowledge, skills, and experiences with assessing student learning and to update or develop program-level assessment plans for all academic programs and selected cocurricular programs/units. The results were also identified by institutional leaders as baseline data to track progress on building a stronger culture of assessment and inquiry at SDSU.

In fall 2018 the surveys were readministered. There were some item modifications. In addition, an administrator's survey was administered. For the second administration of the culture of assessment survey, a total of 131 student affairs professionals were invited to participate and 48 completed the survey (37% response rate). A total of 85 administrators were invited to participate in the administrators' version of the survey and 35 completed the survey (41% response rate). A total of 662 faculty were invited to participate in the faculty version of the survey with 131 completing the survey (20% response rate).

Findings revealed that overall, administrators, faculty, and student affairs professionals understand assessment expectations as part of continuous improvement processes. Many perceptions of assessment are positive, and most respondents think assessment is a good thing for the institution to do. There were several areas that had mixed results, including perceptions of structures, resources, and leadership of assessment, as well as sharing of assessment results. There were also mixed results about the communication and use of assessment results, indicating a continued need to better communicate assessment expectations. The comments also indicated lack of awareness related to assessment processes and activities, which highlights the need to better educate the campus community on assessment of student learning in higher education.

The results reflect an evolving assessment culture. Some individuals recognize institutional efforts to improve assessment processes and expectations. Some survey participants understand assessment as a continuous improvement process. Others seem to have limited understanding of assessment and do not seem to be aware of significant assessment efforts. Faculty continue to connect assessment with course evaluations.

These results also indicate the need for additional communication on the structures, resources, and leadership of assessment. Specifically, awareness of the individuals and offices leading assessment efforts needs to improve. Faculty and staff need to understand assessment responsibilities, processes, and procedures. More effort is needed in sharing assessment results and examples of how information is used to make improvements. Finally, resources for assessment need further examination. There is concern over a lack of resources and increased assessment efforts.

Prior to the administration of the Surveys of Assessment Culture, SDSU had limited information on perceptions and beliefs about assessment. The institution now has a more complete understanding of assessment areas that may need further development. The SDSU assessment subcommittee will utilize the results for professional development opportunities, communication, as well as other campus engagements to improve faculty, staff, and administrator understanding of expectations, purpose, and uses regarding the assessment of student learning.

Online Solutions (Workgroup 2)

Members of Workgroup 2 were tasked with identifying an online solution for gathering assessment plans, data, and reports. Four products were reviewed and one ultimately selected and implemented in spring 2016. The use of a centralized software repository for assessment materials has helped with providing ready access to information for assessment coordinators, faculty, and staff, as well as members of the university assessment committee, which reviews plans and annual reports. Prior to the use of the software platform, assessment information was scattered throughout campus, even though the Office of Institutional Assessment maintained hard copies of documents. The availability of the assessment materials proved invaluable during the November 2019 reaccreditation site visit as peer review team members requested additional examples of plans and reports a few days prior to the visit. Staff could provide files almost immediately, enabling a timely and accurate response. Challenges related to implementation include (a) the need for those who enter and manage data to learn another software platform, (b) the software company continuing to provide updates/changes that require ongoing training and modifications, and (c) ongoing resistance by some users.

Cocurricular Activity Definition (Workgroup 3)

The definition of *cocurricular activities* was developed by Workgroup 3 as follows:

> At South Dakota State University, cocurricular activities promote, encourage and support student learning and success. In partnership with academic curricula, such activities educate the whole student, preparing them as lifelong learners, engaged professionals and engaged citizens of the world. Cocurricular activities typically occur outside the formal classroom.

Based on *Learning Reconsidered 2* and the *Council for the Advancement of Standards of Higher Learning and Development Outcomes* (Keeling, 2006), cocurricular domains were used to guide the development of cocurricular assessment plans, along with identifying possible student learning outcomes and potential assessment methods for each domain.

Transparency in Assessment (Workgroup 4)

Workgroup 4 focused on identifying strategies to make assessment resources more readily available for the university community. The National Institute for Learning Outcomes Assessment (NILOA) Transparency Framework (2011) was used to guide the work on the website, which went live in summer 2016. The group also developed a comprehensive SDSU *Institutional Assessment Handbook*.

Assessment Academy (Workgroup 5)

Workgroup 5 designed the SDSU Assessment Academy. The main purpose of the SDSU Assessment Academy was to foster a culture that values and uses assessment to improve teaching and learning as well as overall institutional effectiveness. The goals of the SDSU Assessment Academy were as follows:

1. Provide a theoretical and methodological foundation to advance the assessment of student learning.
2. Provide assessment training, resources, and ongoing consultation based on research and best practices to facilitate continuous improvement and change.
3. Build and empower campus leaders in the assessment of student learning.

The SDSU Assessment Academy was the cornerstone event for SDSU's quality initiative as it provided an opportunity for participants to build their knowledge base and skills as members of a cadre of individuals focused on building a stronger culture of inquiry in support of student learning and success. The academy was offered for cohorts over 3 academic years (2016–2017; 2017–2018; 2018–2019). Representatives from all academic programs and selected cocurricular units participated over the 3 years with a total of 175 participants. The desired academic participant outcomes were as follows:

1. Identify and describe key elements of the assessment of student learning and success.
2. Use knowledge, skills, and best practices to create or modify student learning outcomes, establish curriculum maps, and design meaningful assessment.
3. Update/create assessment methods, metrics, and procedures to capture student learning outcomes.
4. Integrate program-level assessment plan(s) using assessment management software for each in access and reporting.
5. Provide rationale for program assessment decisions.
6. Integrate, reflect on, and share the assessment process and results.
7. Serve as an assessment champion.

The SDSU Assessment Academy was organized into a half-day opening session at the beginning of the academic year, followed by seven 2-hour workshops, individual meetings in January, and an end-of-year assessment showcase. The opening session featured an external keynote speaker/workshop facilitator with expertise in assessing student learning and time to meet with other participants to review current plans and future goals. Topics for the 2-hour workshops included guiding principles and values of assessment; writing mission statements and student learning outcomes; identifying cross-curricular skills, transferable skills, and cocurricular domains; examining assessment design and methods; analyzing/reporting/using assessment data; closing the loop; sustaining assessment; and making assessment matter.

The final session was titled "Assessment of Student Learning Showcase," a campus-wide event designed to showcase assessment plans/findings for all programs/units in the cohort. All program participants were required to design and present a poster. The purpose of the showcase was to highlight the work of the participants and engage with the campus community on the assessment of student learning.

Participants were expected to participate actively in all sessions; work with department faculty, staff, and leadership to update the current program level assessment plan(s); enter plan(s)/data into the assessment software platform; complete/update program level plan(s) by April of each year; and commit to providing ongoing leadership and continuous improvement for the assessment of student learning and success.

Assessment Academy Outcomes

At the end of each SDSU Assessment Academy, a survey was administered to identify strengths and weaknesses. Findings were used to make changes/improvements for the next year of the academy. For example, the schedule was adjusted to include work sessions to allow programs and units worktime for their assessment plans. Additional trainings for the assessment management software (AMS) were also added. Information on the Assessment Academy showcase posters was provided earlier. Individual meetings were essential, and individuals continued to meet one-on-one with program personnel. Positive comments were shared; for example, one participant stated:

> It [assessment academy] helped immensely with seeing the step-by-step (rather than everything-at-once) approach to assessment that can help make it manageable for my department. It also helped my department effectively navigate the process of writing, committing to, and determining approaches to assessing student learning outcomes.

Another participant said,

> Our faculty have always understood the importance of assessment, but we were not familiar with the actual pieces that make an assessment plan successful. Without a guided program like the academy, we likely would have continued using our previous assessment strategy with poor results. Unfortunately, it is easy for program assessment to fall down the list of priorities due to other more seemingly pressing tasks. After completing the academy, I feel more confident in our ability to systematically review our program.

Overall, faculty and staff felt the SDSU Assessment Academy provided them with direction and resources to create a successful and manageable assessment plan. Among the outcomes of the Quality Initiative/SDSU Assessment Academy are the following:

1. most undergraduate and graduate programs have up-to-date and sustainable assessment plans,
2. additional cocurricular units/programs have up-to-date and sustainable assessment plans,

3. SDSU reestablished the University Assessment Subcommittee (this group reports to the university-level Academic Affairs Committee),
4. academic programs and cocurricular units submit annual reports using the centralized electronic repository and members of the University Assessment Subcommittee review the report and offer feedback,
5. the development of a comprehensive SDSU *Institutional Assessment Handbook* and robust website with assessment resources using the NILOA transparency framework,
6. ongoing education workshops/events on assessment,
7. establishment of an annual assessment event, and
8. the offering of one-on-one meetings with program faculty and staff who serve as assessment coordinators and/or attended the SDSU Assessment Academy.

Strategies and Innovative Approaches

As a result of the last 4 years' work and accomplishments, the planning team identified critical conditions and strategies, which helped foster success of the SDSU Assessment Academy and ongoing efforts into the future focused on assessing student learning. These recommendations will also help ensure sustainability and ongoing improvement.

Use Existing Frameworks and Guiding Values

The SDSU Assessment Academy utilized the nine principles of good practice for assessment student learning (AAHE, 1992), assessment guiding questions, and guiding values and principles. The principles and values were displayed on large poster boards at each session. The facilitator and participants referred to these during the academy workshops.

Garner Central Administration Support

Campus support is essential, particularly from the president, provost, and vice president for student affairs. SDSU is fortunate to have individuals in these positions who truly believe in the value of assessing student learning. They demonstrated this belief by providing financial resources to cover costs including fees for the HLC Assessment Academy and travel to the annual HLC conference and required forums. Funds were also provided to support the SDSU Assessment Academies, including stipends and travel for guest facilitators, hospitality, room rental, and set-up. Funds were also committed for the contract with the company selected to provide the central, electronic repository for assessment plans, data, and reports. These administrators also used a wide variety of venues and opportunities to spread the word (written and verbal) about the SDSU Assessment Academy. Assessment was included as a common topic on regularly scheduled management and leadership team meeting agendas. Campus leaders set the expectation that there would be widespread and active participation in the Assessment Academy activities.

Manage Expectations

While it was clearly communicated that all academic programs and selected cocurricular units would identify individuals to participate in one of the annual SDSU Assessment Academies, the planning and implementation team met the participants where they were in terms of base knowledge of assessment terms, methods, and past experiences with assessment. Participants came with a wide range of levels of knowledge and skills about assessment, which posed challenges throughout the life of the project. One strategy used was to build in worktime during the workshop sessions. By doing so, individuals could focus specifically on the plan for their program, starting with its current state.

Recognize the Differences

It is important to recognize the differences in assessment knowledge, skills, and experiences for individuals from programs that hold specialty accreditation, programs without specialty accreditation, and cocurricular programs. Such differences were noted by Assessment Academy facilitators, identifying those with a strong understanding of assessment to serve as mentors to others. These individuals were also called upon to share their previous experiences and serve as cofacilitators when appropriate. It was also important to communicate that the required outcomes identified by the external accrediting body (if available) were to be used to guide planning.

Create a Growth Mindset Culture for Assessment

The SDSU Assessment Academy team understood that a variety of factors created challenges within the culture of the institution for any new initiative related to assessment including previous university and system initiatives, institutional cultures, accreditation expectations, and individual perception and experiences (or lack thereof) with assessment. Doyle and Zakrajsek

(2013) identify challenges and criticism as characteristics that impact the development of a fixed mindset. A fixed mindset can be created to avoid challenges where potential failure might exist. Understanding the potential for fixed mindsets toward institutional initiatives, and specifically assessment, was important when planning the Assessment Academy. The planning team understood that through intentional curriculum and pedagogical choices in the planning stages, a growth mindset culture could be encouraged. Dweck (2006) notes that an individual's mindset is often context-specific. Thus, it was important for the team to understand that participants may have preconceived, fixed perceptions of assessment and/or assessment initiatives prior to joining the assessment academy. The planning team wanted to create a culture where challenges and criticism were viewed as essential to the growth process. Doyle and Zakrajsek's (2013) ideas as viewed through the Assessment Academy lens reinforce the perspective that challenges allow programs to grow, and that an open perspective toward feedback (criticism) contributes to growth and improvement. To this end, specific curricular and pedagogical decisions were made to create a growth mindset culture for participants, including

- personalized content and outcomes,
- flexible delivery models,
- individual feedback opportunities,
- cohort creation with combination of growth and fixed mindset programs,
- small and large group learning opportunities,
- case study examples—institutional examples of assessment implementation and improvement, and
- recognition of participants and celebration of achievements and successes.

Team Approach

SDSU highly recommended that programs and units identify a minimum of two individuals to participate in the Assessment Academy. Developing and implementing a high-quality assessment plan is hard work. This complex task is easier to manage and helps foster buy-in from colleagues if more than one person is responsible for the plan.

Importance of Regular Communication

Academy participants needed to communicate with program faculty/staff about all aspects of the plan (mission, values, program goals, student learning outcomes, methods, use of data, communication plans, and reports) on a regular basis. Participants were encouraged to add the topic of assessing student learning to department/unit meetings in order to build a culture that addresses the topic often and in meaningful ways.

Accountability Measures

The SDSU Assessment Academy built in monthly tasks and milestones. For example, updated student learning outcomes were due by the third session, typically scheduled for October or November. Without clearly defined, measurable, and agreed-upon student learning outcomes, little progress can be made in mapping the curriculum or identifying assessment methods. Academy participants were also required to design and present a poster outlining their assessment plan at the SDSU Assessment Showcase each May. For all 3 years of the academy, individuals from 100% of the programs and units participated in the poster presentations.

Assessing the Assessment Process

As described previously, information about the current status of assessment plans and processes, as well as the current assessment culture, was gathered to have a basis on which to develop the content and structure of the SDSU Assessment Academy. In addition, and to model the need to inquire and reflect on current practices, feedback was requested from all academy participants and changes were made to the academy based on themes that emerged.

Recognize Contributions and Accomplishments

The culminating event of the SDSU Assessment Academy was the Spring Assessment Showcase. All current and former participants; department, school and unit heads; directors and coordinators; university leadership (president, vice presidents); and assessment leaders from other South Dakota Board of Regents institutions were invited to the showcase.

Next Steps

Academic year 2019–2020 was the first full academic year following the institution's official completion of the HLC and SDSU Assessment Academies. Support, resources and accountability measures for assessing student learning will continue, with a focus on the following:

- Increasing communication with deans and department heads/school directors about the status of assessment plans within their units and strategies to support faculty and staff

- Designing one or more award(s) to recognize contributions and accomplishments related to assessing student learning
- Identifying additional cocurricular units to participate in the ongoing Assessment Academy at SDSU. The 2020–2021 SDSU Assessment Academy will focus on assessing student learning within cocurricular units
- Reviewing performance standards for annual review, promotion and tenure, and rank adjustment to identify the degree to which work related to assessing student learning is included and investigating the degree to which workload is awarded for assessment-related tasks and responsibilities
- Fine-tuning the annual reporting review process conducted by the University Assessment Subcommittee

Over the past 4 years SDSU has made significant progress in continuing to build a stronger culture of assessment in a systematic and intentional manner. Participation in the HLC Assessment Academy provided a structure to guide the work including timelines and accountability measures. The model used over the 3 years of the SDSU Assessment Academy will continue to be used to offer comprehensive information and responsive consultation to develop knowledge, skills, and experiences with assessment processes and sustainable assessment practices.

References

American Association for Higher Education. (1992). *Nine principles of good practice for assessing student learning*. AAHE.

Doyle, T., & Zakrajsek, T. (2013). *The new science of learning: How to learn in harmony with your brain*. Stylus.

Dweck, C. S. (2006). *Mindset: The new psychology of success*. Random House.

Fuller, M. B., & Skidmore, S. (2014). An exploration of factors influencing institutional cultures of assessment. *International Journal of Educational Research, 65*, 9–21. https://doi:10.1016/j.ijer.2014.01.001

Fuller, M. B., Skidmore, S. T., Bustamante, R. M., & Holzweiss, P. (2016). Empirically exploring cultures of assessment in higher education: Results from the administrators' survey of assessment culture, *Review of Higher Education, 39*, 395–442. https://doi.org/10.1353/rhe.2016.0022

Keeling, R. P. (Ed.). (2006). *Learning reconsidered 2: A practical guide to implementing a campus-wide focus on the student experience*. American College Personnel Association.

National Institute for Learning Outcomes Assessment (NILOA). (2011). *Transparency framework*. University of Illinois and Indiana University, National Institute for Learning Outcomes Assessment.

8

INTRODUCING ASSESSMENT-TASK CHOICE IN AN ONLINE BACHELOR COURSE[1]

Ryan Jopp, Keryn Chalmers, Sandra Luxton, and Jay Cohen

> *You are free to make whatever choice you want, but you are not free from the consequences of the choice.—Anonymous*

Drawing on Jopp and Cohen (2020), this chapter summarizes the initiation, implementation, and outcomes of a choice-based assessment regime in an online course in a bachelor business program at Swinburne Business School.[2] Online modality is typically associated with higher attrition rates. Encouraged by the positive effects of "cafeteria-style assessment" (Hanewicz et al., 2017), a faculty member invested time and effort to initiate a choice-based assessment regime with the aim of enhancing learner retention, engagement, and completion. Learners were given agency to select the assessment tasks to complete from within a predefined set.

Swinburne Business School's Bachelor of Business is delivered through various modalities, including online via Swinburne Online (SOL).[3] Based on equivalent full-time student load (EFTSL), online learners account for 23% of learners studying the Bachelor of Business. Through SOL, Swinburne has become the fastest growing provider of online education in Australia.

Swinburne Online enables the Swinburne Business School to reach a broad cohort of learners, many of whom would otherwise not have an opportunity for quality tertiary education. Compared to learners studying on campus, the SOL cohort is older, resides in remote areas, and has a greater representation from the Indigenous population. Consistent with the extant literature (Edwards & McMillian, 2015; Moore & Greenland, 2017), the retention rate for the online modality is lower than for on-campus due to factors including managing competing priorities and socioeconomic status.

Recognizing that retention is more challenging for learners studying online, SOL has developed a program of study dedicated to the online learning environment. This content includes social media and communication technologies, models of online communication, current and evolving learning theories, identifying and evaluating sources of knowledge, critical analysis skills, referencing and attributing sources, creating and publishing in the online environment, and strategies for reflecting on work. Further, all courses have minimum standards of engagement with online learners, with options including digital assessment, mobile content, and community connectivity. SOL also arranges virtual classrooms through the organization of small study and discussion groups and assignment assistants using Studiosity. Initiating flexible assessment was a further investment to encourage online learner engagement and retention.

Consistent with the prior literature, preliminary findings of positive learner feedback and increased learner satisfaction suggest that learners value choice. Learner satisfaction increased slightly with the introduction of assessment-task choice relative to the prior teaching period. Further, a review of learners' qualitative feedback suggests that they are positively disposed toward assessment-task choice. Such findings support the benefits that accrue from empowering learners with a sense of ownership and responsibility related to assessment tasks.

Literature Review and Goal of the Assessment

Learner engagement is necessary for effective educational practices and learning (Biggs, 2012). Increasing learner engagement has focused on enhancing learners' participation in their learning through initiatives such as blended, peer, and experiential learning. Assessment is an influential factor for learner learning (Gibbs & Simpson, 2005; Williams, 2014). Assessment initiatives to drive learner engagement have predominantly been related to introducing authentic assessment tasks. Traditional forms of assessment are essays, tests, and exams. While these remain enshrined in many programs, innovations in assessment tasks have seen more diverse sets of tasks emerging.

The focus of the discussed study is introducing *flexible assessment* (also referred to as *student choice* and *selected assessment*) as a means of promoting learner engagement. Assessments are flexible "if they can accommodate the scope of knowledge and skills encompassed by the assessment criteria, the variations in context in which assessment may be conducted, and the range of needs and personal situations of potential candidates" (Rumsey, 1994, p. 20). Promoting learner choice in assessment regime design is advantageous as it encourages a sense of ownership and control for learners and enables them to self-select based on personal interests and capabilities (Nicol, 2009; Sambell et al., 2012).

Rideout (2018) notes that flexibility in assessment has received relatively scant attention within the literature. Studies that have examined this approach have operationalized flexible assessment through incorporating learner choice in assessment weighting, type, or format (Irwin & Hepplestone, 2012; Varsavsky & Rayner, 2012), timing (McCurdy, 2000), and criteria (Francis, 2008). The study contributes to prior studies investigating how learners can be more actively involved in the assessment tasks through assessment-task choice.

The move to an assessment-task choice regime in the Swinburne Business online bachelor course was motivated by positive learner outcomes reported by prior studies involving flexible assessment projects (Arendt et al., 2016; Cook, 2001; Hanewicz et al., 2017; Rideout, 2018). The early study of Cook (2001) provided learners with four assessment options built around various weighting combinations of final exam, midsemester exam, and computer-managed learning. The aim was to promote learner responsibility for their learning. Learners could elect the number of assessments to attempt—except for the final exam, which was mandatory—with the consequence of selecting less being a reduction in possible marks. The learner choices were interesting, with only 13 students of the 900 enrolled sitting the final exam only, and most of these students (n=11) failing the course. Further, 35 students elected not to undertake the computer-managed learning assessment, thereby restricting their marks to performance in the midsemester exam and final exam. Cook (2001) noted that the flexible assessment regime was positively received by learners and gave them a sense of control of their learning.

Hanewicz et al. (2017) found that learner choice promoted higher rates of engagement, with better exam results and increased student satisfaction reported. The flexible assessment introduced was a points accumulation system, with more points equating to higher grades. They reported that 36% of learners accumulated more points than were needed to enable them to reach the highest available grade. Similar to Cook (2001), the flexibility was positively received, with high course satisfaction and favorable learner comments. Arendt et al. (2016) allowed learners to choose assessments, with points earned according to the assessments selected. The assessment set was varied and included interviews, quizzes, exams, prototypes, and short academic papers. It included nearly 60 assessment options totaling 781 points and is referred to as *cafeteria assessment and grading*. While learners could achieve the maximum grade by accumulating 376 points, the study found that 9% of students completed more assessments than were necessary to maximize their grade. The flexibility afforded by this assessment regime needs to be balanced with its complexity.

Rideout (2018) allowed learners to personalize their learning experience. Learners were presented with the instructor's assessment regime and were permitted to modify the assessment tasks to complete, as well as the assessment weighting. The majority of learners (68%) elected to exercise some choice. The most popular choice was to opt out of larger assessments. Pretorius et al. (2017) introduced a flexible assessment regime where learners were given the choice to invest in within-semester tasks designed to encourage the development of higher order thinking skills. Faced with the decision to complete compulsory summative assessments and two optional tasks focused on the process of learning, they found that the majority of learners (66%) elected to invest extra time and effort to complete all four assessments. Interviews with learners suggested that they appreciated the ability to proactively manage their learning and the scaffolding of learning that occurred.

The prior studies support that learners appreciate being involved in the decision-making process related to assessments and that they are generally receptive to flexible assessment. Given the extant literature, Jopp and Cohen (2020) proposed that assessment-task choice would be favorably viewed by online learners as it allows them to make choices based on their personal and professional interests.

Moving to an Assessment-Task Choice Regime

There were multiple activities involved in support of the goal of introducing flexible assessment. Steps included setting the criteria for course inclusion, selecting the regime, and considering the learners' choices.

Course Selection

Criteria were established to guide the selection of which course in the Swinburne Bachelor of Business would introduce flexible assessment. The course selected had to

- minimize risk if the learner experience was negative (e.g., the number of impacted students was considered),
- be delivered fully online,

- demonstrate scope for improving learner satisfaction based on prior student feedback,
- have faculty's and e-learning adviser's unreserved support for the assessment regime change, and
- have a current assessment regime warranting improvement (e.g., an overreliance on exam).

Applying the selection criteria, the course selected was Business and Society. This is a 2nd-year course in the undergraduate business program with approximately 150 enrollments. The assessment-task choice regime was introduced in teaching period 3 in 2018. The course synopsis reads as follows:

> This unit challenges students to identify and evaluate major socioeconomic issues, the role of various stakeholders, and the potential for business solutions that can drive sustainable development and innovation. A major focus is on gaining a critical appreciation of stakeholder theory, and understanding how this theory frames integrative thinking, across disciplines. It will also cover two important areas that stakeholder theory has helped to shape and define: business ethics and corporate social responsibility.

Given that pedagogical research associated with the introduction of the assessment-task choice regime was to be conducted, Human Research Ethics approval was sought and granted.

Selecting the Assessment Regime

Introducing assessment flexibility is premised on the choice being motivating for learners. Flexible assessment can take a number of forms, including choices related to assessment type, weighting, format, timing, and assessment criteria (Francis, 2008; Irwin & Hepplestone, 2012; McCurdy, 2000; Varsavsky & Rayner, 2012). However, choice also requires cognitive effort and can create additional burden for learners. Choice complexity is a typical feature of prior choice-based assessment studies (Arendt et al., 2016). Simplicity was the guiding principle in designing the assessment choice for Business and Society. It was desirable to maintain the same assessment format and to make the choices easy to understand and less burdensome by restricting the set of alternatives.

The number, type (individual/group), and weighting of the assessments did not change from previous teaching periods. Within the assessment-task choice regime, each assessment had the same weighting and the same due date. The approach did not involve bonus points as learners did not have the option to complete more than the three selected assessment tasks. The assessment regime in the course before and after the introduction of assessment choice is depicted in Table 8.1. There was no change to Assessment Task 1A, with all learners required to complete a quiz in week 4. This assessment task is designed to provide early feedback to learners and assist with identifying learners who are at-risk or not engaged with the learning. Assessment Task 1B moved from an essay to the choice of an essay or article analysis or quiz. The article analysis assessment required learners to compare and contrast creating shared value (CSV) and corporate social responsibility (CSR) based on two articles, one from *Harvard Business Review* and the other from the *European Management Journal*. The quiz involved a variety of true/false and multiple-choice questions, as well as five short-answer questions.

The choices incorporated for Assessment 2 were a review of a documentary or a point and counterpoint as well as the original case study report. For the documentary review learners selected one of the suggested *Four Corners*[4] documentaries and analyzed the particular socioeconomic or environmental challenge or opportunity portrayed. The point and counterpoint involved students working in pairs to develop an academic argument for two sides of an ethical issue or debate. The historical final assessment task in the course was an examination (2 hours) and this was amended to allow learners the option to do an examination (2 hours), business interviews, or a poster. The business interviews involved learners

TABLE 8.1
Assessment Regime Before and After Adoption of Assessment-Task Choice

Assessment Task	Weighting	Nonchoice Assessment Regime	Assessment-Task Choice Regime
Assessment 1A	10% weighting, Individual	Quiz	Quiz
Assessment 1B	20% weighting, Individual	Essay	Essay or Article analysis or Quiz
Assessment 2	30% weighting, Group	Case study report	Case study report or Review of documentary or Point and counterpoint
Assessment 3	40% weighting, Individual	Exam	Exam or Business interviews or Poster

asking the same set of questions to a manager from the not-for-profit and for-profit sectors in order to determine any similarities or differences in their approach to business and stakeholder relations. The poster presentation was an online infographic exploring the value and benefits of a selected public-private partnership (PPP).

Clear communication of the assessment regime, to both learners and faculty, was critical to its understanding and success. The learner communication strategy, enacted via the learning management system, comprised an initial email to all learners after their enrollment into the course advising of the assessment-task choice, an introduction video discussing the features and logistics of the assessment, and frequently asked questions. It did not appear that any learner opted out of the course after receiving advice of the assessment regime. For faculty, a briefing session as well as email correspondences provided the teaching team with clear instructions of the assessment-task choice approach, marking requirements, and responses to anticipated frequently asked questions. The limited questions from learners and the teaching team implied that the communication strategy was well planned, executed, and received.

Learners' Choices

Of the 144 students enrolled in the course at precensus date, 135 students attempted Assessment 1B, 134 students attempted Assessment 2, and 129 students attempted Assessment 3. This compares favorably to prior semesters, suggesting the flexibility had a positive impact on learner engagement and retention. It also indicates that success rates are likely to be higher with more learners completing all assessment tasks.

Learners' assessment-task choices are summarized in Table 8.2. For Assessment 1B the selection was much skewed to the quiz, with 119 of the 135 learners completing this assessment task. Only 13 learners opted for the essay and even fewer (three) for article analysis. This outcome also supports Rideout's (2018) findings of strong learner preference to undertake quizzes when available. A plausible reason is that the choice is based on learner familiarity with quizzes given that they are used in most prior courses and a quiz was Assessment 1A. It may also be due to learners' perception that quizzes are easier and less time demanding for online learners.

Interestingly, the average mark (grade) was higher for the least selected assessment task, being 70 for the article analysis compared to 66.2 and 64.5 for the quiz and essay, respectively. Perhaps learners who are striving to achieve select what is perceived to be the more interesting and complex assessment task, in this case an article analysis. The outcomes also suggest

TABLE 8.2
Learners' Assessment-Task Choices

Assessments	# of Learners	% of Learners	Average Mark
Assessment 1B	**135**		**66.9**
Quiz	119	88	66.2
Essay	13	10	64.5
Article Analysis	3	2	70.0
Assessment 2	**134**		**66.6**
Review of Documentary	65	48	64.8
Case Study	47	35	67.0
Point and Counterpoint	22	16	67.9
Assessment 3	**129**		**63.3**
Poster	77	60	64.2
Exam	38	29	61.7
Business Interview	14	11	64.0

that the learners may not have adequately prepared for the perceived easier task, being the quiz. Fail grades were only recorded for Assessment 1B in the learner cohort electing the quiz.

The choices were more spread for Assessment 2. The documentary review was the most selected task (n=65), followed by the case study (n=47) and then the point and counterpoint. The average marks were similar across each task, being 67.9 for the point and counterpoint, 67 for the case study, and 64.8 for the documentary review. Assessment 2 was a group task, so understanding group decision-making in the selection process would be interesting to investigate further.

Assessment 3 had the highest weighting (40%), with most learners opting for the poster. The poster assessment was selected by 77 learners, with the average mark being 64.2. The second popular assessment was the exam, selected by 39 learners, with an average mark of 61.7. Only 14 learners opted to conduct business interviews, with the average mark being 64. The popularity of the poster may reflect learners' appreciation of the opportunity to be creative or this being the preferred option to avoid an examination. However, if examinations are disliked, it was surprising to see the number of learners still selecting this option and electing it over the business interviews.

A plausible explanation is that for the online cohort, many of whom juggle various commitments, scheduling a 2-hour block to do an examination is preferable to the time commitment and confidence associated with arranging and conducting business interviews.

Learners' Outcomes

Outcomes of the project to introduce assessment-task choice were evaluated using both quantitative and qualitative data. Student performance was analyzed using course grading, and learner satisfaction was considered through survey responses.

Learner Performance

Of the 144 learners enrolled in the course, 126 (88%) passed the course. The majority of learners received a credit grade (n=60, 42%) or distinction grade (n=48, 33%), 17 obtained a pass grade (12%), and only one learner received a high distinction. There were nine students who completed assessments but failed and a further nine students who failed due to withdrawing from the course postcensus date or submitting no assessment tasks. The grade distribution for the online teaching period coinciding with the introduction of the assessment-task choice (teaching period 3, 2018) is compared with that for the immediate prior online teaching period (teaching period 1, 2018) as well as that for the face-to-face delivery (semester 1, 2018), both having a fixed assessment regime. The distributions are shown in Table 8.3. Overall, the grade distribution was similar to previous deliveries, both on campus and online.[5] The inaugural delivery of assessment-task choice does not appear to have enhanced learner results.

Learner Feedback

At the end of each teaching period, Swinburne Business surveys learners about their overall course satisfaction, using a Likert scale of 1 to 10, with 10 being excellent.[6] Learners can also provide qualitative comments on their learning experience. Sixty-five (45%) of the Business and Society learners completed the questionnaire. The overall course satisfaction was 8.1 out of 10, exceeding the Swinburne Business expectation of 7.5. This rating is higher than the ratings for the course in the periods immediately prior to the introduction of assessment-task choice. The previous online delivery of the course in teaching period 1 recorded an overall satisfaction

TABLE 8.3
Grade Distributions for Business and Society Course

	High D* 80–100%	D* 70–79%	Credit 60–69%	Pass 50–59%	Fail 0–49%	Not Assessed	# of Learners
Online Teaching Period 3 (assessment-task choice)	1	48	60	17	9	9	144
Online Teaching Period 1 (nonchoice assessment)	14	78	37	19	10	1	159
Traditional Face to Face Semester 1 (nonchoice assessment)	7	32	33	14	8	0	94

Note. *D = Distinction

rating of 7.9 and the on-campus delivery in teaching period 1 returned a satisfaction of 7.1. While this outcome is positive, it is inappropriate to associate the higher satisfaction with the change in assessment regime given that this was not a controlled experiment. Many other factors could have influenced the rating such as the learner cohort, delivery mode, and teaching faculty.

Learners' qualitative comments provided insights on the value placed on assessment choice. Learners were asked two specific questions: (a) what were the best aspects of this course, and (b) what aspects of this course could be improved? The number of respondents to the questions was 44 (32%) and 57 (41%), respectively. The assessment choice was a common theme when describing the best aspects of the course. This was mentioned by 24 of the 44 respondents with comments.

As expected, assessment choice was also the target for areas of improvement. Consistent with Hanewicz et al. (2017), no learner suggested that the assessment-task choice regime be abandoned. Five of the 57 responses suggesting improvements in the course related to assessment choice. These respondents identified the complexity of understanding the different assessment choices, and a lack of clarity associated with selecting particular assessment tasks. Interestingly, one student stated that "I myself had difficulty deciding which assignment style to choose which created procrastination," indicating that the ability to self-select assessment tasks may not be for everyone. Example comments for both questions are shown in Table 8.4.

Conclusion and Next Steps

The introduction of assessment-task choice in an online course in a business bachelor program at Swinburne Business School was well received by learners. While the results reported are only for the teaching period coinciding with its introduction, the quantitative and qualitative feedback suggests that learners benefit from empowering them with a sense of ownership and responsibility related to assessment tasks. Learners value choice in assessment tasks.

Assessment choice can also deliver benefits for faculty. Wyman (2017) notes that the number of complaints may be reduced due to the choice and the need for more varied assessment aligned to learning outcomes that may be more effective in assuring learning. She also argues that learners can be more effectively assessed, as assessment tasks can be selected to better align with their learning abilities. For example, some learners simply do not perform well under examination conditions. Allowing learners to choose

TABLE 8.4
Example Learner Comments

What were the best aspects of this course?
The options for assessments is a great idea!
The choice of assignments, great to pick based on my strengths and weaknesses. Also gives me a chance to pick something I've never done before such as the Assignment 3 Poster.
Assignment options—option to choose assignment that best fits personal needs is a great addition.
The ability to choose assignments. Go Swinburne!
Assignment options—option to choose assignment that best fits personal needs is a great addition.
The flexibility has really helped me.
Choice and the relevance of the material and assignments to my work life.
Obviously, the new option of choosing where our strengths were in the style of assessment we were to present. Some of us are not strong in exams and the fact that there [were] options to choose an assessment [where] memorization was not a factor, eased my stress levels and I was able to use my strengths.
Having assignment choices and not having to sit for a final exam as I am one that panics when you have to sit for a closed book exam.
Being able to select our own assessments, and opt in or out of the exam, this helped me play to my skillset and gave me confidence.
What aspects of this course could be improved?
Better explanations of the options were required.
Having assignment options is great, but I believe I would have performed better having full clarity across one assignment choice rather than mixed messages about all different choices.

their assessment can also be more rewarding and meaningful for faculty, as it affords opportunities for learners to demonstrate their learning in a manner that a rigid assessment may not.

Reflecting on the introduction of assessment-task choice, a number of key learnings emerge. First, it is important to have clear communications and dedicated discussion boards to enable students to understand the choices available and make better choices to showcase their strengths and maintain their interest and engagement. While assessment-task choice was well received, there was evidence of choice overload. Recognizing the cognitive effort choice requires and not wanting to unnecessarily burden learners, simplification has subsequently occurred. The next phase of the initiative is running with two options per assessment rather than three. To avoid choice overload there are also fewer options within each assessment task (e.g., choice of documentary). This action makes the selection process easier for students as well as reducing faculty preparation and marking workload.

Given the distributed choice and learner performance across different assessment tasks, a review of the assessment instructions and rubric for all assessment tasks has occurred. Faculty felt that this action was important to ensure clarity for learners of the assessment task requirements, particularly for tasks that learners had less exposure to and therefore less familiarity with (e.g., the documentary review and team point and counterpoint assessments).

Continued research in this area will seek to gather more information (e.g., professional alignment, demographics, preferred learning style) that can be used to explore learner choices given the association between such factors and learners' assessment preferences (Gijbels & Dochy, 2006). Another question worthy of further exploration is whether the introduction of a flexible assessment regime adds significant administrative and grading workload to the teaching team. Arendt et al. (2016) note an increase in preparation time due to the variety of assessment tasks. In contrast, Rideout (2018) suggests that grading time reduces as learners do not complete all assessments. Anecdotally, some faculty did comment that this initiative led to an increase in administrative and marking load. However, this was generally perceived as minimal and worthwhile given the positive student outcomes. Additional workload allocations were also provided for marking as part of the pilot.

Notes

1 This chapter is derived in part from an article published in *Teaching in Higher Education* (March 2020) ©Taylor and Francis. Available online: https://www.tandfonline.com/doi/full/10.1080/13562517.2020.1742680

2 Ryan Jopp is a senior lecturer, Swinburne Business School and the convenor of the course where assessment-task choice was introduced.

3 Swinburne University has an associated entity, Online Education Services (OES). OES provides a range of Swinburne's courses online under the Swinburne Online (SOL) brand. Swinburne retains full control and authority for courses delivered through SOL. Students taught through SOL are Swinburne-enrolled students. Business School faculty construct learning outcomes, assessments, and curriculum content and work with SOL learning designers for these to be translated for SOL delivery. They also have responsibility for quality assurance and equivalence.

4 *Four Corners* is an Australian investigative journalism television program.

5 Caution must be exercised when comparing the grade distributions given that the comparisons are not in the same teaching period. Teaching period 3 is the summer semester period and historically the GPAs at Swinburne for this period are lower than in other periods.

6 The learner surveys include a range of questions related to course and teaching quality with responses to the question on overall course satisfaction being a key metric.

References

Arendt, A., Trego, A., & Allred, J. (2016). Students reach beyond expectations with cafeteria style grading. *Journal of Applied Research in Higher Education*, *8*(1), 1–17. https://doi.org/10.1108/JARHE-03-2014-0048

Biggs, J. (2012). What the student does: Teaching for enhanced learning. *Higher Education Research and Development*, *31*(1), 39–55. https://doi.org/10.1080/0729436990180105

Cook, A. (2001). Assessing the use of flexible assessment. *Assessment & Evaluation in Higher Education*, *26*(6), 539–549. https://doi.org/10.1080/02602930120093878

Edwards, D., & McMillian, J. (2015). *Completing university in a growing sector: Is equity an issue?* Australian Council for Educational Research.

Francis, R. (2008). An investigation into the receptivity of undergraduate students to assessment empowerment. *Assessment & Evaluation in Higher Education*, *33*(5), 547–557. https://doi.org/10.1080/02602930701698991

Gibbs, G., & Simpson, L. (2005). Conditions under which assessment supports students' learning. *Learning and Teaching in Higher Education (LATHE)*, *1*(2004–2005), 3–31. http://eprints.glos.ac.uk/3609/1/LATHE%201.%20Conditions%20Under%20Which%20Assessment%20Supports%20Students%27%20Learning%20Gibbs_Simpson.pdf

Gijbels, D., & Dochy, F. (2006). Students' assessment preferences and approaches to learning: Can formative assessment make a difference? *Educational Studies*, *32*(4), 399–409. http://doi.org/10.1080/03055690600850354

Hanewicz, C., Platt, A., & Arendt, A. (2017). Creating a learner-centred teaching environment using student choice in assignments. *Distance Education*, *38*(3), 273–287. http://doi.org/10.1080/01587919.2017.1369349

Irwin, B., & Hepplestone, S. (2012). Examining increased flexibility in assessment formats. *Assessment & Evaluation in Higher Education*, *37*(7), 773–785. https://doi.org/10.1080/02602938.2011.573842

Jopp, R., & Cohen, J. (2020, March 23). Choose your own assessment—Assessment choice for students in online higher education. *Teaching in Higher Education*, Advance online publication. https://doi.org/10.1080/13562517.2020.1742680

McCurdy, D. (Ed.). (2000). The flexible assessment paradigm. *Proceedings of the 13th Annual Conference of the National Advisory Committee on Computing Qualifications* (pp. 227–233).

Moore, C., & Greenland, S. (2017). Employment-driven online student attrition and the assessment policy divide: An Australian open-access higher education perspective. *Journal of Open, Flexible, and Distance Learning, 21*(1), 52–62.

Nicol, D. (2009). *Quality enhancement themes: The first year experience*. The Quality Assurance Agency for Higher Education.

Pretorius, L., van Mourik, G., & Barratt, C. (2017). Student choice and higher-order thinking: Using a novel flexible assessment regime combined with critical thinking activities to encourage the development of higher order thinking. *International Journal of Teaching and Learning in Higher Education, 29*(2), 389–401. https://files.eric.ed.gov/fulltext/EJ1146270.pdf

Rideout, C. (2018). Students' choice and achievement in large undergraduate classes using a novel flexible assessment approach. *Assessment and Evaluation in Higher Education, 43*(1), 68–78. https://doi.org/10.1080/02602938.2017.1294144

Rumsey, D. (1994). *Assessment practical guide*. Australian Government Publishing Service.

Sambell, K., McDowell, L., & Montgomery, C. (2012). *Assessment for learning in higher education*. Routledge.

Varsavsky, C., & Rayner, G. (2012). Strategies that challenge: Exploring the use of differentiated assessment to challenge high-achieving students in large enrolment undergraduate cohorts. *Assessment & Evaluation in Higher Education, 38*(7), 789–802. https://doi.org/10.1080/02602938.2012.714739

Williams, J. (2014). Student feedback on the experience of higher education. In M. E. Menon, D. G. Terkla, & P. Gibbs (Eds.), *Using data to improve higher education: Research, policy and practice* (pp. 67–80). Sense.

Wyman, K. (2017). *Let students choose alternative assessments and watch their creativity Bloom*. Concordia University Portland. https://education.cu-portland.edu/blog/classroom-resources/students-choose-assessments-creativity/

9

EMPLOYING PEER LEARNING AND ASSESSMENT AT SCALE

Brian Harlan, Shawn Moustafa, and Roxie Smith

University of the People (UoPeople) was established in 2009 with the mission of offering affordable, quality, online, degree-granting educational programs to any qualified student. In support of its mission, UoPeople uses open educational resources (OER), employs technology and automation to improve service and accuracy, relies on a community of volunteers/supporters, and maintains highly efficient processes. Peer learning sits at the intersection of efficient processes and automation in support of programmatic quality. Students who meet admissions requirements pay no tuition and are charged only a nominal course assessment fee—$100 per course at the undergraduate level and $200 per course at the graduate level.

The university serves as a natural experiment for exploring the feasibility of utilizing peer learning and assessment as key components of an institution's overall instructional model. This chapter reports on the results of assessing the institution's effectiveness in employing this strategy at scale and explores adjustments necessary to enhance operations.

Goal of Our Assessment

It has long been accepted that learning has a social component—that direct reinforcement does not account for all types of learning and that people learn new information and behaviors through observational learning. Learning from and with one another occurs naturally in all aspects of life and work and serves to enhance understanding and retention (Boud & Fachikov, 2006). Sloman and Fernback (2017) argue that human knowledge is not a product of individual effort, but rather emerges from cooperative efforts within the community. Humans rely heavily on others to share the cognitive load, with the most intuitive approach to knowledge storage and retrieval being cooperation (Wegner et al., 1985). Observational learning is not new. Its roots can be traced to the earliest forms of community, where knowledge from one generation was transmitted to the next through instruction and modeling. Additionally, making judgments about others is an activity in which people engage on a daily basis, in an almost automatic manner, both explicitly and implicitly.

Topping (2005) defines *peer learning* as "the acquisition of knowledge and skill through active helping and supporting among status equals or matched companions" (p. 631). Research on social learning theory has shown peer learning and peer assessment to be effective instructional tools. They provide an environment where students are learning in a mutually beneficial manner from and with each other, what Boud (1988) calls *interdependent or mutual learning*.

Peer learning takes many forms—seminars, discussion sections, study groups, peer tutoring, peer teaching, group projects, and so on. In these structures, it is not a "teacher" passing knowledge but fellow learners sharing what they themselves have just learned—a student-centered rather than teacher-centered approach to learning. Described as "two-way reciprocal learning" (Boud et al., 2001, p. 3), participants share with one another their ideas, opinions, past experiences, and previously and newly acquired knowledge, to the benefit of both parties. Further, the "peer" is a similarly situated individual on the same plane with respect to power, position, and responsibilities.

Peer learning and peer assessment support active engagement and are consistent with the constructivist models of education wherein reality is constructed from sensory input (Carlile & Jordan, 2005; Vygotsky, 1978). Contemporary constructivist theories related to learning emerged out of the work of Jean Piaget (Pritchard & Woollard, 2010). Vygotsky's contributions were to place an emphasis on the interaction between learners and to make clear that those in the role of "knowledgeable others" need not be teachers in the traditional, hierarchical sense.

Research has demonstrated the effectiveness of these tools in small group and individual classroom settings, yet they are used sporadically. Further, no institution has implemented them across its entire instructional program. Experience with the peer review process for journals and scientific projects, one of the few large group applications, demonstrates some of the challenges encountered in using assessment at scale. In those instances, however, scale meant large submission pools (Kotturi et al., 2018), rather than institution-wide usage with smaller pools of subjects as is found in UoPeople's classes.

UoPeople employs peer learning and assessment, alongside readings, supplemental learning aids, and library resources in every course that it offers. Students both peer assess and peer grade, which means that they are engaging in assessment *for* learning as well as assessment *of* learning.

Student as the Grader

Students grade peers based on rubrics. Rubrics contain common criteria that are used by all students to evaluate and score. Rubrics guide the content of the evaluative comments and inform students beforehand about the criteria that peers will be using to assess their work. Rubrics also let students know the nature of the work that is expected of them and help students plan and organize their own work products. A single 10-point rubric is used for grading all discussion forums. Tailored rubrics, with 5–7 elements, are crafted for one-time assignments and projects, with comment fields for each element. Students are required to comment on the posts of three classmates, so the identity of a commenter is known, but the identity of a grader is always masked. Multiple classmates can and do comment, increasing the amount of feedback students receive on their posts. Assignment grading is also done using a blind process, to foster greater objectivity. Assignments are due at the end of Week X, and students are randomly assigned by Moodle to grade the work product of three classmates in the following week. Students have the full week to do the grading, with 10% of their own grade based on the quality of their grading. Students take the grading responsibility very seriously, even if, as shown in the data, their classmates may not necessarily share that view. They tend to be harsher than course instructors and focus more heavily on shortcomings. Their course instructors work with them to understand that it is okay to give satisfactory and even good grades.

Benefits to Peer Learning and Assessment

Students benefit from peer learning and assessment in a myriad of ways. They receive more feedback than would otherwise be the case if only the course instructor were grading their work. The process promotes an exchange of ideas and helps consolidate the assessor's own learning. Content must first be mastered before one can apply it when assessing the work of others, which has the effect of forcing them to engage content in a more penetrating manner. Since students are writing their assessments, it can eliminate the embarrassment associated with public speaking and can free them to participate more actively. Additionally, it gives students time to organize their thinking and assemble their contributions. As discussed previously, they are, in effect, constructing their own knowledge.

Peer assessment also fosters the life skill of working collaboratively. It hones the ability to give and receive feedback, as well as the ability to evaluate one's own learning and work products (Boud et al., 2001). It provides students with partial ownership of the assessment process, thereby contributing to course/program motivation (Gok, 2012), and it treats assessment as part of the learning process, where mistakes are viewed as an opportunity to learn. Creating a sense of community within the student population has been cited as a benefit (Buraphadeja & Kumnuanta, 2011) and, at UoPeople, peer learning and assessment offer the opportunity to build relationships with fellow students from around the globe.

While advantages to students are paramount, institutions report benefits as well. Faculty who use peer learning and assessment have time freed to devote to other components of their courses. Furthermore, employing these methodologies can reduce the need for additional personnel. At UoPeople, its use translates into the ability to attract volunteer course instructors, be tuition-free, and charge only a modest course assessment fee.

Activities/Strategies to Support Achievement of the Goal

UoPeople invests considerable effort and resources in support of its goal of using peer learning and assessment as key components of its instructional approach. The university has found that the success of the endeavor is dependent upon how systematically peer learning and assessment activities are planned and managed and on how effectively the institution both explains the methodology and trains students to be constructive participants.

The process begins at the course design stage. Subject matter expert/course developers for new courses are coached on how to make their assessments fit with UoPeople's established format. They are given sample rubrics, and there is a template for rubrics in the institution's course development guide.

UoPeople recognized from the outset that few, if any, of its students would have had experience with peer-to-peer learning and assessment before coming to the institution. In their previous educational experiences, they would have been recognized for the work that they had done as individuals. Peer assessment can make students uncomfortable; they find it difficult, may have concerns about fairness, and may even object to it. As can be seen in the data tables, UoPeople has encountered all of these issues, with one of the hardest lessons to teach being that peer assessment is a way of engaging with course content, as opposed to something that is distinct from it.

The first course that all students take, UNIV 1001 Online Education Strategies, contains a unit on the topic of peer learning and assessment. This course was also the first one that the institution developed, recognizing that incoming students were going to need training in this process. Students are introduced to the mechanics and benefits and begin to peer assess their classmates from the first week. Why it is an effective instructional tool and the benefits it brings the learner are explained, and students are guided through exercises intended to teach them how to do it. It is also essential that the course instructor proactively monitor grading to identify potentially unacceptable activity. While not a frequent occurrence, excessively punitive or unsupported positive assessments must be addressed. Students are also advised that they can contact their course instructor if they believe that an assessment of their work is out of line with expected norms, and course instructors are evaluated on their support and monitoring of peer assessment activities.

Assessments Used to Determine Progress Toward Goal

Anecdotal feedback and results of surveys of enrolled students and alumni show the extent to which students have both benefited from and struggled with the model. As can be seen, some aspects have been monitored every year, while others have been assessed only in special studies, probed in revised forms, or are no longer followed.

Enrolled Student Surveys

Each year since 2012–2013, students have been asked to indicate their degree of satisfaction with the overall quality of instruction and the institution's assessment and evaluation procedures. They report being satisfied with the overall instructional quality and neutral-to-satisfied with the assessment and evaluation procedures (Table 9.1).

TABLE 9.1
Student Perceptions of Instruction and Assessment

Item	2012–2013	2013–2014	2014–2015	2015–2016	2016–2017	2018–2019	2019–2020
Overall quality of instruction	4.1	4.3	4.2	4.1	4.1	4.2	3.8
Assessment and evaluation procedures	3.5	3.8	3.8	3.8	3.9	—	—

Note. Survey was based on a 5-point scale. Survey was not conducted in 17–18.

In three of the years, students were asked their views on the merits of peer assessment. As shown in Table 9.2, they viewed peer assessment as a reasonably important part of their own studies, but somewhat more important to the learning of others, a theme that also appears in later studies as shown in Table 9.3. There the data suggest that they believe they work harder and do better for their peers than their peers do for them.

TABLE 9.2
Student Perceptions of Peer Assessment

Item	2013–2014	2014–2015	2015–2016
Peer assessment (and feedback) are a valuable part of my studies.	3.8	3.8	3.7
I understand the process of peer assessment and realize that the quality of my feedback to others will affect my overall grade.	4.4	4.2	4.1

Note. Survey was based on a 5-point scale.

TABLE 9.3
Student Perceptions of Peer Assessment

Item	2015–2016	2018–2019	2019–2020
I find it easy to assess the work of my fellow students.	3.8	3.9	3.5
I gain a deeper understanding of what is being taught because I must use it to assess the work of others.	4.1	—	—
The rubrics provide helpful guidance for assessing the work of others.	4.0	4.1	—
I understand that the quality of my feedback helps my fellow students learn more.	4.3	4.3	3.8
I work hard to give fair and helpful feedback to others.	4.6	4.5	—
I understand that the quality of my feedback to others will affect my overall grade.	4.5	—	—
My peers give me meaningful and helpful feedback.	3.4	—	—
I learn from the feedback that is provided by my fellow students.	3.7	3.9	3.4
The peer learning and assessment process is a valuable part of my studies.	3.9	3.9	3.5

Note. Survey was based on a 5-point scale. Survey was not conducted in 16–17 or 17–18.

In May 2018, as part of planning for a student success initiative, the institution conducted a special study of enrolled students to identify areas of the instructional approach that were particularly challenging to them. It found that, of the 2,600 respondents, 51% were satisfied or very satisfied with the peer learning model. Only 31% indicated being dissatisfied or very dissatisfied with it. Nearly two-thirds (64%) reported having encountered at least one challenge using it. While less than half (43%) said that the challenge(s) they had were with a discussion forum, 84% said that they had encountered one or more challenges associated with written assignments. Not surprisingly, the majority of those reporting having had one or more difficulties were students in their first or second terms of study. Those students further along in their studies were less likely to report continuing to encounter challenges. Students were also asked about the nature of the challenges they were encountering. The percent of students citing an item as a challenge is shown in Table 9.4 in descending order.

One gratifying result emerged from this mini-survey. Students were no longer expressing fundamental concerns about peer learning as a pedagogical approach or questioning how it was structured. This fact suggests that some of the adjustments and interventions described are having an impact. Students do remain concerned about the ability of their peers to do an effective job, similar to what was seen in Tables 9.2 and 9.3. Interestingly, the same ordering of challenges was seen whether the students who responded were early in their studies or further along.

TABLE 9.4
Student Perceptions of Challenges With Peer Assessment, 2018 Study

Item	% Citing
My peers did not provide explanations or feedback to explain low grades.	54
My peers' understanding of the class materials was not sufficient to ensure fair grading.	48
My peers' English level was not sufficient to ensure fair grading.	30
My peers cannot evaluate my work properly due to cultural barriers.	27
Instructors were not involved enough and therefore did not review unfair grades.	25
The instructions for peer-to-peer assessments were not sufficient.	16

Alumni Surveys

At various points, input has also been sought from alumni, although, when interpreting results, it must be kept in mind that until about 2015, the number of alumni was relatively small. When asked to indicate to what extent peer assessment contributed to their overall learning, on average they reported it having had a positive impact (Table 9.5).

When asked to indicate their degree of satisfaction with the overall quality of instruction and with the peer learning process, students reported being very satisfied with the overall quality of instruction and neutral-to-satisfied with the ways in which learning was assessed by their peers (Table 9.6).

As discussed, peer learning and assessment are thought to benefit students in a number of ways. In the early years and again more recently, alumni have been asked to indicate to what extent their degree program at UoPeople contributed to the development of a range of skills and attitudes associated with those benefits as presented in Table 9.7. In almost every area, their time at the institution was seen as significantly strengthening their abilities.

TABLE 9.5
Alumni Perceptions of the Impact of Peer Learning

Item	2013–2014	2014–2015
The assessments you did of the written assignments of your classmates	3.3	3.2
The responses that you submitted to at least three postings of your classmates in the Discussion Forum	3.1	3.2

Note. Survey was based on a 4-point scale.

TABLE 9.6
Alumni Perceptions of the Quality of Instruction With Peer Learning

Item	2013–2014	2014–2015
Overall quality of instruction	4.5	4.6
Ways in which learning was assessed and evaluated by your peers	3.8	3.8

Note. Survey was based on a 5-point scale.

TABLE 9.7
Alumni Perceptions of the Impact of Their Degree on Specific Skills

Item	2013–2014	2014–2015	2017–2018
Thinking critically	3.9	3.7	4.2
Ability to reach a conclusion and make a decision	3.9	3.8	—
Constructively resolving interpersonal conflicts	3.6	3.7	—
Judging the merits of arguments based on their sources, methods, and reasoning	3.4	3.6	—
Functioning effectively as a member of a team	3.8	3.4	3.6
Openness to having my own views challenged	3.8	3.6	—
Ability to discuss and negotiate controversial issues	3.8	3.4	—

Note. The 4-point scale was changed to a 5-point scale in 2017. Survey was not conducted in 15–16 or 16–17.

Additional Assessment Methods

Grades on group projects and in capstone courses provide the most direct measures of student abilities. Course instructors monitor grading, and grades on group assignments show that students are functioning as team members and have the ability to negotiate controversial issues. Grades in capstone courses show that students are able to think critically. Of the 513 students who have completed the MBA degree, 81% earned As in the course, 18% earned Bs, and 1% earned Cs.

Finally, UoPeople needs to monitor whether the use of peer learning and assessment might serve as an impediment to degree completion. Its curricula are designed and monitored by disciplinary advisory boards composed of some of the world's leading scholars and practitioners. Advisory boards function as the equivalent of a department's curriculum committee. This structure ensures that academic rigor is built into the curriculum, with program goals, course content, course sequencing, semester credit hours to be awarded, and other degree requirements being set by the advisory board. After individual courses are developed, the advisory board reviews curriculum mapping to ensure that individual assessment activities map to course learning objectives, and course learning objectives map to program goals. Only after the advisory board is comfortable that the mapping reflects a comprehensive curricular offering are curricula and individual courses offered to students.

UoPeople serves an adult population, with students on average being in their early 30s. Nearly three-quarters of the students report working 40 or more hours per week, and 63% report having a spouse/significant other, children, and/or parents for whom they have responsibility. This means that on average, most take only one to one-and-a-half courses per term and typically take double (or more) the customary time to complete the degree. In the early years, UoPeople kept enrollments intentionally low while it developed institutional structures, refined policies and procedures, and obtained accreditation. Only after it had been operating for about 6 years did it begin growing enrollments in any systematic way.

Access and opportunity are core values of the institution and any applicant over the age of 16 with a high school diploma or its equivalent and English language proficiency is admitted as a nondegree-seeking student (NDSS). They demonstrate preparedness for college-level work and subsequently apply to be a degree-seeking student (DSS). More than half of those who begin, for whatever reason, do not convert to DSS standing. While there are many reasons given for withdrawing, some do cite a lack of comfort with peer learning and assessment as one cause. Even within this highly contextualized environment, students are progressing and are earning degrees. To date, UoPeople has awarded 728 associate degrees, 312 bachelor's degrees, and 513 master's degrees.

Use of Findings

In response to input from students and alumni, UoPeople has taken a number of steps to enhance the way in which the peer learning and assessment process is explained and how it functions. For example, ensuring that the institution was being maximally transparent about its use of peer learning and assessment led to the inclusion of more information about it on the website, as well as in other places. In the early years, the labels were thought to be enough to inform prospective students, but that proved not to be the case. In an effort to increase transparency, the website now does the following:

- defines collaborative learning;
- states that every UoPeople course offers opportunities for students to work collaboratively, including discussion forums and peer review groups;
- describes the skills students gain from collaborative learning;
- defines peer-to-peer learning;
- describes how peer-to-peer learning works at UoPeople; and
- describes the benefits to students of teamwork and cooperation in their educational and professional careers.

These same messages are included in various forms in both the undergraduate and graduate catalogs. Prospective applicants and the public can also read descriptions of what it is like to be a UoPeople student under the tabs "Become a Student" and "Student Experience" that can be found on the institution's landing page.

In an effort to provide early training on the methodology, UoPeople started offering an optional noncredit orientation course for students who had been admitted to the institution but were waiting for the new term to begin. Separate versions were developed for incoming undergraduate and incoming graduate students. It is a 3-week course with one unit devoted to peer learning and assessment. (Note: UoPeople did not introduce the two-stage admissions pathway until summer 2015.)

The institution also created the Peer Assessment Center. Through a mix of instructor assistance, articles, student coaching, tips, and tricks, students receive help fine-tuning their skills. A direct link to the center is provided within Moodle, the institution's LMS, when students log into their courses.

In another move intended to increase students' comfort level with these practices, the institution revised downward the percentage of a student's final grade in a given course that is based on peer assessment. Currently, 20% of the grade in an undergraduate course flows from peer assessment of a student's work products. The remaining 80% is based on grades in quizzes and examinations as well as work on the weekly learning journals that are graded by the course instructor. At the graduate level, 45% of a student's grade flows from peer assessment of a student's work products. The remaining 55% is based on portfolio activities and group activities graded by the course instructor.

Two additional strategies currently being advanced for consideration were suggested by the results of the special study done in 2018 (Table 9.4): (a) individuals might be instructed to take a self-quiz on the knowledge/skills/insights to be assessed before starting their assessments and (b) the process might be revised to require the assessor to provide a brief rationale for the grade that is being assigned to a peer's work product.

Conclusion

What the data do not suggest is that the institution should consider abandoning peer learning and assessment as a key component of its instructional model. As noted, students are graduating in ever-increasing numbers, and at a level that is consistent with what would be found at other young institutions. For over a decade, UoPeople has convincingly demonstrated that the use of peer learning and assessment can be done at scale. That being said, it is also committed to continuing to gather data and use that information to refine the model on an ongoing basis.

References

Boud, D. (1988). *Moving towards autonomy: Developing student autonomy in learning* (2nd ed.). Kogan Page.

Boud, D., Cohen, R., & Sampson, J. (2001). *Peer learning in higher education: Learning from and with each other.* Kogan Page.

Boud, D., & Falchikov, N. (2006). Aligning assessment with long-term learning. *Assessment and Evaluation in Higher Education, 31*(4), 399–413. https://www.jhsph.edu/departments/population-family-and-reproductive-health/_docs/teaching-resources/cla-01-aligning-assessment-with-long-term-learning.pdf

Buraphadeja, V., & Kumnuanta, J. (2011). Enhancing the sense of community and learning experience using self-paced instruction and peer tutoring in a computer-laboratory course. *Australian Journal of Educational Technology, 27,* 1388–1355. https://ajet.org.au/index.php/AJET/article/view/897/174

Carlile, O., & Jordan, A. (2005). It works in practice but will it work in theory? The theoretical underpinnings of pedagogy. In G. O'Neill, S. Moore, & B. McMullin (Eds.), *Emerging issues in the practice of university learning and teaching* (pp. 11–26). AISHE.

Gok, T. (2012). The effects of peer instruction on students' conceptual learning and motivation. *Asia-Pacific Forum on Science Learning and Technology, 13*(10), 1–17. https://www.eduhk.hk/apfslt/download/v13_issue1_files/gok.pdf

Kotturi, Y., Kahng, A., & Procaccia, A. , & Kulkarni, C. (2018). *Rising above conflicts of interest: Algorithms and interfaces to assess peers impartially* [Unpublished manuscript].

Pritchard, A., & Woollard, J. (2010). *Psychology for the classroom: Constructivism and social learning.* Routledge.

Sloman, S. A., & Fernback, P. (2017). *The knowledge illusion: Why we never think alone.* Riverhead Books.

Topping, K. (2005). Trends in peer learning. *Educational Psychology, 25*(6), 631–645. https://doi.org/10.1080/01443410500345172

Vygotsky, L. S. (1978). *Mind in society.* Harvard University Press.

Wegner, D., Toni, G., & Hertel, P. (1985). Cognitive interdependence in close relationships. In W. J. Ickes (Ed.), *Compatible and incompatible relationships* (pp. 253–276). Springer-Verlag.

10

MANY BIRDS WITH ONE STONE

Developing a Multipurpose Student Assessment System

David D. Dworak

Looking back, the years 2015–2017 represented a perfect storm of opportunities concerning the assessment of student learning. The U.S. Army War College had received notice from its regional accrediting body that the school needed to improve its system of student assessment (Middle States Commission on Higher Education, 2015). The college was actively assessing students in the classroom, but there was a lack of a systematic or documented system that could inform institutional decision-making. In a separate action, the U.S. Army realized that it had a problem with academic evaluation reports. Students attending Army schools received end-of-course reports (named academic evaluation reports) that documented student achievement; however, the same form had been in use for 52 years, was out of date, and was of little real use to either students or the profession. There was broad acknowledgment that academic evaluation reports did little to inform student developmental needs and were largely discounted by both talent managers and Army selection boards. These two forcing functions—the need to have an assessment system that could provide data for decision making at many levels, plus the need to better document student success for the profession—drove the college to develop a fundamentally new way to assess and document student learning. The result is an approach that provides direct evidence of student achievement, supports student self-development, and aids decision-making at many different levels (Department of Defense, 2020, p. 7).

The U.S. Army War College is a graduate school that takes professionals, already skilled in their craft, and raises them to the master level of the profession. Most of the academic programs deal with developing the cognitive, technical, and interpersonal skills necessary for success at the highest levels of government. Despite being a military educational institution, the efforts associated with this new system of assessing student learning have several possible applications, both for professional programs such as business schools, music schools, and seminaries, as well as for traditional institutions of higher learning. There are a number of features that can be used independently or in concert with one another.

Goals of Assessment

As work progressed on crafting a viable and useful student assessment system, four primary goals eventually emerged. The first was to answer a simple question that accrediting bodies and stakeholders often ask, but can be devilishly challenging to answer: How do you know the students are learning the things you think they are learning? A more precise way of stating this is: Can you demonstrate the degree to which students are attaining the learning outcomes? The college needed a system that provided direct, defensible, and clear evidence that could answer this question for a wide variety of constituents. The old, but common, faculty adage of "I know the students attained the goals of my course; I see it in their eyes" is neither defensible nor adequate in today's educational environment.

A second goal was to develop a system that could help improve courses and programs through evidence-based decision-making. Rather than rely on hunches or subjective opinions to make curricula changes, the college wanted to be able to collect direct evidence of student learning and then combine this data with other indirect feedback to make better decisions. In addition, the approach needed to be systematic and documented, allowing for qualitative and quantitative longitudinal analysis.

A third goal went beyond the War College and dealt with the larger institution of the profession. Unlike never before, the college felt it had an important role in helping the Army make more informed talent management decisions. Rather than just relying on tactical performance appraisals from the field, the Army needed to consider the knowledge, skills, and abilities demonstrated in an academic environment. Only then could the profession make a holistic appraisal of an individual's potential. Why should a promotion or critical assignment be based only on an officer's past performance and not also consider the cognitive and interpersonal skills evaluated in the classroom? Academic programs provide an opportunity to observe and assess skills in the unique context of professional education. This point has significant implications for the profession and involves a change in culture—a fact that was not lost on students, faculty, or administrators.

Lastly, the college wanted to minimize the amount of additional work required of faculty. Any change was bound to involve additional effort, but the goal was to minimize the burden on faculty. The college knew that there were already lots of actions underway regarding student assessments; the challenge was to systematize these activities and build a documented system that captured essential data, while eliminating anything that was either redundant or not especially useful.

Activities in Support of Achieving the Goals

Transcripts and end-of-semester grades tell us the degree to which a student passed a course, but typically lack other details. If a course included four learning outcomes, how did the student do in attaining each of those outcomes? Did the student exhibit any traits that might be especially useful postgraduation, or were there any competencies that the student should consider for additional self-development? In many ways this type of information is more insightful and useful than just an overall grade.

The War College took two important steps to help guide its efforts. First, it created the assessment working group comprising faculty representatives from all teaching departments, centers, and institutes. This working group played a critical role in proposing learning outcomes and assessment strategies, as well as gaining buy-in on proposed efforts. The college worked to include a number of diverse perspectives within the group, which helped generate innovative thinking and enabled the questioning of long-held beliefs and assumptions.

The second initiative was to transition to outcome-based academic programs. Within a year, all programs and courses became outcome-based—meaning that the learning goals of courses and programs were observable, relevant, and appropriate for the academic environment. The college ultimately settled on three levels of outcomes:

- Institutional learning outcomes (ILOs): Provide overarching competencies that are important to the Army as a profession and serve to guide the development of program-level outcomes across the many programs offered at the college
- Program learning outcomes (PLOs): More specific and describe the knowledge, skills, and abilities of graduates of a specific program of instruction
- Course learning outcomes (CLOs): The building blocks upon which students attain larger program outcomes

Long lists of outcomes are not particularly useful; instead, the college found it best to have six to seven outcomes at the institutional and program levels, with three to five outcomes at the course level. A logical nesting of outcomes between the different levels helps allow for an assessment of whether courses and programs are aligned and working to produce graduates that are of use to the profession.

The assessment effort then transitioned to a discussion of academic evaluations and the data needed to inform student developmental needs, aid program improvement, and enable better talent management by the profession. In 2016 the Army started an initiative to revise all academic reports, which was a once-in-a-generation chance to contribute to the talent management effort, and could have significant implications across myriad constituencies. The college's new approach to assessment was to develop a course evaluation report that provided an overall grade, as well as the ability to highlight competencies and key knowledge, skills, and abilities deemed critical for the professional success of its graduates. The data from course evaluation reports would then serve as a basis from which to create an end-of-program report that not only provided information useful to the student and the institution, but could also be used for talent management decisions across the profession.

Building Blocks of Assessment: The Course Evaluation Report

There is a fundamental difference between training and education. Training often involves replicable discrete tasks, with some description of task, condition, and standard. Education, on the other hand, tends to focus on cognitive skills and the application of theory across a wide range of possible environments. The challenge for the college was to develop an assessment system that focuses on development of cognitive and interpersonal skills, while allowing for documentation of critical technical skills as well. The result is an academic evaluation system that includes several distinct areas of assessment, each with a different purpose.

The college created a new course evaluation report with four distinct assessment areas: (a) overall grade; (b) focus areas; (c) knowledge, skills, and abilities (KSAs); and (d) attainment of CLOs (as shown in Table 10.1). The overall grade is no different from assessing student performance for a typical class and required no adjustment from faculty. Faculty determine a student's grade and then have the opportunity to add several lines of narrative comments relating to specific student performance on graded events such as papers, forums, class contribution, and so on.

The second assessment area focuses on three skills viewed as critical to success in the profession: strategic thinking, written communications, and

TABLE 10.1
Course Evaluation Report

Course Evaluation Report	
Demographic data	
Overall	Grade
	Overall Comments
Focus areas	Strategic Thinking
	Written Communications
	Oral Communications
Knowledge, skills, and abilities	Demonstrated
	Areas of refinement or additional development
Assessment of CLOs	

oral communications. Each of the three areas includes a check block indicating a demonstrated level of proficiency (distinguished, superior, performed to standards, or did not meet standards). Additionally, faculty have the opportunity to provide narrative comments highlighting specific attributes in each focus area. A common set of rubrics helps faculty determine student performance in each of the three focus areas.

Practice has shown strategic thinking to be the area most debated among faculty. For the first time, the college was attempting to identify the best strategic thinkers from a cohort that is already distinguished in many ways. A clear definition of the term, combined with a documented rubric and accompanying faculty development, has been essential to implementing the new approach. Table 10.2 shows an excerpt from the course evaluation report, specifically, for strategic thinking.

TABLE 10.2
Excerpt From a Course Evaluation Report

Strategic Thinking: Distinguished Performance
Comments: Comment on the student's strategic thinking competencies. Possible items include the following: ability to comprehend, integrate, apply, and synthesize course content within and between courses; think critically, creatively, and systemically; apply ethical considerations; evaluate contrasting viewpoints; consider historical insights; and draw valid conclusions.

TABLE 10.3
Knowledge, Skills, and Attributes

Strategic Mindedness		Technical		Interpersonal
☐	Synthesizes multiple perspectives and theories into a coherent whole	☐ Understands and respects the importance of civil-military relationships	☐	Works collaboratively as a team member
☐	Recognizes interdependencies and interactions between systems and processes	☐ Understands the dynamics and players involved in the DoD resourcing processes	☐	Displays both confidence and humility
☐	Provides context and perspective that nest arguments within a broader worldview	☐ Applies theory and doctrine to develop feasible, creative solutions to complex strategic problems	☐	Responds unemotionally to criticism or argument; demonstrates self-control
☐	Articulates the long-term implications of decisions, policies, or options	☐ Understands how to integrate all elements of U.S. national power to achieve an objective through unified action	☐	Displays empathy; understands, values, and considers others' equities and agendas; treats others with respect
☐	Challenges assumptions or perspectives that others take for granted	☐ Speaks with substance; communicates clearly, persuasively, and succinctly, cognizant of the audience	☐	Is a good listener
☐	Is intellectually curious	☐ Writes economically, articulately, and persuasively using compelling arguments built on solid evidence, cognizant of the audience		

TABLE 10.4
Example Assessment of CLOs

CLOs	Not Observed	Little or None	Acceptable	Excellent
Analyze the international system and the behavior of actors in it, with a particular focus on the causes of war.	☐	☐	☐	☐
Analyze coercion theory and use its principles to help frame and inform strategic options.	☐	☐	☐	☐
Evaluate the contemporary security environment in its international and domestic contexts, and identify their influence on the development of U.S. national security policy and grand strategy.	☐	☐	☐	☐

The third component of the course evaluation report addresses areas of demonstrated excellence and areas for possible refinement or additional development. Research on desired competencies of general officers across the Army identified specific KSAs that are essential for success. The report includes 17 of these KSAs, divided into three groupings: strategic mindedness, technical, and interpersonal (Table 10.3). Upon the completion of a course, faculty choose from zero to four of these KSAs for a student, identifying those senior leader competencies that were demonstrated during the course. Along the same lines, faculty can choose zero to four KSAs that the student ought to consider for refinement or additional development. The data are especially useful in identifying areas of student strength as well as potential areas for additional emphasis within the curriculum. Individual student data on areas of potential refinement or additional development are not shared outside the college.

The final assessment area of the course evaluation report is attainment of CLOs as seen in Table 10.4. Faculty indicate the degree to which each student demonstrated attainment of each course outcome. There are four possible selections: (a) not observed, (b) little or none, (c) acceptable, and (d) excellent. These data are not shared with students, but are useful in course development and institutional decision-making. The "not observed" section is important because this can indicate possible issues with curriculum design. This approach is a subjective assessment, but useful for course and program review, especially when combined with data from other sources.

When combined, the four assessment areas provide a comprehensive picture of demonstrated student performance. Data can be used at many different levels to identify trends, find opportunities for improvement, and document student success. This direct evidence of student learning can help faculty, curriculum developers, and institutional decision-makers by providing details on learning that were never captured previously. However, this design does come at some cost of faculty time compared to the previous approach for course reports. A deliberate faculty development effort, combined with automated processes and detailed rubrics, help minimize the time needed for data input.

End-of-Program: Academic Evaluation Report

Realizing that the development of future executives begins prior to attendance at the War College, the assessment working group worked with representatives from the Army's intermediate level school and the Command and General Staff College to develop a new evaluation report that captures details on student success. The goal was to develop a common format that the profession could use to identify and track specific competencies related to executives and senior leaders. The result is the Senior Service and Command and General Staff College Academic Evaluation Report (Figure 10.1). Beginning in 2017 the War College began piloting the new form, characterized by the following:

- identifies the top strategic thinkers and communicators among a student body,
- provides specific comments on notable academic performance, competencies, and areas of research that can inform the profession's talent management decisions,
- identifies the overall top performers,
- is evidence based—uses data collected from courses throughout a program of instruction,
- provides information useful for assignment and promotion decisions, and
- only includes comments that are specific, meaningful, and relevant.

Faculty are asked to avoid the urge to fill a block with text that offers little insight.

Figure 10.1. Academic evaluation report.

HQDA#:

SENIOR SERVICE AND COMMAND AND GENERAL STAFF COLLEGE ACADEMIC EVALUATION REPORT
For use of this form, see AR 623-3; the proponent agency is DCS, G-1.

See Privacy Act Statement in AR 623-3.

PART I - ADMINISTRATIVE DATA

a. NAME *(Last, First, Middle Initial)*	b. DOD ID No.	c. RANK	d. BRANCH	e. SPECIALTY/PMOSC

f. COURSE TITLE	g. NAME AND LOCATION OF SCHOOL

h. DURATION OF COURSE		i. COMPONENT	j. NO. OF ENCLOSURES	k. RATED STUDENT'S EMAIL ADDRESS *(.gov or .mil)*
FROM *(YYYYMMDD)*	THRU *(YYYYMMDD)*			

l. REASON FOR SUBMISSION

☐ COURSE COMPLETION ☐ INTERIM REPORT ☐ AHRC DIRECTED ☐ DID NOT GRADUATE

MILITARY EDUCATION LEVEL: ______ ☐ PHASE COMPLETION / PHASE #______ OF ______ ☐ RELEASED EARLY (NO FAULT OF STUDENT)

PART II - ACADEMIC PERFORMANCE (ACADEMIC RATER)

a. DOES SOLDIER FULLY SUPPORT SHARP, EO, AND EEO: ☐ Yes ☐ No *(comments are required)*

b. APFT PASS / FAIL / PROFILE: ______ DATE: ______

c. HEIGHT: ______ WEIGHT: ______ WITHIN STANDARD? ______

Comments required below, for "Failed" APFT, or "Profile" when it precludes performance of duty, and "No" for Army Weight Standards. Reset Item b. APFT / PASS / FAIL / PROFILE

d. OVERALL GRADE POINT AVERAGE: ______ of ______

e1. ASI/SQI AWARDED: SKILL IDENTIFIER: ______ e2. CODE: ______

f. JOINT EDUCATION CREDIT: ☐ JPME I ☐ JPME II

g. Strategic Thinking: Assess the rated Student ability to: think critically, creatively, and systemically; employ an ethical reasoning framework; evaluate contrasting viewpoints; apply historical lessons; and draw valid conclusions.

☐ Distinguished Performance ☐ Superior Performance ☐ Performed to Standards ☐ Did Not Meet Standards

Comments:

h. Written Communication: Assess the rated Student ability to: write clearly, concisely, and correctly; convey ideas convincingly; and use sources skillfully.

☐ Distinguished Performance ☐ Superior Performance ☐ Performed to Standards ☐ Did Not Meet Standards

Comments:

i. Oral Communication: Assess the rated Student ability to: speak clearly, correctly, and confidently; convey ideas convincingly; and negotiate effectively.

☐ Distinguished Performance ☐ Superior Performance ☐ Performed to Standards ☐ Did Not Meet Standards

Comments:

j. Demonstrated Knowledge, Skills, and Abilities Relevant to Future Assignments; Notable Academic Performance:

Comments:

k. SPECIAL PROJECT(S) OR PAPER(S):

1) ______

2) ______

3) ______

PART III - OVERALL ACADEMIC ACHIEVEMENT AND POTENTIAL

a. Overall Academic Achievement:

☐ Distinguished Graduate (limited to 10%)

☐ Superior Graduate (11 % to 30%)

☐ Graduate

☐ Non-Graduate

b. COMMENTS:

DA FORM 1059-2, MAY 2018 PREVIOUS EDITIONS ARE OBSOLETE. APD LC v1.00ES Page 1 of 2

Toward the end of an academic program, faculty begin to prepare an academic evaluation report for each student. These are the formal reports used for creation of transcripts as well as transmission to the Army, documenting student achievement. For decades these reports were typically boilerplate entries with few specifics on observed student competencies.

The new report has four areas of student assessment, each closely linked to those found in the course evaluation reports. This approach allows an automated system to aggregate data from the course-level reports and auto-fill many parts of the program report. Therefore, the program-level reports are based on a record of student achievement from across courses, are defendable, and reflect specific student competencies directly observed by faculty.

As in the course-level report, the first assessment area in the academic evaluation report focuses on strategic thinking, written communications, and oral communications. An automated algorithm determines the level of performance (distinguished, superior, performed to standard, etc.) by averaging the corresponding input from each of the student's course reports. Faculty then add in narrative comments relating to each of the three areas; an automated roll-up report provides faculty with a list of all comments recorded from across the different courses. Faculty can then quickly review comments associated with an area such as oral communications, identify trends, and then make final comments for the end-of-program report.

The second assessment area is for demonstrated knowledge, skills, and abilities. Faculty add narrative comments relating to these competencies and any other notable academic performance, such as participation in special programs. Again, an automated roll-up report lists which KSAs came up most frequently across all the course-level reports, allowing faculty to make informed judgments about the KSAs on which to comment. The college deliberately designed this section to help inform the talent management efforts of the profession.

The next assessment section allows faculty to make mention of any special projects or research papers. It allows for data mining by the profession. For example, if the Army is interested in the impact of artificial intelligence, it now has the means to find students that completed a research effort on the topic. This assessment can also help in talent management efforts of the profession.

The final section is a stratification of the student body into distinct grouping of overall performance (as shown in Figure 10.2). The registrar uses the average of course grades to create a rank-ordered list by GPA of all students in a cohort, to include military, civilian, and international students. This list is used to identify the corresponding level of overall academic achievement. Faculty have the ability to add narrative comments. This section was deliberately designed to be in the same location and appear similar to the senior rater part of an Army officer evaluation report. The intent is to provide Army selection boards with a clear picture of overall student performance in an easily recognizable format.

Figure 10.2. End-of-program report—overall performance and potential.

PART III -	OVERALL ACADEMIC ACHIEVEMENT AND POTENTIAL
a. Overall Academic Achievement: ☐ Distinguished Graduate (limited to 10%) ☐ Superior Graduate (11 % to 30%) ☐ Graduate ☐ Non-Graduate	b. COMMENTS:

Faculty report that completion of the end-of-program academic evaluation report is generally straightforward. The use of an automated roll-up report, along with the use of computer algorithms to identify levels of performance, make for a system that is evidence-based, but still allows for faculty judgment and input. One significant insight from 2 years of using the new approach is that faculty must now truly know the students in order to make useful comments.

Assessments Used to Determine Progress Toward Goal

The development and implementation of this new approach to student assessment took several years of effort and coordination, but early indicators appear promising. Some faculty comfortable with the previous system questioned the need for change, but higher-level guidance from both the profession as well as accreditors made it clear that the old way of documenting student performance was no longer adequate. Feedback from new faculty is positive, indicating that the new approach is logical and not overly burdensome. The vast majority of faculty report that the use of an automated roll-up report of data from course reports makes the end-of-program report much easier to complete.

The effort to develop the new approach also led to unexpected discussions on other opportunities for assessing student learning. For years the college had been conducting oral comprehensive exams at the end of the core block of instruction for all resident course students. These exams typically lasted 90 minutes, after which the student was told whether they passed or failed and the results were recorded in the college's student information system. The work on the new student assessment system prompted the college to reassess the type of data collected from the comprehensive exams. Now, faculty not only record whether a student passed or failed, but also record how they did in terms of strategic thinking, content, and oral communications. Additionally, faculty also record the extent to which each student performed for each of the PLOs that were in evidence during the exam. The data from the comprehensive exams serve as a key element in a student's end-of-program report and the collection of data on demonstrated performance on each PLO enables informed decision-making at many different levels.

Discussions have also started on whether the college needs to reexamine its PLOs. The last review was in 2016; since then faculty and administrators have greater experience in assessing exactly what makes for a useful and appropriate outcome. The college updated its intuitional learning outcomes in 2018; the time is right for a periodic review of outcomes at the program and course level.

As a system, the new approach appears to be functioning as designed. There are opportunities for improvement, but there is now widespread faculty buy-in and the Army's selection boards and talent managers are currently using the new reports. Informal feedback from the Army's Human Resources Command indicates that selection boards are now using the Senior Service and Command and General Staff College Academic Evaluation Reports to make holistic assessments of officers during high-level selection boards and that the use of these reports is helping the profession make more informed decisions.

Use of the Data

This new approach fundamentally changes the nature of institutional student assessment. Now more than ever, the profession has a chance to identify specific qualities and competencies it deems important. Faculty and course developers then consider these elements in student assignments and record performance in a manner that is useful at many different levels.

Students now receive feedback across a variety of areas—informing them of both areas of strength as well as opportunities for additional development. Expert faculty tended to do this anyway, but now there is a systematic process to ensure that this happens across all courses and seminars. The use of guiding (but not regimented) rubrics helps set expectations for students as well as faculty, and aids in the calibration of the faculty's student assessment efforts. Faculty and course developers can review data to assess overall student performance longitudinally or assess a specific year. Department chairs and college administrators now can compare student performance across seminars, across demographics, and across courses. The ability to analyze outcome attainment at course and program levels enables evidence-based decision-making at many different levels and is a key component for program and institutional assessment. Finally, the profession now can consider direct evidence of an individual's specific competencies to aid talent managers and selection panels. The question used to be "Is this person a War College graduate?" Now talent managers can ask, "Is this person a War College graduate, and what are their skills that we ought to consider?" The implications of this change are significant given the nature of the profession. As with any data set, the information from this student assessment system is most effective when combined with data from other sources, allowing for confirmation and triangulation. The systemic and documented nature of the approach enables long-term longitudinal analysis for trend identification.

Insights Gained from the Assessment

Completion of an academic program is more than simply attaining a degree or certificate; it is about learning and development. The environment increasingly demands more information in order to make informed decisions; the challenge is devising a system that is aligned with a profession's needs and fitting it into the culture of the academic environment. Meeting that challenge requires a close coordination between the academic institution and outside constituents.

Faculty can offer valid insights on their students. In fact, faculty often see a side of their students that others will not observe outside the academic environment. For this feedback to be of value, the components of an effective evaluation system need validation against a profession's needs.

Two years of experience with this new approach to student assessment has shown that measuring professional competence is hard, but an institution must try. For example, it took months to agree on a common definition of *strategic thinking* within the War College and additional time to gain concurrence from the Command and General Staff College. Be ready for impassioned discussions, especially among the faculty. The discourse is where faculty involvement is critical—faculty need to be a part of the process and the representation of diverse perspectives is crucial to developing a viable system and obtaining faculty buy-in. The development of a new approach to student assessment does not have to fundamentally change how faculty conduct themselves in the classroom, but it can have implications for those things that a faculty member considers when assessing their students. If there is additional faculty workload, a clear messaging campaign on why the change is needed, along with a discussion on cost and reward, helps answer the question of why an institution is deciding to implement change. Recognize these changes are not easy, and note that it is worthwhile to pilot everything. Test everything from the terminology on forms, to the use of rubrics, to ensure they meet desired goals and are appropriate for the institution. Remember that piloting allows for testing of underlying information technology systems and ease of user interface while also creating conditions for faculty buy-in.

Professional education lends itself to outcomes-based assessment, as there is often significant coordination and oversight of the curricular delivery. These types of programs typically involve structured programs with prescribed courses and clearly defined outcomes. Programs that are more open-ended (i.e., sociology or literature), or where students take vastly different courses, may be more challenging to assess from the approach adopted by the War College.

Used in total or in part, this approach to student assessment has the potential to influence a variety of efforts, from the individual to the professional. A key requirement is a deliberate discussion with representatives of the profession and faculty to identify those attributes that ought to be assessed and whether these are appropriate for the academic environment. This approach focuses the data collection effort, while compelling the profession to pinpoint those skills and competencies that are most important. Whether this strategy will have the desired impact on the Army remains to be seen and will take years to fully institutionalize, but the foundation is set and indicators are positive.

Author's Note

The views expressed are those of the author and do not necessarily reflect the official policy or position of the Department of the Army, Department of Defense, or the U.S. Government.

References

Department of Defense. (2020, May). *Developing today's joint officers for tomorrow's ways of war: The Joint Chiefs of Staff vision and guidance for professional military education and talent management*. https://www.jcs.mil/Portals/36/Documents/Doctrine/education/jcs_pme_tm_vision.pdf?ver=2020-05-15-102429-817

Middle States Commission on Higher Education. (2015). *Standards for accreditation and requirements of affiliation* (13th ed.) https://www.msche.org/standards/

PART TWO

STUDENT LEARNING AND ASSESSMENT IN THE DISCIPLINES

11

ASSESSMENT OF PUBLIC HEALTH COMPETENCIES AT MULTIPLE LEVELS

Sondos Islam

Charles R. Drew University of Medicine and Science (CDU) is a small private, nonprofit university located in Los Angeles, California, in Service Planning Area Six (SPA 6), one of the most socioeconomically and medically underserved communities in Los Angeles County. CDU was founded in 1966 after the McCone Commission cited poor health status and diminished access to quality education, health care, employment, and safety as key factors in sparking the 1965 civil unrest in the local community. The university has evolved and grown, shaped by the needs of the diverse community it serves. CDU has created an academic environment that features the "CDU Advantage" institutional learning outcomes (ILOs) based on five domains—excellence in specialized knowledge and research, social justice, global international experience, community and experiential education, and health policy. These outcomes all serve the university mission statement:

> Charles R. Drew University of Medicine and Science is a private nonprofit student-centered university that is committed to cultivating diverse health professional leaders who are dedicated to social justice and health equity for underserved populations through outstanding education, research, clinical service, and community engagement. (Charles R. Drew University of Medicine and Science, 2017, para. 1)

CDU's (2017) Master of Public Health (MPH) in Urban Health Disparities program continues the university's tradition of addressing the health and education needs of underserved communities. The MPH program mission is "to improve the health of urban populations through graduate education of public health practitioners, urban-relevant scholarship and community service specifically targeting the determinants of health disparities in underserved communities" (para. 2).

As a generalist MPH program with a focus on urban health disparities, the MPH faculty developed eight program learning outcomes that encompassed the five core areas of public content (epidemiology, biostatistics, environmental health, social and behavioral sciences, and health administration) and urban health disparities content. The CDU program is cohort-based with a scaffolded curriculum so that, as students progress through the sequenced curriculum, they gain public health content knowledge and skills required to attain the eight program competencies by graduation. The majority of the previous assessment activities of students' attainment of program learning outcomes were content-based. They included objective exams, final papers, and in-class presentations that demonstrated the student's attainment of public health knowledge covered in the courses, culminating in an MPH portfolio and a capstone project reflecting some of the program learning outcomes.

In October 2016, the Council on Education for Public Health (CEPH), the accrediting body for all public health programs, announced the adoption of revised accreditation criteria for public health schools and programs. The new criteria included the requirement that all CEPH-accredited public health schools and programs adopt 22 foundational public health competencies (FPHCs) that address eight public health domains, and 12 fundamental public health knowledge learning outcomes (FPHK-LOs) that address the profession and science of public health and the factors related to human health. Furthermore, programs that offered a generalist MPH degree were now required to develop at least five additional competencies that were program-specific, and which expanded on or enhanced the foundational public health competencies (CEPH, 2016). CEPH also required that all public health schools and programs indicate at least one assessment activity for each of the foundational competencies, knowledge learning outcomes, and program-specific competencies, and show evidence of compliance through a detailed description of the competency-based assessment activities in the syllabi of the required courses (CEPH, 2018). Public health programs had the option to submit evidence of compliance either by early January 2018 or early January 2019. CDU opted for the 2018 due date.

Overall, the CDU MPH program had a total of 44 program and university competencies and learning outcomes that it needed the curriculum to address. It needed to modify content-based assessment activities to competency-based assessment tools to ensure students can demonstrate attainment of all the new competencies and learning outcomes by graduation.

The director of the MPH program and chair of the MPH Curriculum and Outcome Assessment Committee realized that to be compliant with the new CEPH criteria there was a need to revamp the curriculum and assessment activities, and most importantly, to have faculty buy-in. It should be acknowledged that is was the hard work and commitment of the MPH faculty that resulted in a successful and timely CEPH compliance report. In early 2017, faculty started the first of many committee meetings to revamp the CDU MPH curriculum and competency assessment activities.

Goals of Assessment

The goals of assessment of the MPH competencies include: (a) identifying any issues with students' demonstration of attainment of program competencies based on the course assessment tools and to propose action plans, as needed, to improve student outcomes; (b) ensuring that graduates have the skills to demonstrate the application of public health competencies expected of a highly skilled public health professional; (c) ensuring the achievement of the MPH program and CDU missions; and (d) maintaining continuous CEPH accreditation.

Activities/Strategies to Support Achievement of the Assessment Goals

CDU has a set of procedures and criteria that all academic programs use for monitoring and evaluating student progress in achieving the expected program competencies and ILOs, at the course, program, and university levels. The University Academic Program Review Committee requires that assessment tools must include at least two direct assessment activities based on course assignments, and at least one indirect measure, such as the results of student course evaluation or graduate exit surveys. All assessments must have a benchmark/target outcome, and if the assessment results indicate that the benchmark was not met, program faculty must include appropriate action plans to improve student outcomes the next time the course is offered. The process starts with faculty instructors submitting their assessment results and action plans, as needed, to the program director or chair of their program's curriculum and outcome assessment committee. At the end of each academic year, program directors submit the assessment results to their respective college educational and academic policy committees and include the data in the program's annual progress report to the University Academic Program Review Committee. Although this process is exhaustive, it triangulates the monitoring of program and institutional competency findings, and faculty receive feedback on their assessment results and action plans at the program, college, and university levels.

The CDU MPH program requires two to three courses to assess each competency directly through different course assignments; some assignments may assess more than one competency, and some competencies may require assessments in more than one course. All direct assessments tools must be clearly articulated in the syllabus, including the program competencies and ILOs aligned to the objectives and the assignments that are assessing them. The program uses five different indirect competency assessment tools: (a) student course evaluation of attainment of course objectives aligned to program competencies and ILOs, (b) faculty self-reflection and lessons learned at the end of the semester, (c) graduate exit survey of self-assessment of attainment of program and institutional competencies, (d) alumni survey which includes a self-assessment of application of program competencies in the workforce, and (e) employer survey of graduates' skills and performance of competencies in the worksite.

The assessment target outcome for each program competency, public health learning outcome, and ILO is *at least 80% of students will score 80% or better on the specific assessment tool.* If the target outcome is not met, the faculty instructor proposes action plans to improve the outcome of the assessment the next time the course is offered.

The first meeting was focused on developing five new program-specific urban health disparities competencies that enhanced and expanded on the fundamental public health knowledge learning outcomes. Once all faculty approved the urban health disparities competencies, they were added to a new curriculum map which included the new 22 foundational public health competencies and 12 knowledge learning outcomes, in addition to the five ILOs in the map rows, and the MPH required courses in the order they are offered in the map columns. Each faculty instructor was tasked with the identification of the competencies and learning outcomes they cover in their courses by checking the respective cells and sending the information back to the program director to be compiled in one master MPH curriculum map before the next meeting.

In reviewing the compiled master curriculum map during the next meeting, faculty realized that some of the adopted CEPH competencies and LOs were being addressed numerous times in several courses, while others were either minimally covered or not at all. For example, for foundational public health competency 21, *perform effectively on interprofessional teams,* although students in the Community Engagement in Public Health course did engage with community members to develop a community needs assessment, they did not work with other health professionals in this activity, and there was no assessment tool to evaluate the effectiveness of interprofessional teams. Therefore, the faculty instructor proposed to invite graduate nursing students to join the MPH teams in the community needs assessment planning process, and the program director volunteered to develop a rubric to evaluate the effectiveness of the interprofessional teams and present it to the faculty for feedback and approval.

The faculty also noted that foundational public health competency 22, *apply systems thinking tools to a public health issue,* was minimally addressed. Previously, faculty introduced systems thinking approaches in public health in the 1st-year courses, but students were not required to *apply* system thinking tools to a public health issue. Faculty decided that the 2nd-year course, Program Planning and Evaluation, is best suited to address this competency since students are required to review the literature to identify the systems and risk factors associated with a public health problem impacting underserved communities. Accordingly, the faculty instructor of this course added a new assignment that required students to develop a causal loop diagram of the systems impacting the health issue they were addressing in their public health program proposal, based on their literature review.

Faculty also realized that competencies that addressed public health issues in international settings were minimally addressed; therefore, they voted to develop a new required three-unit global health disparity course to address these competencies in more depth.

The next meetings were focused on faculty mapping their course objectives to the MPH competencies, public health knowledge learning outcomes, and ILOs. Faculty also worked on articulating the assessment tools that will be used to assess the course objectives; hence, the program competencies, and the ILOs. Faculty provided feedback and recommendations to each other on the proposed assessment tools (course assignments) that would better assess student attainment of competencies rather than just attainment of public health content knowledge. For example, instead of using objective exams to assess core public health knowledge, faculty added essay questions that would assess how the student would apply the newly acquired knowledge to address a public health issue. Additional competency-based assessment strategies used included, but were not limited to the following:

- analysis of case studies
- critique of public health articles
- analysis and interpretation of quantitative data outputs
- analysis of a focus group transcript
- creation of data sets using statistical software
- evaluation of the effectiveness of a public health program
- development of a public health program and its budget narrative
- interpretation of health disparities data and presentation using plain language techniques to lay audiences

- development of a policy brief addressing a health equity issue
- comparison of healthcare and public health systems across national and international settings
- planning, developing, and conducting a community health needs assessment in an interprofessional setting

As part of the revamping of the course syllabi, faculty instructors were required to include the aligned competencies and learning outcomes identified in the mapping of the course objectives to program competencies and learning outcomes, to ensure that students are aware of which competencies are being addressed through the course objectives. Figure 11.1 is an excerpt from a syllabus demonstrating this process put into action.

The syllabi must also include a course grading and assessment table identifying which course objectives, program competencies, and ILOs each assessment tool/assignment is measuring. Table 11.1 presents an example of the grading and assessment table that all faculty instructors include in their syllabi. Description of each assessment tool is also detailed in the syllabus.

Figure 11.1. Syllabus excerpt.

The following course objectives have been aligned with the MPH Program Foundational Public Health Competencies (FPHCs), Urban Health Disparities Competencies (UHDCs), and CDU's Institutional Learning Outcomes (ILOs). Please see appendix A for the complete list of the MPH competencies, and ILOs.

Upon completion of this course, students will be able to:

1. Conduct a literature review to identify the prevalence, incidence, morbidity, and mortality rates of a public health issue impacting the health of underserved communities, including the behavioral, psychological, and socioenvironmental factors, and systems associated with the public health issue. (FPHC 1; UHDC 1; ILO 1,2)

2. Develop a causal loop diagram and a logic model of risk based on the literature review results that aid in the planning and development of a public health prog ram to address the identified factors. (FPHC 22; ILO 1)

3. Apply the appropriate methods to assess process, impact, and outcome evaluations in a public health program proposal. (FP HC 2, 11; UHDC 4, 5; ILO 1,2,3)

TABLE 11.1
Sample of a Course Grading and Assessment Table

Assessment Tool	%	Course Objective Assessed	MPH Competency and Learning Outcome Assessed
In-Class Activities	10	3	FPHC 16, 22
Assignment 1	20	1, 2, 4	FPHC 1, 22; UHDC 1; ILO 1, 2
Assignment 2	10	5, 6	FPHC 9; ILO 2, 3
Assignment 3	10	9	FPHC 13, 18; UHDC 3; ILO 3
Assignment 4	10	6, 8	FPHC 2, 11
Assignment 5	10	7	FPHC 2, 11; UHDC 4; ILO 1–4
Final Paper	30	4–12	FPHC 1–4, 8–10; UHDC 1, 5; ILO 1–3

Note. FPHC = Fundamental Public Health Competency. UHDC = Urban Health Disparity Competency. ILO = Institutional Learning Outcome.

Assessments Used to Determine Progress Toward Goal

Once all the assessment tools were selected, articulated, and approved by the MPH Curriculum and Assessment Committee, they were compiled in a competency assessment template/table provided by CEPH. Table 11.2 presents a few examples of the assessment tools used to assess the foundational public health competencies. Please note that even though the table presents the assessment tool of one required course for each competency, the program uses two or three courses to assess the same competency, using different assessment activities to ensure that students' competency attainment by graduation is accurately assessed. In addition, some course assignments, such as final program proposals and evaluation plans, may assess multiple competencies and learning outcomes.

Use of the Findings

Results of the direct assessments of the new public health competencies indicated that the target outcome for a few of the competencies were not met. This finding was supported by the results of the indirect assessments of student course evaluations and the faculty reflections, all of which indicated

TABLE 11.2
Sample of Courses and Their Assessment Tools of the Foundational Public Health Competencies

Domain Competency	MPH Course	Assessment Tool
Evidence-Based Approaches to Public Health		
Apply epidemiological methods to the breadth of settings and situations in public health practice.	Principle of epidemiology	Epiville modules assignments: students apply epidemiologic methods within the context of a mock town that experiences various health issues.
Select quantitative and qualitative data collection methods appropriate for a given public health context.	Research methods	Midterm case study: students are required to select the appropriate data collection method (quantitative and/or qualitative methods) to assess the health issue under study.
Analyze quantitative and qualitative data using biostatistics, informatics, computer-based programming, and software, as appropriate.	Principle of biostatistics	Statistical software assignments: Students analyze data sets and generate plots and graphs using various statistical tests.
	Research methods	Qualitative analysis of a focus group transcript: Student groups interpret and analyze a focus group transcript of a community health issue and submit a report of the emerging themes.
Interpret results of data analysis for public health research, policy, or practice.	Principle of biostatistics	Article critique: Students are required to interpret the results presented in a journal article by connecting the findings to future research, policy, and practice.

Domain Competency	MPH Course	Assessment Tool
Public Health and Health Care Systems		
Compare the organization, structure, and function of health care, public health, and regulatory systems across national and international settings.	Global health disparities	Country case study final paper, criterion 4: Students compare the healthcare and public health systems (organization, structure, and function) of their selected developing country with that of the U.S. systems.
Discuss the means by which structural bias, social inequities, and racism undermine health and create challenges to achieving health equity at organizational, community, and societal levels.	Race, cultural competency, and public health	Short essay assignments 1–12: Students read assignments that analyze institutional barriers to achieving health equity; assignments are created for each group of readings that require students to discuss how systemic racial inequalities are produced at the organizational, community, and societal levels.
Planning and Management to Promote Health		
Assess population needs, assets, and capacities that affect communities' health.	Community engagement in public health	Community needs assessment: student groups plan, develop, and implement a community health needs assessment including community assets and capacities.
Apply awareness of cultural values and practices to the design or implementation of public health policies or programs.	Program planning and evaluation	Assignment 3, criterion 1: Students describe how their target audience's cultural values and practices are incorporated in the theme, delivery channels, scope and sequence, and program material and methods of their proposed public health program.
Design a population-based policy, program, project, or intervention.	Social and behavioral theories in public health	Final take-home exam case scenario 2: Students are required to propose a culturally tailored theory-based program to address the increase in obesity prevalence among an underserved community in an urban setting.

Domain Competency	MPH Course	Assessment Tool
Explain basic principles and tools of budget and resource management.	Program planning and evaluation	Assignment 3: Students submit a line item budget of their proposed public health program, and a budget narrative describing the responsibilities of the program manager in managing human and nonhuman resources to ensure achievement of program outcomes.
Select methods to evaluate public health programs.	Program planning and evaluation	Assignment 4: Students submit the evaluation design and evaluation plan summary of their proposed public health program.
Policy in Public Health		
Discuss multiple dimensions of the policy-making process, including the roles of ethics and evidence.	Health policy and management	Final exam: Students are presented with a case scenario in a public healthcare setting and are required to respond to an essay question describing a healthcare setting's policy-making process highlighting the roles of evidence and ethics, and their impact on the surrounding community.
Propose strategies to identify stakeholders and build coalitions and partnerships for influencing public health outcomes.	Program planning and evaluation	Assignment 2: Student groups propose strategies to identify and engage stakeholders and build coalitions to form their program planning group to collaborate in program planning, development, and evaluation processes to achieve program goals.
Advocate for political, social, or economic policies and programs that will improve health in diverse populations.	Global health disparities	Country case study final paper: Student groups are required to recommend/advocate for political, social, or economic policies and programs that will improve population health in a developing country of choice.
Evaluate policies for their impact on public health and health equity.	Health policy and management	Affordable Care Act repeal and replace issue brief: Students identify key issues in the debate and potential impacts for the nation and California in a 2–3-page policy brief.

Domain Competency	MPH Course	Assessment Tool
Leadership		
Apply principles of leadership, governance, and management, which include creating a vision, empowering others, fostering collaboration and guiding decision-making.	Health policy and management	Final exam: Students are presented with a case scenario of a public healthcare setting and its organizational and community challenges and asked to offer solutions to these challenges through the application of leadership and management principles, mediation and negotiating skills, and community collaboration skills covered in the course.
Apply negotiation and mediation skills to address organizational or community challenges.	Community engagement in public health	Student-led discussions of community engagement methods: Students describe how they would apply their acquired negotiation and mediation skills to address community health challenges.
Communication		
Select communication strategies for different audiences and sectors.	Program planning and evaluation	Assignment 3: Students describe their proposed public health program's culturally appropriate materials and delivery channels.
Communicate audience-appropriate public health content, both in writing and through oral presentation.	Health communication and data visualization	Final project: Students present the results their data analysis of a health disparity issue in two formats: (1) a story board presentation to community members and stakeholders, and (2) a scientific/technical presentation to peers and public health professionals.
Describe the importance of cultural competence in communicating public health content.	Social and behavioral theories in public health	Final exam case scenario 1: Students are required to propose a culturally tailored public health program to improve access to a free community health clinic among an immigrant population, and to discuss why cultural competence is critical in communicating with and impacting the target audience.

Domain Competency	MPH Course	Assessment Tool
Interprofessional Practice Perform effectively on interprofessional teams.	Community engagement in public health	Team project and evaluation rubric: Public health and nursing graduate students work with members of the Watts labor community action committee to plan a community health needs assessment project; students reflect on the interprofessional team experience through an evaluation of the team members' collaboration skills, roles, and responsibilities toward collaborating with community members, and conflict management and resolution skills, using a 4-item scale rubric.

Systems Thinking		
Apply systems thinking tools to a public health issue.	Program planning and evaluation	Assignment 1: Based on their literature review, student groups develop a causal loop diagram of some of the systems impacting the health issue under study and submit a logic model of risk identifying the behavioral and socioenvironmental factors, and personal determinants, associated with the selected health outcome impacting an at-risk urban underserved population.

the need for action plans to improve student outcomes and close the evaluation loop. For example, for the Principles of Epidemiology course, one of the more challenging courses for students, the faculty instructor proposed to administer five or six mini-exams instead of three comprehensive exams to better focus on the interpretation of the epidemiological studies presented in the modules. The faculty instructor also proposed to increase class time spent in reviewing the results of the mini-exams and other assignments. The action plans were implemented the next time the course was offered and resulted in better student outcomes and the achievement of target outcomes.

The Research Methods course, which covers quantitative and qualitative research methods, presented another example of how the findings were used for outcome improvement. The faculty instructor reflected that the previous assessment tool, where students were given a focus group text and asked to translate it and report the emerging themes, can be improved to ensure students have the skills to conduct focus groups rather than just interpreting the results. She proposed a new assessment activity where students are required to develop their own focus group moderator guide, conduct a focus group, analyze the results, and report the emerging themes to the class. The new assessment activity improved students' qualitative research skills and the target outcomes were met. Other faculty proposed to add more peer-reviewed articles to better prepare the students for the development of their own public health program proposals. Still other faculty proposed new required textbooks that have more public health case studies for student analysis.

In conclusion, CDU's Master of Public Health (MPH) in Urban Health Disparities program advocates for direct competency-based assessment tools, indirect assessment activities of student and faculty perceptions of pedagogy, consistent reporting of assessment findings, and use of findings to close the loop and improve student outcomes and program pedagogy. Program personnel believe that the processes described in this chapter ensure attainment of assessment goals, while furthering program and university missions.

References

Charles R. Drew University of Medicine and Science. (2017). *Mission, vision and values.* https://www.cdrewu.edu/COSH/MPH/Vision

Council on Education for Public Health. (2016). *Accreditation criteria School of Public Health and Public Health programs.* https://media.ceph.org/documents/2016.Criteria.pdf

Council on Education for Public Health. (2018). *Building curricula from competencies: Approaches and practical tips from an instructional design perspective.* https://ceph.org/constituents/schools/faqs/pres

12

ELEVATING ASSESSMENT PROCESSES THROUGH STAKEHOLDER ENGAGEMENT

Leigh M. Onimus and Joyce A. Strawser

This chapter describes how the Stillman School of Business at Seton Hall University uses the concept of *engagement*—engagement with external stakeholders, engagement of faculty, and engagement with faculty colleagues across the university—to enhance the relevance and impact of undergraduate and graduate assessment processes. The authors explain the approaches used to engage each distinct group of stakeholders and the benefits that have been realized from connecting these individuals more closely to assessment processes. It is the hope that the narrative will be useful to colleagues at other institutions who seek to elevate the impact of their assessment activities and more meaningfully engage their stakeholders in the learning endeavor.

The Stillman School of Business (Stillman) is the second largest academic unit of the eight colleges and schools that comprise Seton Hall University, the largest and oldest Roman Catholic diocesan university in the United States. Stillman's fall 2019 enrollment totaled 1,864, with 1,478 undergraduate and 386 graduate students, and 60 full-time faculty housed within six discipline-specific departments. The Stillman School maintains accreditation of both its business and accounting programs by AACSB International (Association to Advance Collegiate Schools of Business).

Stillman is located in South Orange, New Jersey, just 14 miles from New York City. The location enables the school to attract talented business professionals to guest lecture in classes, serve as adjunct faculty, and mentor students. Moreover, a majority of Stillman graduates live within commuting distance of the university, making it relatively easy to maintain relationships with alumni and involve them in the students' educational experiences. Stillman's mission is "to enrich each student's life through an ethics-centered education focusing on transforming concepts into business practice." As will be described, the school's mission, and especially its commitment to connecting students with practice, drives the choices made in designing and implementing assessment processes.

Engagement of External Stakeholders (Alumni and Industry Professionals)

The Stillman School uses a variety of approaches to assess student panels learning outcomes, including course-embedded assessments, stand-alone panels, performance-based methods, student surveys, and exit interviews. However, with the mission goal of applied learning in mind, the school's assessment processes are centered on performance-based methods that use industry professionals as coaches and evaluators. The approaches used at both the undergraduate and MBA program levels will be presented.

Although external volunteers serve as both evaluators and coaches, the school refers to them throughout this narrative as *assessors*. These assessors are, in most instances, Stillman alumni who have expressed an interest in being meaningfully involved in the school's activities. When identifying a potential assessor, the process requires that the individual has at least 5 years of work experience. Many of the assessors hold senior or midmanagement positions. While the pool of assessors serves at both the undergraduate and Master of Business Administration (MBA) levels, the MBA program assessors are generally those individuals who have greater professional experience and/or experience with the Stillman assessment process. The assessors come from a variety of industries and represent a wide range of companies, including EY, Horizon, PSE&G, and Prudential.

Undergraduate Assessment

At either the sophomore or senior level, all business students participate in what is referred to as *sophomore/senior assessment panels*. Participation in the sophomore or senior assessment panels is a noncredit-bearing graduation requirement for all business students. Approximately 40% of the students are randomly selected to participate at the sophomore level, and the remaining students participate as seniors. Students are randomly assigned to teams with four or five other business students and are given a case to analyze over a 2-month period. At the sophomore level, the case will generally focus on economics and legal issues, as those are two discipline areas in which students have already completed a number of core classes. At the senior level, the case tends to be more cross-disciplinary, as seniors have completed all of their core business classes. The cases tend to be timely Harvard Business School cases or a series of articles on a particular industry or company. Students are given a series of multipart, open-ended questions that require them to not only read the case, but also to do significant research beyond the scope of the case itself. From there, student teams are required to deliver a 30-minute presentation to a panel of outside business professionals, responding to the case questions and providing a comprehensive analysis of the company or industry they are examining.

Assessment panels are held twice a year on a Friday evening and Saturday, with multiple time slots in which assessors can participate. Each team is evaluated by two or three assessors. Veteran assessors are intentionally paired with those individuals who are new assessors or less seasoned professionals. The assessors evaluate team presentations on the school's learning goals (competencies): business discipline knowledge, business analytics, collaboration, communication, critical thinking, and ethical reasoning. Stillman purposefully designed the process to allow examination of students' achievement level at two different points in the curriculum. The hope is, of course, that seniors demonstrate a higher level of mastery in each of the competency areas than their sophomore counterparts.

The assessors use behaviorally anchored rubrics, developed by the faculty, to evaluate the student teams in each of the competency areas. After the team presentation, the assessors ask the students questions, probing further on particular content areas to more accurately assess their critical thinking and analysis skills. This question-and-answer period also allows assessors to evaluate how well students can respond to questions extemporaneously. Finally, in order to gain more information about the students' teamwork skills, the assessors question students about how they collaborated and the process they undertook to complete the project. After the presentation and question-and-answer period, assessors coach students on ways in which they can improve their presentation and analysis proficiencies. Assessors provide this feedback immediately after the team presentations and submit additional written feedback on the rubrics they use to evaluate the presentations.

MBA Assessment

The school's MBA curriculum includes two course experiences that serve as critical bookends for the program. These two courses deliver the applied learning that characterizes the Stillman MBA experience, while providing effective vehicles for collecting learning outcomes data. These courses also are designed to offer unique opportunities for engaging stakeholders in student development and learning outcomes assessment activities.

The first bookend course, the Launch Experience, is an onboarding course that is generally completed in the first semester of the MBA program. While the class runs in a hybrid format throughout a 7-week session, the most significant component of the experience is an immersive weekend event that runs from Saturday evening through late Sunday afternoon. Students, working in newly formed groups, are required to develop strategic recommendations for a specific company. They derive these recommendations from their analysis of the organization through the lenses of a strength, weakness, opportunity, threat (SWOT) analysis, Porter's five forces (Porter, 1980), and the Boston Consulting Group matrix (growth-share matrix) (Henderson, 1970). Using presentation software, they deliver their analyses to a small group of faculty and external assessors. The full-day Sunday program is divided into two distinct sessions—the morning session during which student teams develop their analysis and recommendations and the afternoon session, during which teams present their analyses. Stillman stakeholders play pivotal roles in both sessions.

During the 3-hour morning session, an external assessor serves alongside a faculty member as both an evaluator and a coach. For the 1st hour or so, the pair of assessors simply observes the dynamics of the team, evaluating each individual student on his or her teamwork and leadership competencies. To help align their expectations and scoring, the assessors work from detailed rubrics with behaviorally anchored trait descriptions. Assessors are asked to provide written comments in support of the scores they assign for teamwork and leadership, specifically identifying those areas of strength and those areas that might require further development.

About halfway through the morning session, assessors shift their focus from evaluating the student teams to coaching them through the final stages of analysis and presentation development. At this point, assessors might answer questions from the team or serve as a sounding board for the team's ideas. They also might provide feedback on the team's presentation slides or even observe and critique a rehearsal of the team's presentation.

In the afternoon session, a second set of assessors (again, one faculty member and one business professional) observe the student team presentations, asking probing questions during and after the formal presentation. Each student is required to deliver a portion of the group presentation, so that assessors can evaluate the communication skills of each individual learner.

The evaluation of students' performance in the Launch Experience accomplishes two goals. First, data are captured and used for program-level assessment of the MBA curriculum. Because this data reflects competency levels of students who are beginning their MBA studies, it provides information that can be used to evaluate absolute competency levels at that point in time as well as baseline results that can be compared with similar assessments administered at the completion of the students' program (in the final bookend course). This pretest/posttest structure enables the school to identify the change in learning goal mastery that occurs during students' MBA studies.

The second objective of the evaluation is to provide students with feedback they can use to enhance their own personal and professional development. Students are given assessors' scores and written feedback for purposes of self-reflection and development. A subsequent assignment in the Launch Experience course requires students to prepare a written reflection paper that compares their perceptions of their performance in the weekend immersion exercise with the performance feedback provided by assessors. From that comparison, students develop an action plan for improving any performance gaps.

The culminating bookend course, the Business Consulting class, includes a similar assessment activity that leverages Stillman stakeholders. As its name indicates, this course gives students an opportunity to work as consultants for a local organization—generally a small business or nonprofit. Students work throughout the semester to help their "client" resolve a specific business question or issue, with a final deliverable that includes actionable suggestions for improvement. As with the Launch Experience class, external business practitioners serve as both coaches and assessors, evaluating team and individual student behaviors and coaching students as they develop their client analysis and recommendations. However, in contrast to the accelerated pace of the Launch Experience, the Business Consulting class meets regularly throughout a 15-week semester, with assessors participating in several distinct student-team working sessions. External assessors also observe students' final presentations to clients, evaluating students on multiple learning goals, including communication skills, critical thinking, teamwork, social responsibility considerations, and functional business knowledge.

Benefits of External Stakeholder Engagement

Using external stakeholders in the assessment processes provides several distinct benefits, some of which were not anticipated when the process was designed. First, and perhaps most importantly, the assessors provide students with developmental feedback on skills that are essential as they progress through their curriculum and enter the workforce. While the quantitative feedback from the rubrics is certainly important, this developmental feedback, which ultimately makes Stillman students more "job-ready," is invaluable. Interestingly, students, particularly graduate students, tend to view the feedback that is provided by business professionals as being more credible and relevant than similar feedback provided by their faculty members.

External assessors frequently relate their comments to business trends or experiences in which they are currently involved, providing a richer context for their observations. For example, in a recent Launch Experience presentation, a student team made a recommendation related to the structure of the company's pension benefit plan. The external assessor, a seasoned human resources executive, was able to provide insights on benefit programs that caused students to reconsider their recommendation. Students often view courses that incorporate stakeholder participation as more impactful than those that are delivered solely by academics. Consequently, the use of external stakeholders as assessors, whether it is in the stand-alone undergraduate assessment panels or the course-embedded graduate assessment activities, is viewed by students as a unique and valuable learning experience. In fact, in the program annual survey of rising seniors, in response to an open-ended question about their "most valuable" educational experience, students frequently cite their participation in the sophomore/senior assessment panels. Likewise, in the MBA exit interviews students often comment on the value that the participation of external coaches and assessors provided to their overall experience in the program.

The engagement of alumni in the assessment processes has an important impact on the program curriculum. Alumni appreciate the opportunity to share their views with faculty and administrators on students' career readiness and on possible curricular improvements to enhance student development. Feedback from the assessors each semester provides informal input on the skills employers are seeking and what the industry demands of graduates. While the data collected through the assessment process are important in driving curricular changes, the informal conversations with the assessors who evaluate student presentations are equally valuable.

Specifically, assessors have provided feedback on students' oral communication and presentation skills and students' ability, through their presentations, to "tell a story" that holds the attention of the audience. This feedback comes through to some extent on the evaluation rubrics, but conversations with the assessors are helpful in identifying important areas for student development. Through this sharing, the school obtains a deeper understanding of its success in delivering on program learning objectives, especially those related to career preparation.

Engaging external stakeholders in the assessment process also increases meaningful interaction and information sharing between business professionals and faculty members, giving the latter the opportunity to enhance their knowledge of current industry practice in an unstructured, casual manner. In other words, the faculty, like the students, benefit from the insights that the program's business practitioners share in their evaluation of student performance. With the Stillman mission goal of connecting concepts to applications, the school greatly values opportunities for faculty to engage regularly with business practitioners.

Finally, Stillman has found that engaging alumni and employers in assessment processes helps to forge strong relationships with these stakeholders, to the ultimate benefit of the school and its students. Alumni enjoy connecting with students, and external assessors become more engaged with the school, extending their volunteer service to other areas and increasing their level of financial support to the school and its programs. For example, Stillman assessors are more likely to get involved in other initiatives, at the school, including hosting student dinners, serving as guest lecturers and recruiting students to their respective organizations. Given the flexible schedule of the assessment panels and the relatively limited preparation and time commitment involved, service as a Stillman assessor is a relatively easy, but very impactful, approach to engaging alumni. Indeed, many of the younger alumni have fond memories of their experience participating in Stillman assessments and are eager to experience the other side of the process through service as an assessor.

In some cases, the external assessors have become adjunct professors for the school, with the role of assessor providing a bit of an onboarding experience for the new hire. In other cases, students who have performed well in the assessment process have made connections with assessors who subsequently offered students internship or full-time job opportunities. In all, the Stillman use of external assessors has been of significant value in advancing the school's mission goal of connecting students to industry and "transforming concepts into business practice."

Of course, input from alumni and employers should not be limited to the evaluation of student performance. These stakeholders can provide important insights on appropriate learning goals and essential curriculum content as new programs are developed. Alumni and industry professionals also are an excellent source of feedback on the continued relevance of learning goals that may have been developed at an earlier date. Best practice would dictate that academic units regularly review program learning goals, and practitioners can provide valuable perspectives on the current applicability and relative importance of specific goals. Alumni and other stakeholders also are valuable participants in the process of identifying curriculum or pedagogical improvements that would be helpful in addressing cases where learning outcome results do not meet the institution's expectations.

Engagement of Business Faculty

Faculty have always played a critical role in the school's assessment processes. Over the years Stillman has worked diligently to shift the nature of faculty participation from a department/discipline-centered approach to a collaborative approach that spans discipline domains. To accomplish this goal, the Stillman School encourages faculty collaboration in several unique ways. All of these approaches have the potential to provide significant value to faculty's teaching and course development activities as they work to meet their responsibilities for assuring student learning.

Prerequisite/Subsequent Course Assessments

The school relies on several course-embedded assessments to test students' mastery of functional business knowledge, which include analytical tools such as statistical analysis and spreadsheet skills as well as fundamental principles of individual business disciplines such as accounting, finance, management, and marketing. Some of these assessments are formative in nature, with measurements that evaluate knowledge or skills that are introduced or developed in the course in which the testing occurs. For example, faculty teaching the Business Statistics class have used a quiz to evaluate students' understanding of several statistical concepts and methods.

In contrast to the formative assessments described, a number of the program's course-embedded assessments are summative. An upper-level course tests knowledge or skills that were introduced or developed in one or more prerequisite courses. In most cases, this type of summative assessment involves application of previously acquired knowledge or skills in the context of a new business discipline area. For example, in the core Business Finance class, faculty assess students' work on a quiz that requires their use and interpretation of regression analysis, a technique that they learn in the prerequisite Business Statistics class. Similarly, faculty assess students' ability to apply microeconomic concepts related to supply and demand curves and equilibrium prices (taught in the freshman Principles of Economics course) through a quiz that is delivered in their Principles of Marketing class (a class generally taken in the sophomore year). Macroeconomic concepts related to the impact of tariffs on global trade, generally taught in the freshman year, are tested through an assessment conducted in the Global Business course, frequently taken in the junior year.

The Stillman approach of testing knowledge delivered in prerequisite courses through assessments conducted in subsequent courses has provided several benefits. First, from a learning outcomes perspective, this approach allows testing the extent to which learning persists over time and in application across different contexts. Thus, the faculty believe that the measures obtained from this analysis provide them with greater insight into the learning that has taken place than would a similar assessment conducted during the period in which the concepts or skills are being introduced. Beyond these insights, the school believes that the approach used provides significant benefits in terms of engaging faculty and elevating school-wide discussions of learning goals and curriculum content.

In order to design theses course-embedded assessments, faculty representing two distinct discipline areas or departments must collaborate to identify the manner in which the school's existing learning goals can be tested through the combination of their two courses, one of which serves as a prerequisite for the other. The two faculty representatives agree, with input from their departmental colleagues, on the concepts or skills from the prerequisite course that are most relevant to topical coverage and learning goal development in the subsequent course. After the specific concepts and/or skills are identified, the pair must work together to identify an assessment approach that measures the relevant learning outcome(s) by leveraging existing assignments or course-level assessments. These discussions are often quite illuminating, because they require departments to reexamine and reaffirm the key concepts and skills that are required for upper-level courses. This reflection has caused departments to revisit their expectations of prerequisite course coverage and, in some cases, to recommend changes to the sequencing of business core coursework.

Once the course-embedded assessment has been implemented, results are reviewed and discussed by representatives of both departments. In cases where results fall below established benchmarks, the two departments work together to identify changes in curriculum or pedagogy that they believe would improve future learning outcomes. These recommendations are then forwarded to a curriculum committee for further consideration and approval.

Faculty members who are involved in these discussions come away with an enhanced understanding of how the courses in the various discipline areas contribute to the development of Stillman students and, ultimately, the achievement of the school's mission. Curriculum discussions that were previously confined to departmental/discipline "silos" are discussed in a collaborative fashion, with a greater appreciation of how individual courses interrelate to create a shared core curriculum. The school has found that this team approach to assurance of learning has increased faculty comfort with, and engagement in, the assessment process. Stillman is confident that the insights obtained through this collaborative approach will be helpful to the school as it prepares to undertake a comprehensive review of its undergraduate curriculum.

MBA Colloquium

The Stillman School launched a redesigned MBA program in August of 2017. As part of the redesign, faculty aimed to create a "community of practice" (Lave & Wenger, 1991) promoting cross-departmental communication and sharing of best practices. To that end, the school's faculty and dean's office implemented a monthly colloquium (MBA Colloquium) in which faculty teaching MBA core classes, two associate deans, and partners across campus connect virtually through Microsoft Teams for an hour-and-a-half meeting. This virtual platform allows for robust faculty participation and makes for an interactive presentation and discussion forum.

As part of this colloquium, teaching faculty and colleagues in the Teaching, Learning, and Technology Center have led development-focused presentations on topics such as collaborative learning, engaging students in online classes, and tools for preventing academic integrity breaches. Perhaps most importantly, the MBA Colloquium provides the opportunity to share and discuss results from the direct and indirect assessment methods utilized in the MBA program on a consistent basis with faculty across all departments.

The school conducts MBA exit interviews once a semester with students who are completing their degree program. During the exit interviews, at least one faculty member and one member of the dean's office probe students on their experiences inside and outside of the classroom. The MBA Colloquium provides a sound forum in which to share the feedback from these exit interviews as soon it is summarized. Prior to the implementation of the colloquium, there would often be a lag between the time of the exit interviews and the time during which feedback was shared. Now, this immediate sharing allows faculty to respond to the feedback and consider possible improvements or modifications to their respective courses and the program as a whole.

Stillman utilizes course-embedded assessments in MBA core courses on a rotational basis to evaluate the extent to which students are meeting expectations with respect to program learning goals. Results from the course-embedded assessments are summarized by an associate dean and shared with faculty each semester during the MBA Colloquium. During this meeting, faculty begin to identify corrective actions that can be taken to address the results from the course-embedded assessments. Thus, one of the benefits of the MBA Colloquium has been improved cross-departmental communication and collaboration. Now faculty more frequently reflect on what students are learning in a specific discipline area and discuss how those concepts and skills can then be reinforced and built upon in subsequent courses.

Scoring Sessions

Once each semester, faculty from all departments are encouraged to participate in MBA *scoring sessions*. During these sessions, faculty use the school's standard MBA learning goal rubrics to evaluate a number of student artifacts from the MBA core courses. Sessions include at least eight to 10 faculty from the various business discipline areas, as well as one or more associate deans.

During the scoring sessions, faculty use a set of standard rubrics that are introduced to students at the beginning of the MBA program and subsequently reinforced throughout their core courses. The rubrics have clearly delineated behavioral anchors. Because faculty are working in a room together and discussing the artifacts and elements of the rubric as they are scoring, there is an informal calibration that takes place. Thus, the likelihood of variability in scoring decreases and interrater reliability increases. As faculty score the artifacts, they discuss their rubric ratings and engage in a collegial dialogue. It is important to note that faculty are not "scoring" assignments from the classes that they teach. The artifacts being scored are selected from a number of core courses and distributed so that faculty score assignments from another instructor's class.

One of the incidental benefits of these scoring sessions is that faculty are able to see the type of assignments their colleagues in other departments are using in their courses. Faculty who have designed the assignments that are being evaluated comment on how well they have worked for their courses and describe the revisions that they have made over time to improve the assignments. This sharing of best practices, which can spark new ideas for many of the participants, is the element of the scoring sessions that faculty enjoy most. Faculty members appreciate the opportunity to engage across disciplines and reflect with one another on the work they do as teachers.

Engaging Colleagues Across Campus

As with most business schools, Stillman relies on the work of colleagues in other academic units to assist in developing the learning outcomes that have been established for the undergraduate business program. The school believes that its program is unique, however, in the extent to which it involves nonbusiness colleagues in the assurance of learning process. Several general education courses are critical to developing the undergraduate student competencies, with the most prominent of these being classes in finite mathematics, business ethics, oral communication, and business writing. All these classes are housed in units other than Stillman and are delivered by instructors who are not business faculty. However, because the courses serve the business students, the course content is developed in collaboration with Stillman faculty and is driven by the learning goals established for the business students.

As part of the sophomore and senior assessment panels, in addition to the team presentation they make, students are also required to prepare a writing sample. Colleagues in the Department of English, the department that teaches the core Business Writing course, score students' writing samples each semester using a rubric jointly developed by business and English faculty. Once the results of the assessment are summarized, they are shared not only with the business faculty, but also with faculty in the Department of English. When benchmarks are not met in a particular area or there is a noticeable decline in scores, business faculty meet with faculty representatives from the Department of English and discuss options for corrective action. As an example, when results indicated that students were not properly formatting their writing samples, business faculty asked colleagues in the Department of English to increase the amount of time spent on formatting business communiques. An additional class module and assignment were added to the core Business Writing course to reinforce the importance of properly formatting business documents.

The College of Communication and the Arts delivers a series of communication courses for business students. Over time, business faculty and colleagues in the College of Communication and the Arts have worked together to identify the most suitable communication courses for business students given the school's learning goals. Beyond that, in recent years as the school observed a decline in assessment scores in the area of oral communication, faculty collaborated across the units to modify the content in the required Oral Communication course to address the deficiencies the assessors observed. In addition, a faculty member who teaches the Oral Communication course for business students led a development workshop for business faculty to share how she teaches oral communication skills and the type of feedback she provides students after their presentations.

In line with the school's mission of providing an "ethics-centered" education, one of the Stillman undergraduate learning goals centers on ethical reasoning. The Department of Philosophy (College of Arts and Sciences) delivers the core course that provides the foundation in ethical reasoning. The chair of the Department of Philosophy delivered a training workshop for business faculty to share the framework for analyzing ethical issues that is taught in the core Business Ethics course. Through participation in this workshop, business faculty gained confidence in teaching their students to apply the same framework of analysis to the types of ethical dilemmas that arise in their specific discipline domains.

Beyond the significant benefits associated with strengthening student learning outcomes, the assessment work with colleagues across campus helps to advance the university's strategic imperative of greater cross-campus collaboration and cohesion—an initiative referred to as One Seton Hall. Discussions with these colleagues open minds to new ideas and approaches as best practices are shared with one another. This work is helping to create an environment in which interdisciplinary cooperation can flourish. In fact, Stillman is proud to report a significant achievement that is a direct result of these shared assessment activities. A Stillman faculty member recently collaborated with a colleague in the Department of Philosophy to secure a National Endowment for the Humanities Connection Planning Grant. The grant will fund an initiative to more fully integrate business and the humanities at Seton Hall. Specific goals of the initiative include the development of multiple disciplinary case studies that combine philosophical, historical, literary, religious and spiritual, artistic, and business perspectives, as well as the creation of an advanced interdisciplinary, team-taught course in the business humanities.

Conclusion

The Stillman experience has demonstrated that assessment programs can be greatly enriched through a focus on engaging a variety of relevant stakeholders—both internal and external. Increasing the engagement of stakeholders has made the school's assessment program more effective in enhancing student learning outcomes, increasing student connections to practice, and fostering faculty development. The business assessment work with university colleagues has ignited a new enthusiasm for cross-campus initiatives that provide great promise for curriculum enhancement. The benefits experienced are significant and extend well beyond the domain of assurance of learning.

References

Henderson, B. (1970, January 1). *The product portfolio.* Boston Consulting Group. https://www.bcg.com/publications/1970/strategy-the-product-portfolio

Lave, J., & Wenger, E. (1991). *Situated learning: Legitimate peripheral participation.* Cambridge University Press.

Porter, M. E. (1980). *Competitive strategy: Techniques for analyzing industries and competitors.* Free Press.

13

COMPETENCY-BASED STUDENT ASSESSMENT IN ONLINE AND IN-PERSON MASTER OF PUBLIC HEALTH PROGRAMS

Kimberly Krytus, Sarah Cercone Heavey, and Gregory G. Homish

Assessment of student learning is a foundation of the U.S. education system. Student assessment in graduate education in particular has an essential role in ensuring that individuals who obtain a degree have the knowledge and skills necessary to perform as competent practitioners in their profession. As public health program administrators seek ways to best assess student learning, the focus in recent years has turned from assessing students in a content-based curriculum to assessing students in a competency-based curriculum (Calhoun et al., 2011). Competency-based learning and assessment focuses on how well students apply knowledge and demonstrate an ability to perform professional skills. This approach is in contrast to traditional assessments in content-based learning, which measure student knowledge and understanding of content, rather than skill attainment (United States Department of Education, 2002).

Competency-based education is new to public health. In past years, there was widespread support among public health education institutions for basing the Master of Public Health (MPH) program, the standard degree for public health practice, on five core knowledge areas: (a) biostatistics, (b) environmental health, (c) epidemiology, (d) health policy and management, and (e) social and behavioral health, while also including cross-cutting areas of communication, leadership, professionalism, program planning, diversity, and systems thinking (Association of Schools and Programs of Public Health [ASPPH], 2014; Calhoun et al., 2011; Council on Education for Public Health [CEPH], 2011). A pivotal step toward competency-based education in public health occurred when the Council on Linkages Between Academia and Public Health Practice (Council on Linkages), a collaboration of national public health agencies, formed in 1992. The Council on Linkages aimed to bridge efforts between public health programs and the practice community. In order to strengthen public health education to meet knowledge and skill needs of the workforce, they proposed a set of core competencies for public health curricula (Council on Linkages Between Academia and Public Health Practice [Council on Linkages], 2010, 2014). The core competencies were offered in part to provide a standard framework for educating future public health practitioners (Institute of Medicine, 1988; Public Health Functions Steering Committee, 1995). The competencies were also introduced to strengthen practice-based skills in the labor market where workforce shortages and skill gaps have yet to be fully addressed (Barna, 2019). The number of public health professionals in the market has not met employer demand in recent decades, and many of those in the workforce were not trained in public health, lacking essential skills for practice (Castrucci, 2019; Gebbie et al., 2002; Halverson, 2019).

Following the Council on Linkages (2001) introduction of core public health competencies, the Association of Schools of Public Health (ASPH, 2006) proposed a wide-ranging set of competencies that spanned the traditional five core knowledge areas and cross-cutting areas for MPH programs. While ASPH (2006) recommended that institutions integrate the competencies into their curricula, adoption was not compulsory. At that time, the CEPH, the accrediting body for public health education, required programs to focus on core knowledge and cross-cutting areas in their curricula, in addition to competencies. However, each institution could adopt any competencies they chose, such as those from the Council on Linkages (2001) or ASPH (2006), or they could design their own competencies for each program (CEPH, 2011). At that time, no standard existed.

Public health institutions recognized the need for a standard education framework, and in 2014, the Association of Schools and Programs of Public Health (ASPPH), ASPH's successor, established the Framing the Future Task Force charged with advancing public health education to meet workforce needs for the 21st century (ASPPH, 2014). Around this time, the National Board of Public Health Examiners (NBPHE) conducted a job task analysis to strengthen the Certified in Public Health (CPH) credential, a certification earned through successful completion of a national public health exam that measures public health knowledge and skill application (NBPHE, 2019). The job task analysis team surveyed over 4,500 public health employers who prioritized 200 essential public health job tasks (Breidenbach & Irwin, 2016).

Recommendations made by the Framing the Future Task Force and findings from the NBPHE job task analysis led to two key changes in MPH education. First, the data led the NBPHE to strengthen the CPH exam to better align with knowledge and skills employers prioritized for practice. In addition, the findings led CEPH to strengthen the MPH curriculum by developing 22 foundational public health competencies required for accredited programs (Breidenbach & Irwin, 2016; CEPH, 2016a; Kurz et al., 2017; NBPHE, 2019). The 22 foundational MPH competencies introduced by CEPH (2016a) also aligned with practice-based competencies from the Council on Linkages (2014). Further, CEPH's foundational MPH competencies aligned with the essential public health services a national steering committee identified in 1994, which provided a mission and framework for public health practice that is still used today (Centers for Disease Control and Prevention [CDC], 2018; Council on Linkages, 2014).

Developing a Competency-Based MPH Curriculum

The University at Buffalo, which is the largest campus within the State University of New York (SUNY) and a research university ranked as a top public institution in the United States (Andrei, 2019; U.S. News and World Report, 2019), offers an MPH program in six concentrations. MPH concentrations are housed across three departments in the university's School of Public Health and Health Professions. Each concentration has a director; however, because multiple departments offer MPH concentrations, an MPH program director in the dean's office centrally administers the program.

In 2012, following the introduction of public health program competencies by ASPH (2006) and the Council on Linkages (2010), University at Buffalo MPH concentration directors began to integrate select competencies into core curricula. This strategy proved challenging as there were many competencies to select from, no standard set to integrate, and little guidance on how to assess competencies that were integrated. In addition, at that time competency-based education was new to faculty. Consequently, many instructors did not include competencies in their courses or modify course assessments to measure how well students attained competencies that were included (University at Buffalo School of Public Health and Health Professions [UBSPHHP], 2014). The MPH curriculum continued to focus on content from the five core knowledge areas: biostatistics, environmental health, epidemiology, health policy and management, and social and behavioral health, and cross-cutting content (UBSPHHP, 2014).

In 2016, CEPH required accredited schools and programs to integrate the new foundational MPH competencies, developed in part from tasks employers prioritized in the NBPHE job task analysis (Breidenbach & Irwin, 2016; CEPH, 2016a; Council on Linkages, 2014). MPH programs were tasked with fully integrating the 22 foundational competencies into their curricula and assessing student attainment of each competency in order to better prepare students to meet employer needs. While some institutions developed new curricula to address the foundational competencies, the MPH program at the University at Buffalo needed to maintain its existing courses focused on core knowledge and cross-cutting areas, as many of the courses were required for other master's and doctoral degrees. The MPH director and concentration directors worked within the existing core curriculum to integrate and assess the new foundational competencies.

Implementing and Assessing a Competency-Based MPH Curriculum

The University at Buffalo's MPH program established a curriculum revision implementation team consisting of two concentration directors, the MPH director, one faculty instructor, and one graduate program director, all of whom taught in the program; two MPH students also joined the team. The team worked with instructors to review course syllabi and content, mapping each of the 22 foundational MPH competencies to an existing core course in the curriculum. The resulting map was a matrix of the 22 competencies, individually linked with one or more of the five core MPH courses that covered material related to the competency. Some competencies had no courses mapped to them, and those competencies were flagged for further discussion. For competencies mapped to an existing core course, the team reviewed and ranked how well the course covered its respective competency (ranging from 1=weak to 5=strong). Through this ranking process, the team identified competencies that were directly addressed by multiple courses, competencies that were indirectly addressed in a core course, or competencies that were not addressed at all. Table 13.1, a map of select foundational competencies to core courses, depicts sample outcomes of this mapping process.

Of the 22 foundational competencies reviewed, eight were directly and comprehensively covered by existing content and were integrated into the applicable core course. Three competencies were indirectly covered in a

TABLE 13.1
Map of Select MPH Foundational Competencies

Competency Number and Description (from 22 foundational competencies; CEPH, 2016a)	Core Course	Course Coverage Average Rating: (1—weak to 5—strong)	Note About Specific Areas Requiring Course Revisions
1. Apply epidemiologic methods to the breadth of settings and situations in public health practice	Epidemiology	5 (no variation)	Prioritize *apply* and *calculate* learning objectives over *describe* or *understand*
3. Analyze quantitative and qualitative data using biostatistics, informatics, computer-based programming, and software, as appropriate	Statistics	5 (quantitative, no variation); 0 (qualitative, no variation)	*Quantitative* is well covered; no course addresses *qualitative* content
15. Evaluate policies for their impact on public health and health equity	Health Care Systems	3 (range 2–4)	Policies are evaluated for impact on public health, but not *impact on health equity*
17. Apply negotiation and mediation skills to address organizational or community challenges	Health Behavior	1 (range 0–1.5)	*Understanding community challenges* is covered, but not *negotiation/mediation*
21. Perform effectively on interprofessional teams		0 (no variation)	No course addresses
22. Apply systems thinking tools to a public health issue	Environmental Health	2 (no variation)	Ecological health is covered, but not *systems thinking tools*

course, and the implementation team asked course instructors to strengthen their content to directly cover those competencies. In addition, instructors were asked to revise content in their core courses to cover seven more competencies that had not been directly or comprehensively covered elsewhere in the curriculum, but that logically flowed from the core course content.

To address the remaining four competencies that were not covered by a core course (collaboration, leadership, negotiation and mediation, and interprofessional teamwork), the team worked with instructors to develop two new courses totaling four credits. While these competencies were the most challenging to integrate into the curriculum, they aligned well with each other, facilitating development of the new courses. One new course covered collaboration, leadership, and negotiation and mediation, and one new course covered interprofessional teamwork. Through the mapping process, the implementation team identified one three-credit core course that did not address any of the 22 foundational competencies. This course also duplicated a significant amount of content that was delivered in another core course. To make room in the curriculum for four more credits from the new courses, this three-credit course was removed.

Once all foundational competencies were mapped to a course, instructors included the competency language in their syllabi and in course material, exposing students to language that aligned with specific tasks and skills employers sought (Breidenbach & Irwin, 2016). This change was important so students could become familiar with the vernacular employers use to describe public health practice. Instructors also identified an assessment in their core courses that addressed each foundational competency they covered. Course assessments included homework assignments, quiz or exam questions, projects, group activities, interactive exercises, papers, or presentations.

Challenges in Assessing Competency Attainment

Selecting an assessment activity in a course that appropriately addressed each competency was difficult. Most courses introduced and progressively strengthened competencies over the duration of a semester. Instructors had to consider when to assess a competency that required higher-order cognitive processes or actions. In addition, many of the 22 foundational competencies are comprehensive, include multiple or complex concepts, and focus on a specific skill or skill set. To best assess competencies such as those described in Table 13.1, instructors had to consider the level of skill students should be able to demonstrate for each competency, and how well their course assessments addressed a competency's comprehensiveness or complexity.

Assessing Higher Order Educational Objectives

The 22 foundational MPH competencies were developed to employ higher order cognitive processes on Bloom's taxonomy of educational objectives (Anderson & Krathwohl, 2001; Bloom, 1956; CEPH, 2016a). Assessing students on their ability to *describe* or *define* a public health concept, which are basic cognitive processes on Bloom's taxonomy (Anderson & Krathwohl, 2001; Bloom, 1956), can be reasonably addressed by quiz or exam questions. In contrast, assessing students on their ability to *apply* knowledge or methods, or *perform* a skill, which are higher order cognitive processes (Anderson & Krathwohl, 2001; Bloom, 1956), requires more in-depth student assessments.

Competency assessments in the MPH program needed to meet the specific cognitive process and action a competency required (CEPH, 2016a, 2016b). Faculty frequently assessed students by asking them to *describe*, *define*, or *identify* information from course material on homework, quiz, or exam questions. However, revising an assessment question from *define* or *identify* to *apply* a skill or *evaluate* a concept required instructors to conceptualize course content differently. This effort took time, practice, and often multiple iterations. For example, asking students to *define* systems thinking or *describe* how systems thinking relates to a public health issue (competency 22) in a quiz question does not address the action required by this competency. Students needed to apply a systems thinking tool, such as a stock and flow map, which illustrates how parts of a system influence each other, or a root cause analysis, which identifies direct and indirect causes of an issue (CDC, 2019). Assessing students on applying a stock and flow map or a root cause analysis required more time and focus than a quiz question would allow, as well as more instructor and student engagement with the tools during class for students to apply them effectively.

Assessing Comprehensive and Complex Competencies

Instructors also had to consider how well assessments addressed comprehensive competencies such as applying epidemiologic methods to the breadth and depth of public health scenarios (competency 1). One course assessment often was not sufficient to fully assess a competency, and multiple assessments were needed. For example, faculty needed more than one homework, quiz, or exam question to assess students' ability to apply epidemiologic methods, which required more than one method, to multiple public health settings (competency 1).

Competencies that were complex, covering more than one concept or requiring interaction and engagement, were also challenging to assess.

Competency 15, evaluate policies for their impact on public health and health equity, is a complex competency. The instructor for the course addressing this competency asked students to evaluate a policy and its impact on public health as a short-answer exam question. Yet this task did not allow for students to further evaluate the policy's impact on health equity. Revising the exam question to include health equity required a more comprehensive response from students, becoming a long-answer question worth more points on the exam. In addition, other competencies that addressed multiple concept such as analyzing quantitative and qualitative data (competency 3), or that required significant engagement with others such as performing on interprofessional teams (competency 21), required more than one course to fully cover and assess them.

The implementation team worked with instructors throughout these processes to help revise or create appropriate assessments for each of the 22 foundational competencies. Once instructors revised existing assessments or developed new ones, they were tested to ensure each assessment fully assessed its respective competency. Assessment reviews were completed by the implementation team, and instructors integrated the revised or new assessments into courses over two or three semesters. In some cases, guidance from public health academic organizations such as ASPPH communities or CEPH was sought to ensure assessments fully assessed a competency.

Assessing Students in Creative Ways
Competencies 17 and 21 proved to be particularly challenging, as assessing negotiation or mediation skills (competency 17) and interprofessional teamwork skills (competency 21) requires instructors to observe students as they apply each skill. However, in courses with many students, instructors had limited opportunities to observe them. Following the mapping process, competencies 17 and 21 were integrated into the two new MPH courses, providing an opportunity for instructors to develop creative ways to measure how well students attained these competencies. Students negotiated in small groups in class, and students worked interprofessionally in small groups outside of class with faculty observation, allowing instructors to observe multiple students at one time. Instructors also gave students rubrics or activity guides before their small group work and asked students to prepare a group-level summary after their discussion that followed the rubric or activity guide instructors provided. This process documented knowledge and skills students applied in their discussions for instructors to review, supplementing the instructor's observations and providing performance verification for student grading. Table 13.2 provides

TABLE 13.2
Assessment of Select MPH Foundational Competencies

Competency	Core Course	Assessment
1. Apply epidemiologic methods to the breadth of settings and situations in public health practice	Epidemiology	Three multipart quiz questions calculating prevalence, mortality rate, and risk ratios for public health issues across three different settings
3. Analyze quantitative and qualitative data using biostatistics, informatics, computer-based programming, and software, as appropriate	Statistics (quantitative)	Compute ANOVA and regression analysis using statistical software package
	New course: Contemporary Public Health Issues (qualitative)	Collect and analyze qualitative interview data
15. Evaluate policies for their impact on public health and health equity	Health Care Systems	Policy evaluation paper
17. Apply negotiation and mediation skills to address organizational or community challenges	New course: Contemporary Public Health Issues	Student small group negotiation for a public health scenario
21. Perform effectively on interprofessional teams	New course: Public Health Teamwork	Online modules assessing foundational interprofessional collaborative practice knowledge
	New course: Contemporary Public Health Issues	Observation of student performance on interprofessional teams applying content learned in the Public Health Teamwork course
22. Apply systems thinking tools to a public health issue	Environmental Health	Final paper: analysis of an environmental health issue, including a root cause analysis

assessments that addressed these challenges for select foundational MPH competencies.

Assessing Competencies in Online Courses
Online courses presented unique challenges for instructors to assess how well students attain competencies. Instructors can view students taking quizzes and exams, working on group projects, or delivering presentations during courses that students attend in person. However, instructors must use different tools and techniques for online course assessments. In moving coursework online, instructors had to start fresh in many ways. Although course content was often preexisting, every activity, quiz, test, or project needed revision. To provide lecturelike structure in an online course, instructors divided material weekly and then posted a weekly roadmap at the start of each week. This format provided an overview for the student, included all weekly requirements, and allowed students to see how they were gaining competencies throughout the course.

Critically, instructors needed to incorporate active learning opportunities for students to master competencies. Generally, a recorded lecture video is passive, while a discussion board post or reply is active. Instructors embedded questions in recorded lecture material to check content comprehension, emphasize key points in course material, and incentivize student participation. Some examples of active learning in an online environment included technology allowing video posts from students, as well as discussion boards, collaborative documents, blogs, and journals. To assess competencies that required instructor observation, such as competencies 17 and 21, instructors used web conferencing programs such as WebEx to view student engagement with each other and with the course material. Conferencing programs allowed instructors to view and assess students during negotiations or interprofessional discussions. In addition, instructors encouraged students to use collaborative programs such as Google Drive to work on documents, presentations, and spreadsheets together. Opportunities for students to work collaboratively on a document also provided instructors with excellent ways to meet and assess higher-order educational objectives. Students were kept engaged by using varying techniques such as discussion board posts, which are individual student activities, and collaboratively editing a document, which is a group activity. Using a variety of techniques also provided instructors with flexibility in delivering competency-related content and assessing how well students attained a competency.

Testing, whether through quizzes or exams, in an online course presented a new challenge for instructors, as well. Remote proctoring services, such as ProctorU or Respondus Monitor, offer additional security for test-taking settings. Remote proctoring services require students to have a video camera that can record while they take the assessment through learning management software used for the course. Generally, these services require students to verify their identity with a state-issued form of identification, show their setting to ensure that no hidden resources are available to the student, and then record the testing session. In some cases, these services also provide live proctors who watch students remotely complete an assessment and can immediately intercede, should an issue of academic integrity arise. While not all assessments require a live proctor, it can be particularly useful for a high-stakes exam such as a comprehensive final exam worth a large portion of a student's final course grade.

Measuring Student Attainment of Foundational MPH Competencies

All students who began the MPH program at the University at Buffalo in fall 2018 or later receive the competency-based curriculum and are assessed on their level of competency attainment. To evaluate how well students attain each competency, instructors record student performance on each quiz/exam question, homework assignment, paper, or presentation that assesses a competency. Each competency assessment differs in number of points it contributes to a student's grade, based on the course instructor's grading structure. Some assessments, such as quiz questions, are worth as few as 2 points on a course quiz, while other assessments such as final student projects are worth as much as 30 points of the student's final course grade. Each core MPH course addresses between one and five competencies. Course instructors track and provide student performance data for an average of three competency assessments per course. The MPH director reviews aggregate student performance data for each competency assessed.

To understand how well MPH students attain each competency, the MPH director applies a cut-off between 80% and 84% to the aggregate assessment data instructors provide for their course. This cut-off represents the percentage of students in each course who obtained a passing grade on the competency assessment. Competency assessment grade cut-offs are equivalent to a letter grade of B or better in the respective course. This approach aligns with University at Buffalo's MPH requirement of a grade of B or better in each foundational MPH course, and a B or better for a student's cumulative grade point average to earn the MPH degree (University at Buffalo, 2020). The MPH director also analyzes assessment data to identify correlations between a student's performance on competency assessments and the student's final course grade.

Use of Assessment Findings

The percentage of students who attain each competency, and correlations between student competency performance and final course grade, are shared with each course instructor. When the percentage attaining a competency falls below a course's B-equivalent cut-off grade, the MPH director discusses ways to strengthen competency-related material with the course instructor. In addition, the correlational data allows directors to identify courses where the majority of students receive a passing course grade, but do not demonstrate attainment of the foundational competency in the course. The MPH program aims to assure that all MPH students attain each of the 22 competencies. However, students who pass a course but do not do well on the competency assessment may graduate without obtaining skills employers seek (Breidenbach & Irwin, 2016). In these cases, the assessment may not effectively measure competency attainment, or the competency may not be sufficiently integrated with course material. The MPH director works with instructors, program directors, and department chairs to enhance competency attainment in core courses where needed, ensuring that the program produces MPH graduates who have demonstrated the foundational competencies.

The initial MPH competency assessment evaluation in 2019 showed that a small number of students in core courses did not complete competency assessments, yet those students still passed the course. In these courses, instructors were assessing a foundational competency through a bonus question on a quiz/exam, an extra credit homework assignment, or an optional course activity. Once these gaps were identified, program directors worked with instructors to ensure all students completed assessments that addressed a foundational competency. Instructors moved bonus questions to be part of the graded quiz content, or changed optional course assessments to required assessments.

Summarizing a Process for Assessing Competencies in an MPH Curriculum

By establishing a curriculum revision implementation team to integrate new competencies into the MPH program, the University at Buffalo's MPH program effectively migrated from a content-based to a competency-based curriculum. Strategies the team implemented to facilitate this change, such as mapping competencies to courses and ranking competency coverage in courses, helped identify gaps in the curriculum. Program directors worked with instructors to address the gaps, ensuring that students receive training on the 22 foundational MPH competencies employers identified as essential (Breidenbach & Irwin, 2016). While identifying assessments in the core courses that addressed each competency proved to be challenging in some cases, instructors had flexibility in revising existing assessments or creating new ones. This flexibility was particularly important in online core courses where a variety of teaching techniques and platforms were used.

Performance data on competency assessments for each of the 22 foundational competencies (select set is shown in Table 13.1) are collected each semester and evaluated by the MPH director. The evaluation provides data to assess three main areas of the MPH continually. First, the data shows foundational competency assessments that not all students complete, such as optional homework assignments. Once these assessments are identified, the MPH director works with instructors to move the assessment from optional to required. Next, evaluation results show competency assessments with an average student grade below the passing grade for the course. In these cases, the MPH director works with instructors to ensure relevant content is directly covered in the course for students to attain each competency. Finally, courses that have low correlations between students' competency assessment grade and final course grade may indicate that competency assessments are not effective measures of competency attainment. Alternately, low correlations may indicate that students pass a course and earn their MPH without demonstrating that they have gained competencies required for public health practice (Breidenbach & Irwin, 2016; CEPH, 2016a). Program directors and instructors work together to revise course content or competency assessments to assure students attain each competency required for the program.

References

Anderson, L. W., & Krathwohl, D. (2001). *A taxonomy for learning, teaching, and assessing: A revision of Bloom's taxonomy of educational objectives.* Longman.

Andrei, M. (2019, September 9). *UB rises to 31 among public universities in U.S. news rankings.* University at Buffalo. http://www.buffalo.edu/ubnow/stories/2019/09/us-news-rankings.html

Association of Schools and Programs of Public Health. (ASPPH). (2014). *Framing the future.* https://www.aspph.org/teach-research/framing-the-future/

Association of Schools of Public Health. (ASPH). (2006). *Master's degree in public health core competency development project.* https://s3.amazonaws.com/aspph-wp-production/app/uploads/2014/04/Version2.31_FINAL.pdf

Barna, M. (2019). More public health grads being drawn to private sector jobs. *The Nation's Health, 49*(6), 1–12. https://www.thenationshealth.org/content/49/6/1.2

Bloom, B. S. (1956). *Taxonomy of educational objectives: The classification of education goals by a committee of college and university examiners.* David McKay.

Breidenbach, D. H., & Irwin, Z. (2016). *A job analysis of the certified in public health* (Conducted for the National Board of Public Health Examiners). AMP and National Board of Public Health Examiners.

Calhoun, J. G., Wrobel, C. A., & Finnegan, J. R. (2011). Current state in U.S. public health competency-based graduate education. *Public Health Reports, 33*(1), 148–167.

Castrucci, B. C. (2019). Perceptions from professional and accrediting organizations. In S. Maitin-Shepard & C. Alvarado (Eds.), *Dialogue about the workforce for population health improvement: Proceedings of a workshop* (pp. 13–34). National Academies Press. https://www.nap.edu/read/25545/chapter/1

Centers for Disease Control and Prevention (CDC). (2018). *The public health system and the 10 essential public health services.* https://www.cdc.gov/publichealthgateway/publichealthservices/essentialhealthservices.html

Centers for Disease Control and Prevention (CDC). (2019). *Thinking in systems overview.* https://www.cdc.gov/policy/polaris/tis/index.html

Council on Education for Public Health (CEPH). (2011). *Accreditation criteria: Public health programs, amended June 2011.* https://media.ceph.org/wp_assets/SPH-Criteria-2011.pdf

Council on Education for Public Health (CEPH). (2016a). *Accreditation criteria: Schools of public health and public health programs.* https://media.ceph.org/wp_assets/2016.Criteria.pdf

Council on Education for Public Health (CEPH). (2016b). *FAQs: 2016 criteria—Competencies.* https://ceph.org/constituents/schools/faqs/2016criteriafaq/competencies/.

Council on Linkages Between Academia and Public Health Practice (Council on Linkages). (2001). *Core competencies for public health professionals* (original version). http://www.phf.org/resourcestools/Pages/Core_Public_Health_Competencies.aspx

Council on Linkages Between Academia and Public Health Practice (Council on Linkages). (2010). *Crosswalk of the core competencies for public health professionals with the essential public health services.* http://www.phf.org/resourcestools/Documents/Crosswalk_corecompetencies_and_essential_services.pdf

Council on Linkages Between Academia and Public Health Practice (Council on Linkages). (2014). *Core competencies for public health professionals.* http://www.phf.org/resourcestools/Documents/Core_Competencies_for_Public_Health_Professionals_2014June.pdf

Gebbie, K., Merrill, J., & Tilson, H. H. (2002). The public health workforce. *Health Affairs, 21*(6), 57–67.

Halverson, P. K. (2019). Ensuring a strong public health workforce for the 21st century: Reflections on PH WINS 2017. *Journal of Public Health Management and Practice, 25,* S1–S3. https://doi.org/10.1097/PHH.0000000000000967

Institute of Medicine. (1988). *The future of public health.* National Academies Press.

Kurz, R. S., Yager, C., Yager, J. D., Foster, A., Breidenbach, D. H., & Irwin, Z. (2017). Advancing the certified in public health examination: A job task analysis. *Public Health Reports, 132*(4), 518–523. https://doi.org/10.1177/0033354917710015

National Board of Public Health Examiners. (2019). *Why get certified?* https://www.nbphe.org/why-get-certified/.

Public Health Functions Steering Committee. (1995). *Public health in America*. U.S. Public Health Service.

United States Department of Education. (2002). *Defining and assessing learning: Exploring competency-based initiatives* [Report]. National Postsecondary Education Cooperative Working Group on Competency-Based Initiatives in Postsecondary Education. https://nces.ed.gov/pubs2002/2002159.pdf

U.S. News and World Report. (2019). *Top public schools: National universities.* https://www.usnews.com/best-colleges/rankings/national-universities/top-public

University at Buffalo. (2020). *The graduate school: Policy library.* https://grad.buffalo.edu/succeed/current-students/policy-library.html

University at Buffalo School of Public Health and Health Professions (UBSPHHP). (2014). *Self-study report: August 2014.* http://www.buffalo.edu/provost/oia/initiatives/Accreditation/middle-states/self-study-report.html

14

DESIGNING AND ASSESSING COCURRICULAR STRATEGIES TO PROMOTE PERSONAL AND PROFESSIONAL DEVELOPMENT

Burgunda V. Sweet, Katherine A. Kelley, Melissa S. Medina, and Marianne McCollum

In 2008, the National Survey of Student Engagement (NSSE) published a list of what is known as high-impact practices, or HIPs (NSSE, n.d.). Together, these practices correlate with high retention and graduation rates and support student success and learning. HIPs include practices such as learning communities, service learning, internships, other experiential learning opportunities, portfolios, and capstone courses. Traits shared across HIPs are that they "demand considerable time and effort, facilitate learning outside of the classroom, require meaningful interactions with faculty and students, encourage collaboration with diverse others, and provide frequent and substantive feedback" (NSSE, para. 1, as cited in Kuh, 2008).

Writing about disruptive moments in teaching, Randy Bass raises the issue of how these high-impact practices might be affecting the formal curriculum in education (Bass, 2012). While some courses may capture some HIPs (e.g., capstones and experiential learning), most HIPs reside primarily outside the classroom in the cocurriculum. The cocurriculum includes "activities, programs, and learning experiences that complement, in some way, what students are learning in school—i.e., experiences that are connected to or mirror the academic curriculum" (Great Schools Partnership, 2013). The greatest impact on learning in higher education arises from the coupling of learning-intensive activities of the cocurriculum with capstone and experientially oriented courses in the formal curriculum. Students gain knowledge and skills and develop personally and professionally, while learning in and outside of the classroom.

The importance of cocurricular activities is also stressed by higher education institutional accreditors advocating for student success through development and assessment of cocurricular activities and student services. Expectations are that schools foster learning and achievement of program outcomes through the formal curriculum as well as promote activities designed to help students acquire affective skills, ensuring they have the resilience to succeed in their programs (e.g., HLC [3.E.1] and SACS [8.2.c.]) (HLC, 2019; SAC, 2018).

Merging curricular and cocurricular activities supports meaningful learning and personal and professional development both in the general higher education environment and in the professional programs. Similar to undergraduate education, professional programs are charged with preparing students to take positions in challenging fields such as health care. Clinical knowledge and skills can be taught in the classroom, but the development of professionalism is best supported through the cocurriculum. For example, the Doctor of Pharmacy (PharmD) degree provides the necessary academic training for students to pass knowledge and skills-based licensure requirements and to develop personally and professionally. This training is best met through the thoughtful and intentional development of the formal curriculum and the cocurriculum in order to meet the needs of the profession and the public. The Accreditation Council on Pharmacy Education (ACPE) provides guidance similar to that of other higher education institutional accreditors, supporting creation of an enriched educational approach among colleges and schools of pharmacy. The principles of developing and assessing cocurricular activities are applicable to both general higher education programs as well as professional programs leading to the PharmD degree; this chapter will focus primarily on the latter.

The curricular programs that lead to pharmacy professional licensure are typically 4 years in length, encompassing approximately 3 years of didactic coursework as well as 300 hours of early experiential training occurring alongside this didactic coursework. The program is completed by a year of full-time advanced experiential training. PharmD programs are generally lock-step and students progress through the program in cohorts. Additionally, PharmD programs are subject to specialized accreditation from ACPE.

Accreditation guidelines specify the knowledge, skills, and attitudes necessary to become generalist, entry-level pharmacy practitioners. The 2016 ACPE Standards (ACPE, 2016) specifically state that cocurricular activities should augment, complement, and advance the learning that occurs in the formal didactic and experiential curriculum and that they should be implemented in a manner that provides an array of opportunities for students to develop in the affective domain (ACPE, 2016; Zeeman et al., 2019b). The affective domain includes areas such as leadership, professional development, and community service (ACPE, 2016).

In pharmacy education, there is a distinction between extracurricular and cocurricular activities, with the former defined as activities that students may partake in that are optional and not related to program outcomes, and the latter requiring activities that are designed to complement the formal curriculum and are directly related to program outcomes (ACPE, 2016). Often, cocurricular activities include a reflective component where the student considers how the experience supports their overall learning and personal and/or professional growth (e.g., communication, professionalism, problem solving). Service provides an example of how an activity can move from extracurricular to cocurricular. Service-learning is distinct from service much like extracurricular differs from cocurricular. When a student engages in service, they complete activities that serve others. In order to move service into service-learning, there must be a reflective element on how engagement in the performed service connects to didactic learning. The same is true for cocurricular activities that are linked to classroom learning via a reflective element. Students reflect, and receive regular feedback from faculty or peers, on how the activity they completed enhanced their growth in the affective domain. Through this high-impact practice, development of the affective domains emphasized by ACPE, which are thought to be critical for successful pharmacy practitioners of the future, can be strengthened.

Cocurricular Goals

Historically, pharmacy students completed cocurricular activities on a voluntary basis, which resulted in some students frequently participating in activities and others participating in no activities. ACPE's most recent PharmD accreditation standards transitioned student completion of cocurricular activities from voluntary to mandatory (ACPE, 2016). Although ACPE gives programs the flexibility to determine the amount and types of activities their students complete, ACPE's goal is clear: All students must participate in cocurricular experiences that foster students' development in the affective domain (e.g., self-awareness, leadership, entrepreneurship and innovation, and professionalism) (ACPE, 2016). To accomplish this objective, all colleges and schools must formally and systematically plan, implement, and evaluate their cocurricular programs and student learning outcomes related to professional knowledge, skills, and attitudes.

As the emphasis on the value of cocurricular experiences in advancing pharmacy students' professional development and identity has increased, programmatic assessment of student learning outcomes from the activities has remained largely undocumented (Zeeman et al., 2019a). Therefore, in addition to requiring student participation in cocurricular activities, ACPE's second goal requires programs to systematically assess student outcomes for these activities. The previous lack of assessments allowed students to complete activities without a focus or reflection on what developmental outcomes they should have received from the activities connected to their professional goals. Relatedly, the lack of assessments also hindered colleges and schools' ability to understand and document what students have gained from activities, and if the students have achieved the intended learning outcomes. Overall, the two main cocurricular goals are to (a) ensure that all students are completing activities related to their personal and professional development, and (b) require students to engage in reflection about how the activities have impacted and advanced their personal and professional growth. Together these goals assure the evaluation and documentation of the affective learning outcomes.

Activities and Strategies to Achieve Cocurricular Goals

There are many different ways in which programs may choose to implement their cocurricular strategies. The approaches used by four different colleges of pharmacy are summarized in Table 14.1.

While these schools developed their cocurricular programs independent of each other, there are several similarities in the general approach, including overall expectations of students and definitions of cocurricular domains or themes. Differences in how each school achieves its cocurricular program also exist. For example, some schools hold students accountable by awarding course credit for the activities, while others have made completion of the activities a programmatic requirement where students cannot progress to the next level of the curriculum without successful completion. The key is that each school is thoughtful and intentional in how it holds students accountable using a process that works within the program.

Similarly, all programs have defined learning outcomes for the cocurriculum. Some schools chose to define specific cocurricular domains while others mapped the learning back to the programmatic outcomes. In either case, the cocurriculum was intentionally designed to provide students with

TABLE 14.1
Cocurricular Programs of Four PharmD Programs

College of Pharmacy	Mechanism to Track/ Accountability	Person Monitoring Program Requirements	Learning Domains	Course Credit Awarded	Structure/ Requirements
Ohio State University	Activity log thru guided reflection that highlights what was learned	Associate Dean for Outreach and Assessment	<ul><li>Career</li><li>Innovation/ entrepreneurship</li><li>Leadership</li><li>Professionalism</li><li>Self-awareness</li><li>Wellness</li></ul>	Embedded in a course in each program year	<ul><li>Longitudinal</li><li>Self-directed learning within defined requirements by learning domain</li></ul>
Oklahoma	<ul><li>Activity log</li><li>Quiz</li></ul>	Associate Dean for Assessment and Evaluation	<ul><li>Community service</li><li>Health and wellness</li><li>Leadership</li><li>Patient education</li><li>Professional development</li></ul>	One course per semester per professional year awards a quiz grade for the cocurriculum quiz	<ul><li>Longitudinal</li><li>Students can choose activities within each of the five areas; one activity per area must be completed</li></ul>

College of Pharmacy	Mechanism to Track/ Accountability	Person Monitoring Program Requirements	Learning Domains	Course Credit Awarded	Structure/ Requirements
Regis	• Cocurricular documentation (self-assessment instrument) • Student reflections in professional e-portfolio • Tracked using computer-based testing software	Office of Assessment and Academic Affairs	Activities mapped to Program Learning Outcomes and CAPE Outcomes	• No course credit; program-level accountability thru tracking completion of cocurricular self-assessment reflection • faculty/student portfolio review • development of student action plan	• Longitudinal • Mandatory and optional activities each semester recorded using cocurricular self-assessment instrument
University of Michigan	Cocurricular log	Course coordinator	• Advocacy • Career exploration • Health promotion • Leadership • Professional/career development • Service	0.5 credit per academic year	• Longitudinal • Self-directed learning within defined requirements by learning domain

opportunities to build skills and attitudes in the affective domain. Table 14.2 provides examples of the types of cocurricular activities that programs consider acceptable in each of the domains. ACPE and the American Association of Colleges of Pharmacy (AACP) recognized that development of these attributes is essential to successful pharmacy practitioners of the future. The 2016 standards hold pharmacy programs accountable while simultaneously allowing them the flexibility to define the process that best works within their individual curricula. For example, programs may allow students to self-select activities within predefined domains or they may require similar activities be completed by all students; some programs use a combination of these approaches. The key is that students are offered the opportunity to choose within a range of options, but they cannot opt out of cocurricular activities.

Assessments Used to Determine Progress Toward Cocurricular Goals

The assessment plans for each of the school's cocurricular programs are outlined in Table 14.3. A critical element to ensure that cocurricular activities promote learning and development in the affective domain is the student's ability to reflect on the activity and connect it to prior learning.

For all four of the programs illustrated here, the elements of participation in cocurricular activities are assessed via feedback on students' reflections. Different activities can be incorporated into or added onto the cocurricular experience so that students can reflect on and receive feedback from faculty regarding what they learned from the experience. Self-reflection is a common method used to allow students to connect the learning opportunity to their personal and professional growth. It is important that faculty review student reflections to ensure learners are not just telling a story of what they did, but are speaking to how they are different because of the experience, or the lessons learned and insights gained from the activity. Similarly, faculty advisers can play a key role in helping students identify cocurricular activities that align with their individual career goals. This alignment supports an experience that is meaningful to the student rather than simply being a check-the-box requirement. Ingraining the skill set of lifelong learning through reflective practice is critical for health professions students who will need to routinely self-assess and keep abreast of the continuously changing healthcare environment.

One alternative option to using reflection papers may be to ask students to respond to a Likert-type rating scale reflection question. This is a newer concept, but the approach may be beneficial to programs with personnel

TABLE 14.2
Examples of Cocurricular Activities by Domain

Cocurricular Domain	Definition	Examples of Activities in Domain
Advocacy	Activities to learn about advocating for the profession or for patients, including diversity, equity, and inclusion events that improve cultural competence.	• Pharmacy day at the capitol • Attending state/national/regional meetings • Participating in events relating to diversity, equity, and inclusion
Career exploration	Activities involving shadowing a pharmacist, upper class student, or other healthcare professional to learn about their roles and responsibilities.	• Shadow of upper class student • Rho Chi shadow program • Shadow of pharmacist or other licensed healthcare professional
Fitness/wellness	Activities intended to improve student wellbeing in one or more of the following domains: career, social, financial, physical, mental health, and community.	• Book club • Fitness class/event • Art class/program • Financial workshop/seminar • Wellbeing seminar
Innovation/entrepreneurship	Activities that focus on creating change at any level, such as practice advancement or service implementation.	• Local professional organization meeting on service implementation • Local professional organization webinar on status of cannabidiol legislation

Cocurricular Domain	Definition	Examples of Activities in Domain
Leadership	Activities where a leadership role is assumed or a leadership development event is attended.	- Leadership position in student organization - Leader for an event - Student ambassador - Attend legislative day - Attend leadership seminar
Patient care/health promotion	Activities with direct interactions with an audience of one or more people in the community to provide education or health services. A licensed preceptor must be present.	- Health fair - Immunization clinics - Educational event on health topic - Mission trip - Brown-bag medication review - Skills/counseling competition
Professional/career development	Activities that contribute to professional growth and career development.	- Attend professional or clinical seminar - Attend national/regional pharmacy meeting - Volunteer research - Etiquette dinner
Self-awareness	Activities focused on self-reflection and growth emphasizing student desire for growth in an area of personal interest.	- Book club on empathy - Reflecting on impact on potential pharmacy students
Service	Activities providing service to the community, college, or university. The goal is to tie learning to the service.	- Community food bank - Habitat for Humanity - Volunteer community service (charity event, free clinic) - Service to college or university - Church/community outreach

TABLE 14.3
Assessment of Cocurricular Programs of Four PharmD Programs

College of Pharmacy	Student Requirements	Student Assessment	Faculty Assessment
Ohio State University	• Guided worksheet for each cocurricular activity • Minimum of 6 activities annually	• Self-assessment/reflection via guided worksheet • Student-defined action plan in the form of SMART goals statements	Faculty feedback annually on SMART goals and reflective worksheets in writing or in small group discussion sections.
Oklahoma	• Complete 1 activity for each of the 5 cocurricular areas • Receive cocurricular log signature	Twice yearly knowledge quiz and Likert-type student reflections quiz	Review students' grades on quiz and ensure students have completed all required activities by verifying uploaded completed activity logs.
Regis	Longitudinal portfolio and reflections, including reports, artifacts, documents from coursework, experiential education, teamwork, professionalism, and cocurricular activities	• Student-level cocurricular self-assessment, including reflections on development based on cocurricular activities • Student-defined action plan (developed with faculty adviser)	Adviser meetings annually to review portfolio; students develop an action plan with faculty adviser to define goals for the coming year to meet student's long-term goals (including supportive co curricular activities). Cocurricular activities included in final portfolio defense and reflections.
University of Michigan	• Complete minimum number of activities for each domain as defined by academic year • Annual SMART goals • Cocurricular log	Twice yearly reflections • Fall term: group reflection that includes peer feedback • Winter term: individual reflection reviewed with faculty adviser	Twice yearly adviser meetings to review progress on cocurricular requirements, SMART goals, and student reflections.

constraints for reading reflection papers, as well as programs wanting to easily summarize outcomes data related to reflections. Two sample questions are as follows:

1. How much has your confidence in your leadership skills grown as a result of participating in the leadership activity?
   A. High growth in confidence
   B. Moderate growth in confidence
   C. Low growth in confidence
   D. No growth in confidence

2. Select all that apply: By participating in this community service activity my perspective grew and I gained insights about:
   A. how many different groups in my community need help
   B. how pharmacists can serve their community
   C. the disparities and inequities that exist in my community
   D. how I can help serve the needs of my community
   E. the rewards of serving my community
   F. Other:

Use of the Findings

Once programs assess the learning outcomes students achieved as a result of participating in their cocurricular experiences, they can use the findings to evaluate: (a) the impact of the activities on student learning (knowledge, skills, and attitudes) and professional development and/or if there are opportunities for improvement, and (b) whether or not the activities augment program outcomes and/or if there are gaps found or changes needed in the cocurriculum.

The requirement for all students to complete cocurricular activities and for programs to assess the outcomes is relatively new in pharmacy education. As programs gain experience, it is important for them to evaluate the data to ensure that the cocurricular requirements are making a difference in the growth of their student learners, and that students are not simply treating the requirement as another activity that must be completed to meet graduation requirements. One way to accomplish this objective is for faculty or a mentor to review the students' reflections to evaluate if students explain the lessons they learned, the insights they gained, or the growth they achieved from the activity. Faculty can provide students with feedback about the reflection as well as have a dialogue about the students' future goals and identify which new cocurricular activities can assist with their continuous professional development. This feedback and dialogue could be used to help students create a cocurricular program of study to align with their career goals. It is important to reinforce to students that intentionally selecting activities with demonstrated outcomes related to their professional goals is essential in the cocurricular process, especially given that students are being asked to do increasingly more with their limited amount of time. An iterative feedback and dialogue process can help programs use students' data to make ongoing adjustments as needed.

Curriculum review and mapping is an accreditation and quality improvement requirement in pharmacy education. However, the concept of mapping the cocurriculum is in its nascency. Engaging in cocurricular review and mapping can help programs determine if their activities augment their program outcomes and/or if there are gaps or changes needed in the cocurriculum. Accomplishing this map could be challenging because programs would need a mechanism to tag a cocurricular activity to a program outcome. For example, if leadership is a program outcome, then cocurricular leadership activities are logically tagged to that outcome. Programs would then need to use their existing curriculum mapping mechanisms or identify new contrivances to create their cocurriculum maps. This process would allow programs to use the student cocurriculum activity completion data to determine where the cocurriculum is augmenting the curriculum and where there are deficiencies.

In addition to programs using data to evaluate where the cocurriculum complements the curriculum and where adjustments can be made, in the future it may also be helpful for programs to collect data about student learning outcomes from the activities that could be quantified and aggregated. Programs could then use this data to document levels of learning and track students' advancement across a program. While reflection papers are useful for determining student learning attainment, it is difficult to collate and summarize these outcomes for all students. If an activity could be tagged to an outcomes achievement level, the level of learning could be counted and summarized in a map. For example, the learning outcomes for attending a health fair activity could be considered exposure, low level, or introductory. In contrast, the learning outcome achieved from creating a health fair activity including finding volunteers, advertising, securing funding and space could be considered transformational, high level, or advanced.

Creating a map of cocurricular learning outcomes is a new concept in pharmacy education, but it could be a useful strategy to ensure that students' learning is advancing throughout the program. In the future, in order for programs to fully capture what knowledge or skills students gain from a cocurricular activity, beyond students' perceptions and reflections, programs could consider offering students a knowledge test or a performance-based assessment. Test questions could be aligned with the program outcome tags described previously, as well as to activity learning objectives. These learning objectives for activities could be designed and distributed to students prior to completing the activity. While this type of assessment is conceptual, it would allow programs to document learning outcomes that result from completing a cocurricular activity.

Conclusion

Cocurricular programs embedded in the curricula of both undergraduate and professional degree programs support student growth and development by creating an enriched educational environment. Cocurriculum program similarities and differences between undergraduate and professional programs exist. As part of the PharmD program, the cocurriculum provides a means for students to transition from their identity as a student learner to one as a practicing healthcare professional. Embedding this requirement over these 4-year programs instills in students the importance of lifelong learning, an essential habit of mind. PharmD accreditation standards outline cocurricular requirements but allow programs the flexibility on how to implement. This flexibility allows pharmacy students to choose experiences that are meaningful to their career paths. Tables 14.1–14.3 offer examples of cocurricular programs at four distinct institutions, along with specific activities and methods of assessment.

References

Accreditation Council for Pharmacy Education (ACPE). (2016). *Accreditation standards and key elements for the professional rogram in pharmacy leading to the doctor of pharmacy degree: Standards 2016.* https://www.acpe-accredit.org/pdf/Standards2016FINAL.pdf

Bass, R. (2012). Disrupting ourselves: The problem of learning in higher education. *EDUCAUSE Review, 47*(2), 23–33. https://er.educause.edu/articles/2012/3/disrupting-ourselves-the-problem-of-learning-in-higher-education

Great Schools Partnership. (2013). *Glossary of education reform.* https://www.edglossary.org/cocurricular/

Higher Learning Commission. (2019). *Higher Learning Commission criteria for accreditation.* https://www.hlcommission.org/Policies/criteria-and-core-components.html/

Kuh, G. D. (2008). *High-impact educational practices: What they are, who has access to them, and why they matter.* Association of American Colleges & Universities. https://www.aacu.org/node/4084

National Survey of Student Engagement (NSSE): (n.d.). *High-impact practices.* https://nsse.indiana.edu/nsse/survey-instruments/high-impact-practices.html

Southern Association of Colleges and Schools Commission on Colleges (SAC). (2018). *Southern Association of Colleges and School principles for accreditation.* http://sacscoc.org/app/uploads/2019/08/2018PrinciplesOfAcreditation.pdf

Zeeman, J. M., Bush, A. A., Cox, W. C., Buhlinger, K., McLaughlin, J. E. (2019a). Identifying and mapping skill development opportunities through pharmacy student organization involvement. *American Journal of Pharmacy Education, 83*(4), Article 6950. https://www.ajpe.org/content/83/4/6950

Zeeman, J. M., Bush, A. A., Cox, W. C., McLaughlin, J. E. (2019b). Assessing the cocurriculum by mapping student organization involvement to curricular outcomes using mixed methods. *American Journal of Pharmacy Education, 83*(10), Article 7354. https://www.ajpe.org/content/83/10/7354

PART THREE
FACULTY ENGAGEMENT AND ASSESSMENT

15

GIVING LIFE TO INSTITUTIONAL STUDENT LEARNING OUTCOMES

Dan Shapiro

More institutions of higher education are developing institution-level student learning outcomes intended to communicate what their students know and can do at graduation; align assessment, curriculum, and pedagogy; and improve student learning (Jankowski et al., 2018). However, it is far too easy to invest considerable time and resources in crafting outcomes statements that do little beyond filling space on institutional websites. This chapter is about creating more cohesive and effective learning systems for our students (Jankowski & Marshall, 2017) by giving life to institutional student learning outcomes. "Giving life" includes engaging the campus community in developing outcomes, assessing student achievement, using results to improve student learning, and providing professional development that helps all educators connect and align assessment, curriculum, and pedagogy (Driscoll et al., in press).

This chapter tells an assessment story (Jankowski & Baker, 2019) about how California State University, Monterey Bay (CSUMB) gave life to its institutional learning outcomes. The experience is shared as a story rather than as an analysis of institutional dos and don'ts, because no two institutions are the same. Therefore, any change effort must be tailored to each institution's unique context (Kezar, 2018). The hope is that reading this story will spark ideas for advancing assessment and student learning at your institution—ideas that could only be generated with an understanding of your particular institutional context.

Three Themes

This story has three intersecting themes, which are highlighted because of the important role they play in connecting and advancing assessment and student achievement at CSUMB. The first theme has to do with leveraging accreditation. CSUMB's accreditation agency, the Western Association of Schools and Colleges Senior College and University Commission (WSCUC) is a particularly important protagonist and ally. This story tells how CSUMB leveraged the accreditor's directives and expectations—as well as their educational programs—to develop and give life to institutional learning outcomes.

The second theme has to do with faculty engagement and what Metzler and Kurz (2018) have coined *Assessment 1.0* and *Assessment 2.0*. Metzler and Kurz characterize Assessment 1.0 as the standard, linear, accreditation-motivated assessment process employed by many institutions across the nation: write outcomes, align outcomes, design student assignments, assess student work, report on assessments, and then make changes in response. Metzler and Kurz (2018) tell us,

> In order to conduct learning outcomes assessment systematically across schools, programs, and disciplines at university, it is necessary to devise a standard process that can be employed by faculty assessors who may have little or even no experience with assessment. ... And yet, the very system that enables schools to perform assessment at a high level brings with it inflexible processes that can result in compromised data, frustrated or alienated faculty, and ultimately the subversion of the very purpose of learning outcomes assessment. (p. 4)

The authors raise the concern that "the focus on collecting quantifiable data at the expense of meaning often yields spreadsheets of data and plentiful reports that are nevertheless seldom used to improve student learning" (p. 9).

Metzler and Kurz argue that we should emphasize Ewell's (2009) assessment for improvement paradigm and focus on "assessment *methods and questions that are meaningful for the faculty* who will be conducting the assessment" (p. 17). That is, on one hand, we have routinized assessments designed to generate student achievement data that can be compared over time and across institutions (Assessment 1.0). On the other hand, we have diverse assessments designed to answer specific questions that in some cases might even be one-offs never to be repeated (Assessment 2.0). Engaging faculty is much easier in the latter and in many ways embodies the approaches Maki (2017) describes in *Real-Time Student Assessment*. Real-time assessment, Maki tells us, shifts from a delayed use of assessment results, often extended well beyond when student work is collected, scored, and analyzed, to an immediate synchronous use of assessment results to address continuously the range of obstacles or persistent challenges that students face as they progress toward a degree. (p. 17)

Ultimately, however, Metzer and Kurz (2018) argue both are important for improving student learning and that Assessment 1.0, done in the right way and for the right reasons, complements Assessment 2.0.

The third theme is the central role professional development has played in advancing assessment and student learning at CSUMB. Kinzie et al. (2019) point out,

Faculty development has evolved in ways that underscore the power of constructive, evidence-informed exchange among faculty, moving beyond individual instructor improvement to focus on the establishment and exploration of shared goals for student learning and the collaborative design of courses and curriculum that advance those goals, how those outcomes are assessed, and how faculty and staff use assessment results to align and improve student learning in general education and the disciplines. (p. 53)

Professional development, the right kind, ensures learning outcomes do what they are supposed to do: improve student learning.

Readers are encouraged to keep these three themes in mind—leveraging accreditation, engaging faculty, and professional development—while reading the CSUMB story.

CSUMB's Story

CSUMB is a 4-year, public, Hispanic-serving institution (HSI) founded in 1994 on the former Fort Ord Army Base. CSUMB currently serves approximately 7,000 students. The institution's mission is to "prepare students to contribute responsibly to California and the global community by providing transformative learning experiences in an inclusive environment" (CSUMB, n.d.-a). CSUMB was founded as an outcomes-based education (OBE) institution, which from the beginning integrated assessment of learning outcomes into all curricular and cocurricular programs (Driscoll & Wood, 2007). In fact, Driscoll, the founding director of CSUMB's teaching and learning center, successfully argued that it be called the Center for Teaching, Learning, *and Assessment* to highlight the essential connections among teaching, learning, and assessment.

This particular story, about institutional learning outcomes, begins in the middle of CSUMB's history. The many challenges associated with CSUMB's start-up initially limited the extent to which the institution could develop and align program-level and institution-level processes for assessing student learning (Driscoll & Wood, 2007). Consequently, much of the early institutional assessment work focused on course-level assessment, which fortuitously fostered an assessment culture focused on improvement (Driscoll & Wood, 2007). Subsequently, in 2011, following CSUMB's comprehensive Educational Effectiveness Review for reaccreditation, WSCUC recommended,

> the use of direct evidence of student learning and multiple measures of learning to inform decisions about academic offerings . . . continued alignment of assessment and data-driven decision making in support of both program review and CSUMB's plans to use "data to improve both programs and services as part of continuous improvement." (WSCUC, 2011)

Further, WSCUC requires all institutions it accredits to "ensure the development of core competencies including, but not limited to, written and oral communication, quantitative reasoning, information literacy, and critical thinking." (WSCUC, n.d., para. 2). Institutional accreditation reports must explain the following:

- What methods are used to assess student learning and achievement of these standards?
- What evidence is there that key learning outcomes are being met?
- What steps are taken when achievement gaps are identified?
- How are teaching and learning improved as a result of assessment findings? (WSCUC, 2015, p. 31)

In response, CSUMB strategically leveraged WSCUC's recommendations and accreditation standards to create an assessment infrastructure intentionally and strategically designed to be faculty-driven and student-learning-centered (CSUMB, 2014, para. 2). First, academic affairs started funding faculty associates for each college who together provide collective institution-level assessment leadership, while also supporting assessment within their colleges. Next, in spring 2012, the institution invited nationally recognized assessment scholar Peggy Maki to campus to facilitate a university-wide assessment retreat for faculty and administrators. At this retreat, Maki guided discussions about how to create an assessment committee, how to structure the committee's work, and how to cultivate partners in assessment work from across campus. Soon after, the academic senate created an ad-hoc assessment committee with representation from all colleges. The committee first met in May 2012, followed by a summer retreat during which short- and long-term assessment priorities were established. In 2013, the senate bylaws were amended to make the ad hoc committee a standing body of the academic senate. Among the assessment committee's first priorities were developing an institutional assessment plan, initiating assessment of the five "core competencies" (critical thinking, information literacy, quantitative reasoning, written communication, and oral communication), and developing institution-level student learning outcomes.

Assessment Goals, Activities, and Use of Findings

In 2012, prior to the institution adopting any institution-level learning outcomes, the assessment committee, with funding from the provost's office, selected a faculty member to develop and implement an institution-level approach to assessing critical thinking. Knowing this first institution-level assessment would be a valuable, but largely experimental process, the critical thinking coordinator (CT coordinator) designed an assessment that prioritized faculty engagement over generating assessment results meeting professional standards for validity and reliability. The primary goal was to create a positive assessment experience for faculty, one that fostered evidence-based discussions about how to better facilitate student learning (Driscoll et al., in press). At the same time, the CT coordinator and other faculty participated in several WSCUC workshops on assessing the core competencies. These workshops were critical for helping the CT coordinator design an assessment that would meet institutional goals for engaging faculty and staff in institution-level assessment, while also meeting accreditation expectations and requirements.

Undergraduate Learning Outcomes (ULOs)—Round 1

The assessment committee and CT coordinator put out a call for eight faculty members to participate in a fall 2012 and a spring 2013 faculty learning community (Cox, 2004) on assessing critical thinking. These faculty members were later referred to as the critical thinking scholars (CT scholars). It is important to note that using faculty learning communities to conduct this work was critical for fostering an improvement-focused assessment culture grounded in engaging, student-centered discussions about teaching and learning. After studying several critical thinking assessment rubrics, the CT scholars adopted the Association of American Colleges & Universities critical thinking VALUE rubric (AAC&U, n.d.) in its entirety and without revision. Then, after attending one of the WSCUC workshops on assessing the core competencies, the CT coordinator and scholars recommended to the assessment committee that critical thinking and information literacy be assessed together. In fall 2013, an information literacy coordinator (IL coordinator) and eight information literacy scholars (IL scholars) were selected. As was the case with the critical thinking group, they participated in semester-long faculty learning communities that developed an institution-level information literacy rubric. The CT and IL coordinators and scholars then designed the first institution-level assessment of critical thinking and information literacy, which was conducted in the summer of 2014.

Subsequently, a process and timeline were determined for assessing each of the five core competencies, with the goal of assessing all five core competencies at least once prior to the next accreditation visit in spring 2019. A core competency coordinator (CC coordinator) and six to eight core competency scholars were selected for each of the remaining core competencies. As before, each CC coordinator and the scholars participated in a faculty learning community during which they created an institution-level rubric for assessing student work, determined an assessment question—of interest to faculty—and planned a summer assessment (i.e., Assessment 2.0). Each CC coordinator next facilitated, with support from the Center for Teaching, Learning, and Assessment, summer assessments that lasted from 3 to 5 days.

Initial assessments of each of the five core competencies occurred between 2014 and 2016. Each assessment was followed by a semester-long faculty learning community during which the coordinator and scholars discussed the assessment results and generated ideas for improving student achievement. As with the faculty learning communities, assessments were designed to maximize faculty engagement. The assessments included professional development for faculty on scoring student work with a rubric, implicit bias training, frequent opportunities for faculty to collectively reflect on what they were learning from reading assignment guidelines and scoring student work, and lots of good food (Canner et al., 2020; Driscoll et al., in press). In total, over 800 samples of student work from over 150 different courses were scored by 40 faculty representing 16 different programs. Conclusions drawn from those initial assessments included the following:

- Assignment prompts appeared to have a significant impact on the level of student achievement as measured by the rubric. Because assignments were typically only partially aligned with the rubrics, the core competency scholars were often not able to determine whether lower-than-expected levels of proficiency were the result of students not being proficient or the assignment not prompting students to demonstrate the skills being assessed. This is a common finding among institutions that have engaged in this kind of work and a finding later

highlighted in McConnell and Rhodes's (2017) AAC&U report *On Solid Ground: VALUE Report 2017.*
- To improve students' ability to apply and demonstrate the core competencies across different contexts, the kinds of assessments now being implemented at the institutional level should be encouraged at the program levels.
- The assessment scholars had generally positive responses to the assessment work, including finding the work rewarding and engaging. Evidence further suggested participating in the assessments helped them generate ideas on how to better facilitate student learning in their own classes (Canner et al., 2020; Driscoll et al., in press).
- It was difficult to separate written communication, oral communication, and quantitative reasoning skills from critical thinking and information literacy skills.

In response to these insights, the core competency coordinators did the following:

- Created three "integrated" rubrics—one for written communication, one for oral communication, and the third for quantitative reasoning—each of which incorporated critical thinking and information literacy criteria (CSUMB, n.d.-b).
- Created three assignment guides—one for each rubric—that translated the rubric criteria into questions faculty could use to create better assignment prompts (CSUMB, n.d.-b).
- Facilitated assignment design workshops for faculty based on the integrated assignment guides and rubrics.

ULOs Assessment —Round 2

Between the first assessments of critical thinking and information literacy and the second round of core competency assessments, the academic senate facilitated the development of institution-level ULOs. Following a series of town halls that engaged students, faculty, and staff, the following ULOs were approved by the academic senate:

- Intellectual skills: critical thinking, information literacy, quantitative reasoning, written communication, and oral communication;
- Personal, professional, and social responsibility;
- Integrative knowledge; and
- Specialized knowledge.

With the new integrated rubrics, the next round of ULO assessment could be reduced from five to three assessments (written communication, oral communication, and quantitative reasoning, each integrated with critical thinking and information literacy). All three assessments occurred over the summer of 2017. This second round of assessment focused on student capstone work and work from lower division general education courses on writing, critical thinking, and quantitative reasoning.

As with the 2014–2016 assessments, following each day of assessment and after the entire assessment was complete, the core competency coordinators and scholars were asked to reflect on their experiences conducting institution-level assessment. Their reflections provided information not only on how to improve the validity and reliability of assessment results, but also what faculty gained from the experience. As with the 2014–2016 assessment projects, the core competency scholars found the work rewarding and engaging, and it helped them generate ideas on how to better facilitate learning in their own classes (Canner et al, 2020; Driscoll et al., in press).

CSUMB's two rounds of ULO assessment highlighted and created interest in multiple areas of professional development. The assignment design workshops using the ULO Assignment Guides (CSUMB, n.d.-b) were supplemented with additional workshops on Winkelmes's transparent assignments framework (TILT, n.d.). In addition, CSUMB launched a major effort to provide professional development on implementing reading apprenticeship routines and strategies designed to improve students' reading, critical thinking, and problem-solving skills (Schoenbach et al., 2012).

Program Review

While the processes for assessing institutional learning outcomes and using assessment results were being refined, an important development at the program level had started: revision of the program review process. In 2015, CSUMB's new associate vice president for academic planning and institutional effectiveness (AVP-APIE) began asking academic programs what they found most useful and least useful about the program review process. She also solicited recommendations for improving program review. In response, the AVP-APIE, following the direction of a subgroup of faculty from the assessment committee, significantly revised the program review procedures manual. Changes included the following:

- Placing more emphasis on annual assessments of student learning
- Requiring all program learning outcomes be assessed at least once during every 7-year program review cycle, while also encouraging

programs to limit the number of program outcomes to a reasonable number
- Requiring assessment of institutional learning outcomes, while also encouraging programs to align program learning outcomes with institutional outcomes so additional assessments are not needed
- Reducing the amount of work for faculty preparing the program review self-study (e.g., provide program with easier access to more user-friendly institutional research data dashboards rather than having them gather the data on their own)
- Allowing programs a full year (as opposed to one semester) to develop a program improvement plan (PIP) informed by annual assessments of student learning, the program self-study, and external and internal reviews (the extended timeline enables more faculty and staff to contribute to developing the PIP)

Placing more emphasis on annual program assessments of student learning based on program-generated questions helped transform program review from a tedious, bureaucratic task conducted by one or a few people, to a more engaging, collaborative, and creative task with a greater emphasis on gathering and using assessment results to improve student learning. All annual assessment reports and plans are reviewed by at least two assessment committee members who provide programs with a set of commendations and recommendations. The assessment committee also conducts an annual meta-analysis of all annual assessment plans and reports for the purpose of assessing institutional assessment processes and program support. To help assessment committee members better support the institution and its programs, they participate in ongoing professional development activities on topics such as evaluating assessment reports and plans and using assessment results.

Requiring programs to assess institutional learning outcomes ensures those outcomes are more than just words on a webpage. At the same time, CSUMB works to avoid the perception that institutional learning outcomes are top-down mandates that add to, or detract from, assessment of program learning outcomes. Rather, the assessment committee presents the institutional learning outcomes and their associated assignment guides and rubrics as tools programs can choose to use to help their students better achieve program learning outcomes. Programs are encouraged to identify which of their program learning outcomes most closely align with each of the institutional learning outcomes. Once aligned, programs are then encouraged to use the institution-level assignment guides, rubrics, and rubric guides (CSUMB, n.d.-b) to develop program-specific assessment tools that can be used to support student achievement of disciplinary learning outcomes.

ULOs Assessment—Round 3

By the time CSUMB had completed the second round of ULO assessment, institution-level assessment had progressed significantly. The institution had a solid assessment infrastructure in place: a robust and engaged assessment committee with multiple representatives from each college; faculty associates from each college with significant assessment experience; experienced ULO coordinators and scholars for each ULO; tools for assessing student work; and an improved program review process that placed greater emphasis on direct assessment of student achievement. Additionally, the assessment committee selected ULO coordinators for the new ULOs to facilitate faculty learning communities and institution-level assessments following the processes developed by the CC coordinators.

Most of this assessment fell into the category of Metzler and Kurz's (2018) Assessment 2.0 rather than Assessment 1.0. Assessment results, while clearly useful, could not be reliably used to detect changes over time since results were typically not comparable year to year. For the third round of ULO assessment, an attempt was made to implement Assessment 1.0. All programs were asked by their faculty associate to identify where in their curriculum each of the core competencies could be similarly assessed, using student work from the same or similar courses and assignments, year after year. That would better enable the institution to determine if changes were improving student achievement. However, few programs were willing to respond to those requests. Common reasons included the curriculum being under revision, program learning outcomes being under revision, not yet having appropriate rubrics, not yet having assignments adequately aligned with institutional rubrics, and so on. That is to say, most programs, and the institution, were not yet ready for Assessment 1.0.

In response, the ULO coordinators decided to conduct the third round of assessment as they had previously, focused on specific issues faculty felt were most relevant to challenges they and their students were currently experiencing. Focus went back to Assessment 2.0 and confirming Metzler and Kurz (2018) claim that "when faculty have control and agency over the assessment process and how the data will be used, their natural interest in student learning is activated and assessment becomes an interesting and energizing activity" (p. 19). Further, because the institution had just revised the general education curriculum, several of the ULO coordinators decided to focus on the connection between the ULOs and the new general education learning outcomes and courses. Examples of the faculty learning community descriptions used to attract ULO Scholars are shown in Table 15.1.

TABLE 15.1
Examples of the Faculty Learning Community Descriptions

Call for Oral Communication ULO Scholars—GE Area A1 Oral Communication Faculty Learning Community
Instructors interested in developing and teaching new A1 (Speaking/Listening) GE courses across campus will collaborate on refining course design and course materials (assignment prompts, class activities, grading rubrics) across the spring semester. The community will also identify an area for A1 assessment, to be carried out in the summer and fall of 2019.
Call for Critical Thinking ULO Scholars—GE Area A3 Critical Thinking Faculty Learning Community
One's understanding of the term *critical thinking* is hugely influenced by discipline and academic background. This faculty learning community will focus on eliciting how campus groups use the term differently with the intention of developing an understanding of the similarities and differences in the ways we understand critical thinking. These understandings will be used to develop assessment questions for critical thinking.
Call for Quantitative Reasoning ULO Scholars—Quantitative Reasoning Faculty Learning Community
With the recent revisions of GE B4 that lay the foundation of quantitative reasoning, we want to think more deeply about supporting quantitative reasoning in the courses after B4 (e.g., new Upper Division Area B GE courses, courses with a specific B4 prereq). We will be considering task and assignment design and preparing for assessment for design of current classes and the development of new courses.
Call for Integrative Knowledge ULO Scholars—Integrative Knowledge Faculty Learning Community
Participants in this faculty learning community will determine what we want to know about integrative knowledge and how we, as faculty, can facilitate students' attainment of integrative knowledge. Part of the faculty learning community's work is to develop assessment questions for the 2019 Summer Integrative Knowledge Assessment. This participant-guided faculty learning community is open to anyone who has an interest in assessing how our students address new and complex situations by synthesizing and connecting knowledge, skills, and experiences across disciplines.

Each of these faculty learning communities was designed to provide faculty with professional development and structured time to reflect on prior assessment results, develop new assessment questions, conduct new assessments, reflect on results, and propose actions. Observation of the faculty learning communities and assessments revealed a high level of faculty engagement and a commitment to improving student learning and quality of work. While as an institution CSUMB is not quite ready for Assessment 1.0, it is still a goal worth aiming for because of the ways it would complement ongoing Assessment 2.0 work.

WSCUC Assessment Leadership Academy

Underlying all the work described here is the WSCUC Assessment Leadership Academy (ALA). The ALA (WSCUC, 2020) is the crown jewel of assessment professional development. The ALA draws administrators and faculty in assessment leadership positions at institutions from across the globe. The program runs from March to January, during which time cohorts of approximately 30 participants learn about assessment and leadership directly from national leaders such as Peter Ewell, Jillian Kinzie, and Adrianna Kezar. They study assessment structures and practices at other institutions and complete a project designed to advance improvement-focused assessment at their own institutions. The program, which has been running for over a decade, currently has a network of over 300 graduates who stay connected through a listserv. Five CSUMB faculty and administrators have completed the ALA (with a sixth entering the next cohort). Collectively they have had an enormous impact on assessment at CSUMB and have played some role in every activity described here.

Is It Working?

"Is it working?" refers to the ultimate goal of improving student learning. While it would be helpful to have reams of evidence demonstrating that CSUMB's assessments of institutional learning outcomes improves student learning, that kind of evidence is difficult to generate. However, there are some examples to share. CSUMB's information literacy assessment coordinator and CSUMB's program in Social and Behavioral Sciences (SBS) worked together to address gaps in information literacy skills revealed by the 2017 ULO institutional assessment of SBS capstone reports. In response, SBS invited librarians to facilitate information literacy sessions with all SBS capstone students. The librarians and SBS faculty then assessed student capstone reports and oral presentations and were able to demonstrate a statistically significant increase in students' information literacy skills (Dahlen & Leuzinger, 2020).

Additionally, research suggests that just participating in assessment coupled with faculty development prompts faculty to make changes to their own courses and how they work with their students (Canner et al., 2020). There are many examples of creative changes that were made in response to faculty participating in assessment and discussing assessment results, ranging from improved assignment prompts, targeted curricular changes, and revision to course and program outcomes. However, there is a big difference between documenting *changes* and documenting *improvements*, with the latter being much harder (Smith et al., 2015). At the same time, not moving forward because of such challenges is short-sighted, in part because of the many different ways assessment results can be used. Jonson et al. (2014) point out, "Assessment is also responsible for transforming thinking of stakeholders about teaching and learning through the use and discussion of learning evidence" (p. 27). CSUMB's experience leads us to fully agree with Kinzie et al. (2019),

> of course, it is reasonable to inquire about the impact of collaboration and assess if integrated models actually contribute to changed courses, data-informed improvement plans, and most important, increased student achievement. In the meantime, from where we sit, bringing assessment and faculty development closer together just makes sense. (p. 53)

It makes sense to us too.

Conclusion

This story communicates one model for giving life to institutional learning outcomes. While still a work in progress, CSUMB is seeing evidence that our institutional learning outcomes are helping faculty improve curricular coherence and alignment—within and among our general education and disciplinary programs—and in ways that improve student achievement. Current efforts to extend this model include the recent approval of institution-level GLOs for our graduate programs and a proposal for a new general education program with two central program learning outcomes—critical thinking and integrative knowledge—directly aligned with the ULOs. CSUMB is also developing institution-level cocurricular learning outcomes. CSUMB is certainly not the first institution to engage in such work. For example, the University of San Diego, a small, private, faith-based institution and one of the inspirations for CSUMB's model, is further along a similar path (USD, n.d.).

As was pointed out at the beginning, every institution is unique, with its own history, mission, culture, and cast of characters. There is no one correct or best approach to using assessment to improve student learning. CSUMB uses a combination of leveraging accreditation, engaging faculty, and professional development to give life to institutional learning outcomes. That approach, in turn, helps CSUMB advance assessment for student success in ways tailored to the institution's unique history, culture, and context. To the extent that any generalizable advice can be drawn from this experience, it might be to (a) identify the existing drivers and support mechanisms at your institution, (b) maintain a unwavering focus on improving student learning, and (c) create as many opportunities among as many institutional stakeholders as possible to engage in evidence-based discussions about improving student learning. Roscoe (2017) captures it well: "The assessment paradigm has been successful in demanding that [collective conversations about curricula and instruction] take place on a regular basis" and that this is "the most important achievement of the assessment movement" (p. 18).

References

Association of American Colleges & Universities (AAC&U). (n.d.). *VALUE rubrics.* https://www.aacu.org/value-rubrics

California State University Monterey Bay (CSUMB). (2014). *WASC interim report.* California State University, Monterey Bay. https://csumb.edu/academicaffairs/wscuc-re-accreditation-2019

California State University Monterey Bay (CSUMB). (n.d.-a). *About CSUMB: Mission and strategic plan.* https://csumb.edu/about/mission-strategic-plan

California State University Monterey Bay (CSUMB). (n.d.-b). *Undergraduate learning outcomes assignment guides, rubrics, and rubric guides.* https://csumb.edu/tla/ulo-assignment-guides-rubrics-and-threshold-concepts

Canner, J., Dahlen, S., Gage, O., Graff, N., Shapiro, D. F., Waldrup-Patterson, V., & Wood, S. (2020). Engaging faculty in assessment of institutional learning outcomes. *Assessment Update, 32*(3), 1–16. https://doi.org/10.1002/au.30210

Cox, M. D. (2004). Introduction to faculty learning communities. In M. D. Cox & L. Richlin (Eds.), (New Directions for Teaching and Learning, no. 15, pp. 5–23). Wiley.

Dahlen, S., & Leuzinger, R. (2020). *Impact of library instruction on the development of student skills in synthesis and source attribution: A model for academic program assessment.* Library Faculty Publications and Presentations, California State Univ California State University, Monterey Bay. https://digitalcommons.csumb.edu/lib_fac/12/

Driscoll, A., Graff. N., Shapiro. D. F., & Wood, S. (in press). *Advancing assessment for student success: Supporting learning by creating connections across assessment, teaching, curriculum, and cocurriculum in collaboration with our colleagues and our students*. Stylus.

Driscoll, A., & Wood, S. (2007). *Developing outcomes-based assessment for learner-centered education: A faculty introduction*. Stylus.

Ewell, P. T. (2009). *Assessment, accountability, and improvement* (Occasional Paper No. 1). University of Illinois and Indiana University, National Institute for Learning Outcomes Assessment (NILOA). https://www.learningoutcomesassessment.org/wp-content/uploads/2019/02/OccasionalPaper1.pdf

Jankowski, N. A., & Baker, G. (2019, August). *Building a narrative via evidence-based storytelling: A toolkit for practice*. University of Illinois and Indiana University, National Institute for Learning Outcomes Assessment (NILOA). https://www.learningoutcomesassessment.org/wp-content/uploads/2019/10/EBST-Toolkit.pdf

Jankowski, N. A., & Marshall, D. W. (2017). *Degrees that matter: Moving higher education to a learning systems paradigm*. Stylus.

Jankowski, N. A., Timmer, J. D., Kinzie, J., & Kuh, G. D. (2018). *Assessment that matters: Trending toward practices that document authentic student learning*. University of Illinois and Indiana University, National Institute for Learning Outcomes Assessment (NILOA). https://files.eric.ed.gov/fulltext/ED590514.pdf

Jonson, J. L., Guetterman, T., & Thompson, R. J., Jr. (2014). An integrated model of influence: Use of assessment data in higher education. *Research & Practice in Assessment, 9*, 18–30.

Kezar, A. (2018). *How colleges change: Understanding, leading, and enacting change* (2nd ed.). Routledge.

Kinzie, J., Landy, K., Sorcinelli, M. D., & Hutchings, P. (2019). Better together: How faculty development and assessment can join forces to improve student learning. *Change: The Magazine of Higher Learning, 51*(5), 46–54. https://doi.org/10.1080/00091383.2019.1652076

Maki, P. (2017). *Real-time student assessment: Meeting the imperative for improved time to degree, closing the opportunity gap, and assuring student competencies for 21st century needs*. Stylus.

McConnell, K. D., & Rhodes, T. L. (2017). *On solid ground: VALUE report 2017*. Association of American Colleges and Universities. https://www.aacu.org/publications-research/publications/solid-ground-value-report-2017

Metzler, E. T., & Kurz, L. (2018). *Assessment 2.0: An organic supplement to standard assessment procedure*. University of Illinois and Indiana University, National Institute for Learning Outcomes Assessment (NILOA). https://www.learningoutcomesassessment.org/wp-content/uploads/2019/02/OccasionalPaper36.pdf

Roscoe, D. D. (2017). Toward an improvement paradigm for academic quality. *Liberal Education, 103*(1), 14–21. https://www.aacu.org/liberaleducation/2017/winter/roscoe

Schoenbach, R., Greenleaf, C., & Murphy, L. (2012). *Reading for understanding: How reading apprenticeship improves disciplinary learning in secondary and college classrooms.* Wiley.

Smith, K. L., Good, M. R., Sanchez, E. H., & Fulcher, K. H. (2015). Communication is key: Unpacking "use of assessment results to improve student learning." *Research & Practice in Assessment, 10,* 15–29. http://www.rpajournal.com/dev/wp-content/uploads/2015/12/A2.pdf

TILT Higher Ed. (n.d.). *Transparency in teaching and learning.* https://tilthighered.com/

University of San Diego (USD). (n.d.). *Student outcomes: Institutional learning outcomes.* https://www.sandiego.edu/outcomes/student-learning/learning-and-assessment/learning-outcomes/

Western Association of Schools and Colleges Senior College and University Commission (WSCUC). (2011). *Acceptance letter of the CSUMB interim report.* https://csumb.edu/academicaffairs/wscuc-accreditation-2011

Western Association of Schools and Colleges Senior College and University Commission (WSCUC). (2015). *2013 handbook of accreditation, revised.* https://www.wscuc.org/resources/handbook-accreditation-2013

Western Association of Schools and Colleges Senior College and University Commission (WSCUC). (2020). *WSCUC assessment leadership academy.* https://www.wscuc.org/ala/overview

Western Association of Schools and College Senior College and University Commission. (WSCUC). (n.d.). *Educational quality: Student learning, core competencies, and standards of performance at graduation.* https://www.wscuc.org/book/export/html/956

16

ASSESSING FOR LEARNING

The Scholarship of Teaching and Learning and Campus Assessment Culture

Kristina A. Meinking

Despite increasing faculty awareness of assessment's ubiquity on college and university campuses, it remains commonplace to lament that many instructors resent or resist data collection measures as perceived intrusions to, or implicit criticisms of, their teaching and threats to their autonomy. This response may be in part due to the connection between assessment and accreditation. For example, campus-wide or programmatic (e.g., general education) assessment initiatives required by accreditors may be interpreted as imposed from the top down, with little if any faculty buy-in or contribution to the design process. Similarly, the absence of a closed loop once data have been collected, analyzed, and submitted leaves faculty wondering about the purpose and utility of their efforts.

Cumulatively these and other elements of a broad-level assessment can lead faculty to assume a compliance mentality toward the process as a whole, adopting a frame located in the external motivation of obligation. However, assessment remains a significant way of discovering, discussing, and developing an institution's better understanding of student learning. Personnel in assessment roles need to adopt or create strategies that encourage faculty participation and ownership; a great deal of literature addresses how this can happen (Walvoord, 2010). While these approaches and principles are critical to the development and support of an effective assessment plan, questions may still remain about how wider shifts in campus culture and attitudes towards assessment might be fostered and encouraged.

This chapter will explore how the scholarship of teaching and learning (SoTL) both offers a lens through which faculty might approach assessment responsibilities and suggests a frame for changing campus culture and conversation around assessment in the broader sense. This story begins with a brief history of how SoTL came to be a defining feature of the Elon University campus culture and moves to a discussion of a series of decentralized campus programs that foster SoTL on the campus. Next, the relationship between assessment and SoTL is explored. Finally, the Elon story illustrates how participation in the campus SoTL programs suggests evidence of changed attitudes toward assessment by hypothesizing how approaching assessment as a process *for* learning might look, and how institutions might create opportunities to cultivate this kind of campus culture.

A Story of SoTL at Elon University

As a midsized liberal arts university where teaching is the faculty's primary responsibility, SoTL appears in and across a variety of contexts at Elon University. These contexts are discussed later. However, it is worth noting here that the university's Center for the Advancement of Teaching and Learning (CATL) is the longest-standing and the most generative campus space for SoTL projects and researchers. CATL's mission is threefold: "to promote intentional, evidence-based, and inclusive teaching and learning practices, contribute to university-wide initiatives related to teaching and learning, and foster the scholarship of teaching and learning at Elon University" (WSCUC, 2011, p. 2). The third component of the mission statement, which explicitly identifies SoTL as a defining feature of CATL's mission, clearly embeds SoTL within the center's dedication to teaching and learning as well as reflects the center's origins and evolution at the institution.

CATL's roots extend to Elon's involvement with the Carnegie Foundation's multi-institutional CASTL project in the late 1990s. Created as the Carnegie Academy for the Scholarship of Teaching and Learning, the CASTL Program

> sought to support the development of a scholarship of teaching and learning that: fosters significant, long-lasting learning for all students; enhances the practice and profession of teaching, and; brings to faculty members' work as teachers the recognition and reward afforded to other forms of scholarly work. (WSCUC, 2011, p. 2)

These roots extend to the establishment of Project Interweave, a program in which faculty explored learning in their own classes and then talked with colleagues about these explorations, what they were seeing and noticing, and what in their courses made them curious about student learning. Conceived as a space where faculty could weave together the fabric of teaching and learning, Project Interweave was distinguished through its inclusion of students as members of the conversation, whose insights into what was happening on campus and in the classroom, what they saw, and what sense they made of the learning experience, were incorporated and valued as essential pieces of the project.

As a precursor to CATL, Project Interweave served in part to underscore the variety of faculty members' relationships to studying and thinking critically about teaching and learning on campus. The foundation of CATL in 2005 presented an opportunity to build upon the work of this initiative by bringing together faculty who were already practiced in the study and public sharing of teaching and learning with faculty who were aware and interested in getting involved but unsure about how to start. In addition to its other central contributions to campus, CATL's role in creating a space for these individuals to connect, learn, and develop as teacher-scholars laid the groundwork for the emergence of SoTL as a recognizable area of inquiry and professional development at Elon.

On the one hand, early CATL programs and initiatives made public to the campus community the work in which individual faculty members were already engaged, such as service-learning and other high-impact pedagogies. On the other hand, specific programs fostered relatively low-stakes opportunities for faculty members who had a burgeoning interest in studying teaching and learning to gather and develop projects. What became (and continues to be) an annual writing residency, a 4-day SoTL-focused writing retreat at the close of each academic year, was arguably the greatest support for this limb of the center's work. Each spring, faculty are invited to apply to the residency to spend dedicated time on a SoTL project in any stage of development. Over the course of the 4 days, participants placed in cohorts engage in setting goals, writing, sharing, offering and responding to feedback, and reflecting on the writing process individually and with one another.

The writing residency supports faculty work in and around SoTL in three important and interconnected ways. First, the small annual community of approximately 20 coinquirers and teacher-scholars encourages support, dialogue, and camaraderie for participants. Providing meals and a stipend also encourages participants' focus. The structured and scaffolded frame of the 4 days provides participants with disciplined time for writing and an opportunity to gain momentum on that writing. Unlike the often fits and bursts of semester- and academic-year-based writing projects, the individual writing time and scaffolded communal or group moments create a framework for iteration, development, and progress on a specific writing project. Finally, and perhaps most importantly, the space of the residency, with its focus on an eventual outcome, helps faculty to work through one of the most challenging pieces of SoTL: going public. For many participants, the residency clarifies distinctions from, as well as connections between, SoTL and their disciplinary scholarship. It offers a sense of the potential audience for their projects, helps them tell compelling stories about their teaching, leads to a first article, and opens up a pathway for future work and publications in one or more areas. Now in its 15th year, approximately 65% of participants have published residency-supported SoTL projects in peer-reviewed journals.

Recognizing SoTL: Support and Opportunities for Engagement

As a program, the writing residency represents one model of SoTL engagement that requires a singular investment of time, but instills habits of mind through which faculty can continue to work in the future. Faculty can participate once (though many come back a second or third time) and take the knowledge, resources, and experience gained into their next SoTL project. Other programs offered through CATL provide a similar structure for project incubation. These include course design and assignment alignment groups of three-to-five faculty who meet three or four times throughout a semester, reading groups around specific approaches and pedagogies, one-off workshops (e.g., on discussion techniques, the intentional use of technology, inclusive teaching), and more. Often collaborations arise in response to a specific change, trend, or immediate need (e.g., transitioning to online learning during the 2020 COVID-19 pandemic). Individually and collectively, these opportunities for engagement on topics and questions centered on teaching and learning contribute to developing and sustaining a community of faculty and staff who are dedicated to deepening their knowledge, adopting new or refining already-practiced pedagogies, and sharing their work, experience, and ideas with campus colleagues.

The campus culture that emerges from this model is one that values teaching and learning and the discussion, critique, and innovation thereof. While the previously mentioned CATL programs do not constitute SoTL per se, the ethos and environment they foster is one that leads to more reflective and observational teaching, a quality essential in an institution that embraces a teacher-mentor-scholar model for faculty identity and development. This second piece, of faculty and professional development, remains central to faculty buy-in for SoTL; an institution at which the record of faculty promotion and tenure includes individuals with SoTL publications as part or the whole of their *curriculum vitae* communicates clearly that SoTL is a valued and valuable marker of professional activity.

CATL offers a series of programs and opportunities to support the work of faculty engaged in the scholarship of teaching and learning. These programs range from a series of teaching and learning grant opportunities, to semester-long SoTL communities of practice, to the CATL Scholar Program. Perhaps the most obvious and dedicated source of support for faculty, the competitive CATL Scholar Program, selects two or three applicants each year to embark upon a 2 year SoTL research project. Critical to the success of the scholars are the availability of annual conference and materials funds, two course reassigned times for each year of the project, and engagement with others across a few years of their cohort. As another of the earliest programs offered by the center, former and current CATL scholars have published in peer-reviewed SoTL and disciplinary contexts, given national and international presentations on their projects, created resources for faculty wishing to adopt their pedagogies, and shifted their 2-year projects into multiyear inquiries and research. CATL Scholars likewise create a space for SoTL conversations on campus, leading or facilitating workshops on topics related to their projects or pedagogies, organizing and facilitating departmental retreats, and serving as campus experts on the pedagogies they have studied or developed.

Over the last several years, the contexts and sources of support for both scholarly teaching and SoTL have broadened and deepened across Elon. A variety of programs and initiatives have come out of CATL. Others developed in response to the multiyear writing in 2013. Two new centers on campus support and sustain SoTL in significant ways: the Center for Research on Global Engagement (CRGE) and the Center for Engaged Learning (CEL). It should be noted that faculty in programs and departments across campus, to varying degrees of scale and breadth, are also consistently involved in SoTL. Each of these centers support and encourage faculty development especially by bringing together faculty in interdisciplinary contexts from disparate programs and departments on campus as well as from international institutions.

Created in 2015 in order to "facilitate, support, and promote scholarship on global engagement," CRGE (Elon University, n.d.) encourages faculty and students to explore research and especially SoTL at the intersection of their global experiences and scholarship. Funding and stipends in support of student research (disciplinary-based) and faculty research (SoTL-based) have led to numerous conference presentations nationally and internationally as well as articles and book chapters. CRGE also invites applications for and supports annual communities of practice in which faculty explore topics related either to mentoring undergraduate research in global contexts or intercultural learning and development. Worth underscoring here is CRGE's intentional inclusion and encouragement of student-centered SoTL projects and its celebration of collaborative research and engagement opportunities. Community of practice participants, grant awardees, and those who engaged with CRGE in other capacities have published in peer-reviewed and disciplinary contexts and have presented their work nationally and internationally.

Founded in 2012, the CEL expands institutional conversations around SoTL and "brings together international leaders in higher education to develop and to synthesize rigorous research on central questions about student learning" (CEL, n.d., para. 1). Through a multitude of programs, including multiinstitutional research and practice-based initiatives, conferences, seminars, and scholars programs, CEL works to bring together educators to understand more deeply how high-impact practices might be done well, can be scaled to reach many students, and demonstrate "how students might integrate their learning across multiple high-impact experiences" (CEL, n.d. para. 2). The center's focus on high-impact practices and experiences together with its international reach serves to deepen participants' foundation and implementation of evidence-based practices and to broaden their circles of conversation and community. Just as the CATL scholars and CRGE conduct research, faculty and staff who have worked in and alongside CEL programs show a strong record of publication in peer-reviewed journals, presentations at conferences, and continued engagement even after their term as a CEL scholar, the multinational seminar, or the annual conference.

Although space prevents a fuller discussion of other important areas in which centers, programs, and other entities on campus are engaging faculty and staff around SoTL, it is worth noting that several departments have regular discussions and campus-wide workshops about SoTL. Recent topics have included partnering with students on a SoTL project, how to navigate the IRB process, tips for preparing for publication or other methods for going public with SoTL work, and strategies for integrating qualitative and quantitative evidence. In addition, the provost's office supports and funds course reassigned times, sabbaticals, and summer projects dedicated to SoTL work, and many departments explicitly include SoTL in their departmental scholarship statements, documents which outline departmental parameters and expectations around scholarship and professional activity for the purpose of preparing faculty for the promotion and tenure processes.

Taken collectively, this broad overview of three significant spaces in which SoTL happens on the Elon campus brings to light the range of SoTL activity on campus and the decentralized ways in which SoTL happens and might be assessed. Faculty can find their niche, focusing on individual or collaborative projects, and find other community members with whom to engage as they work through an inquiry. For these instructors (and others who might wish to pursue these or similar opportunities), SoTL work is integrated into the fabric of their teaching and scholarship; supported across levels of the administration, often with funding or other material support; is often community-based; and is often made public in one or more ways.

SoTL and Assessment

As discussed previously, faculty members' attention to scholarly teaching—what might be considered as the consultation and use of scholarly resources as well as colleagues in teaching—already encompasses a series of intellectual moves and reframing of perspective that are likely to nudge faculty members toward a shift in their opinions on assessment. By approaching teaching as scholarly inquiry as an effort to "think of teaching practice, and the evidence of student learning, as problems to be investigated, analyzed, represented, and debated" (Bass, 1999, p. 1), instructors are already changing their relationship with student work. Faculty members' willingness (and even eagerness) to look critically at the ways in which their decisions and practices can best support student learning in their classes refocuses conversations away from grades and toward an evidence-based approach to assessing students' skills and understanding.

Scholarly teaching also offers an entry point to the scholarship of teaching and learning, which can be distinguished by the significant step of making public (in any one of a variety of ways) the results of a systematic inquiry into questions about student learning. Further, this making-public invites others to evaluate, critique, and review the analysis and results of that inquiry, aligning the production and products of SoTL with those associated with disciplinary research. This critical move, as already hinted, often entails the greatest need for an adjusted perspective for faculty, involving as it does the learning of a new scholarly genre replete with different terminology, methods, conferences, journals, and at times murky borders. Faculty who navigate their way from scholarly teaching to working in SoTL might wrestle with this often unfamiliar scholarly genre and practice.

Both scholarly teaching and SoTL focus on student learning and evidence-based approaches to studying teaching and learning. The practice of SoTL particularly encourages faculty to bring their scholarly training and habits of mind to their pedagogical context and is sparked by a question or perceived problem in their class. Further, SoTL seeks to make public and share or distribute findings related to teaching and learning; it aspires to the improvement of teaching and learning in contexts both specific and general.

In describing SoTL this way, one might detect some parallels to assessment, which is similarly concerned with studying and sharing publicly the outcomes of student learning; adopting an evidence-based approach to inquiries and discussion of teaching and learning; and formulating a plan to deepen, enhance, or otherwise improve upon the reported findings (Hutchings et al., 2011).

SoTL and assessment share a similar set of goals that begin with an inquiry about student learning, involve intervention by applying a strategy for improvement, and are shared by the making-public of the results of that intervention. Although points of contact exist between SoTL and assessment, important distinctions do as well. SoTL is classroom-driven (i.e., it arises from the practitioner's identification and investigation of a teaching "problem") and it seeks to be in dialogue with faculty who make use of findings for their own teaching and learning contexts. Assessment, however, often lacks a ground-up ethos. As a practice required by institutions and implemented by administrators as part of a cycle of identifying and articulating student learning (itself often connected to a need to demonstrate the value of higher education), its results tend to be perceived as most relevant to educational stakeholders external to the classroom (Cain & Hutchings, 2015).

These differences, perhaps more vast and irreconcilable in theory than reality, foster two significantly distinct attitudes among faculty and staff. While faculty onboarding for SoTL, especially in institutional contexts where SoTL is explicitly valued and supported, can invite curiosity and engagement, faculty onboarding for assessment processes can instigate concern, mistrust, and resentment. Faculty perceptions of assessment as top-down, administrative, and driven by bureaucratic compliance can result in a diminished sense of agency and independence while stirring up mistrust. Many faculty view assessment as a process that yields results which "would be used for evaluative purposes, with potentially negative implications for individual faculty and specific programs" (Cain & Hutchings, 2015, pp. 98–99; Linkon, 2005). As a further distinction, many faculty and staff experience assessment as a process wherein the loop is never closed: Results are sent off to the requisite administrative office, accrediting agency, or other interested and invested entities (e.g., the board of trustees) but fail to be shared, intentionally and meaningfully, with instructors as starting points for discussion and planning for classroom- or program-level improvements to student learning.

How might these two diverse attitudes be reconciled? In a book chapter about the relationship between SoTL and assessment, Hutchings et al. (2011) explore this possibility, noting both the shared areas of engagement as well as the distance between both the origins of each and the perspectives that faculty hold toward them. In reflecting on opportunities both existing and potential, the authors argue that "the two movements stand to gain from the work of the other, but also, and more important, that higher education *needs* their combined strengths" (p. 71, emphasis in original). Surveying the current landscape, Hutchings et al. offer examples of a range of colleges and universities wherein SoTL and assessment initiatives complemented one another, where a campus culture that values SoTL has reframed its approach to assessment as one of opportunity, and others where assessment has been guided and informed by SoTL questions and efforts (Hutchings et al., 2011).

Amongst the variety of models and reflections shared, a central theme develops: that SoTL and assessment can perhaps best support and benefit one another by encouraging each to move slightly closer to the other. Assessment efforts, for example, might be shaped by the scholarly activity and SoTL projects of faculty, while SoTL's profile itself might garner more public and nuanced attention for the ways in which it can teach us about student learning and what is happening in our classrooms. In short, the techniques and qualities that help to define each practice can be usefully and insightfully woven into one another: Scholars of teaching and learning in the midst of a project might seek more information in the form of institutional data (e.g., enrollments, persistence in the major, etc.) while those leading broad-level assessment efforts might develop more holistic and specific reports on student learning (e.g., in a general education program or a department) based on the work of faculty pursuing SoTL projects.

Assessment for Learning

These pages have shared a brief narrative about the evolution of SoTL on Elon's campus focused through the lens of the Center for the Advancement of Teaching and Learning. The decentralized nature of SoTL activity and the assessment thereof on campus has been highlighted by noting the important work of other campus centers and partners. It was suggested that both SoTL and assessment share a similar set of qualities and attributes that posit them as likely complements to one another. In these last pages, examples are provided as to how SoTL has informed assessment on Elon's campus and ways in which one might cultivate an even broader campus culture of assessment for learning.

If faculty are invited to think deeply and critically about their teaching and their courses, and if the products of that labor are systemically and programmatically supported, a campus culture of thinking, communicating, and writing in and about the scholarship of teaching and learning might flourish.

But how might SoTL influence how those faculty think about assessment? Although we have already considered the commonalities shared by SoTL and assessment, one wonders if having several faculty who have some experience with SoTL might allow for a certain kind of assessment conversation that is less about proverbial bean counting and more about the actual learning. Indeed, might a campus culture of SoTL encourage faculty to recognize and embrace the messiness of learning? In other words, if we perceive assessment culture to be about the neat and tidy, we might see in SoTL a practice that enables or supports a faculty culture of critically examining learning.

Evidence from ongoing work across areas of Elon's campus suggests that this cultural shift is a valid possibility. Within the context of externally motivated assessments such as those required by accrediting bodies (e.g., SACS), faculty in programs and departments have explored ways of complying with institutionally mandated assessments in ways that are compelling. Members of the Philosophy Department, for example, devote time at their retreats to collectively and collaboratively reading an assortment of ungraded student work. As a community, they work to puzzle out what that student work is indicating and what it might mean for student learning in their courses. Initiatives relevant to their curriculum find their start in these conversations and inform the department's pedagogical perspectives for the upcoming academic year. Similarly, the World Languages and Cultures (WLC) Department, which houses faculty who teach eight different languages, both in its section (i.e., language-specific) meetings and as a full department, routinely employs thematic analysis and other strategies for analyzing qualitative data to understand student learning across the levels of their curriculum. Multiyear, assessment-focused endeavors showcase their commitment both to improving student learning and to iteration. These projects include departments redesigning learning goals, tracking students' progress in a goal through the curriculum, and devoting multiple semiannual retreats to the development of curricula and assessment practices.

Two observations are worth noting here: first, the activity of each department's faculty in SoTL and, second, the community-based approach to making sense of student learning. In both departments, a majority of permanent faculty are active in SoTL (Philosophy: 62.5%; WLC: 54.5%), some of whom are current or former CATL scholars (Philosophy: 25%; WLC: 27.2%), with projects that encompass a range of SoTL topics including student-as-partners, flipped classrooms, competency-based learning, social justice, literacy, and democratic discussion. SoTL practitioners bring to their teaching a habit of noticing and investigating student learning in their courses with an eye toward data collection, data analysis, and the implementation of evidence-based changes and strategies. Having a department with faculty who are already engaged in thinking about evidence of student learning from this perspective is likely to influence, encourage, and support a broader level adaptation of a generative-focused view of assessment.

These departments' community-based approach to assessment emerges as a significant attribute. Rather than tasking individual faculty with performing assessment or using a top-down assessment tool, they are locating assessment conversations at the departmental level and putting faculty at the center of a community activity. Faculty buy-in for assessment is greater when faculty have control over elements of the process. That faculty must engage in assessment is a given, but the shift in mindset from one of compliance to one of curiosity might be best facilitated in an environment where faculty are already oriented to SoTL. While the departments and areas discussed here offer only a few examples, they do suggest ways in which faculty can find or make meaning through the assessment process. If the scope is broadened, we are invited to wonder: What might a campus culture of assessment look like if all, or a majority of units, programs, schools, and departments could shift from the assessment of learning to assessment for learning?

In order for both scholarly teaching and SoTL to feel relevant for faculty, institutional support and the articulation of the activity's value are necessary. According to a recent essay, this kind of support can include "the involvement of an academic developer, collegial support from research team members, encouragement from department leaders, and funding" (Shephard et al., 2020, p. 8). These and other types of supports and incentives can invite faculty to allocate their own resources of time and energy to studying their courses and working to understand a perceived problem (Bass, 1999) in those courses. These sources of support are not purely funding-related, though funding has been found to be a significant motivator (Shephard et al., 2020). Support also encompasses varying levels of university and administrative offices, and these loci of affirmation further emphasize the ideas that both a sense of community and administrative recognition are galvanizing factors.

An institution's recognition of SoTL's place and value might be seen in the availability of resources such as teaching centers or academic developers' presence, in sources of financial support or reassigned time for SoTL projects, and in other spaces and centers on campus where SoTL is explicitly invited or encouraged. Programmatic opportunities in which faculty might be encouraged to think critically about a "real" question or "real" data about student learning and to become student-centered teachers are frequent precursors for becoming involved in SoTL (Shephard et al., 2020). Other opportunities might take the form of orientation programs or workshops. SoTL's acknowledgement might also come in the form of departmental statements for promotion and tenure that specifically list the scholarship of teaching and learning as an acceptable space for publication and professional presentations according to the same criteria as disciplinary scholarship (e.g., high-quality and peer-reviewed journals). Similarly, faculty who successfully navigate the promotion and tenure processes with a record of scholarship partially or even fully entrenched in SoTL offer proof of concept regarding SoTL's place on campus. "Top-down" spaces like those just discussed affirm an institution's commitment to SoTL as an important scholarly activity that is a valuable, worthwhile investment of faculty members' time and resources. In the absence of these types of systemic supports and resources, those involved with assessment across multiple areas of an institution might seek other ways of encouraging a SoTL-framed approach to the task of assessment.

Specific strategies outlined by Kuh et al. (2015) offer inspiring starting points. And as a more generalized approach, campus leaders and faculty might look for opportunities for SoTL and assessment to complement one another. When, for example, might an instructor's inquiry into student learning in their course, or a department's commitment to a shared learning goal, benefit from the data, methods, and habits of mind that drive assessment and its practitioners? When might assessment planning benefit from discussion among faculty? In what contexts might assessment be enhanced and deepened by an embracing of the messiness of learning and the messy processes of making sense of that learning? What voice might students have in these processes, and in what capacities might they contribute and cocreate? In short, cultivating community around both teaching and learning as well as the scholarly study of teaching and learning can begin to shift the tenor and tone of conversations and campus culture, encouraging an ethos in which assessment for learning is understood and explored as a collaborative and valued endeavor.

References

Bass, R. (1999). The scholarship of teaching: What's the problem? *Inventio, 1*(1), 1–10.

Cain, T. R., & Hutchings, P. (2015). Faculty and students: Assessment at the intersection of teaching and learning. In G. D. Kuh, S. O. Ikenberry, N. A. Jankowski, T. R. Cain, P. T. Ewell, P. Hutchings, & J. Kinzie (Eds.), *Using evidence of student learning to improve higher education* (pp. 95–116). Jossey-Bass.

Carnegie Academy for the Scholarship of Teaching and Learning. (n.d.). *Higher education*. http://archive.carnegiefoundation.org/scholarship_teaching_learning/CASTL_highed.html

Center for the Advancement of Teaching and Learning, Elon University. (n.d.). *Mission and annual reports*. https://www.elon.edu/u/academics/catl/about-us/

Center for Engaged Learning, Elon University. (n.d.). *About CEL*. https://www.centerforengagedlearning.org/about-cel/

Elon University. (n.d.). Center for Research on Global Engagement. https://www.elon.edu/u/academics/crge/

Hutchings, P. M., Huber, T., & Ciccone, A. (2011). *The scholarship of teaching and learning reconsidered: Institutional integration and impact*. Jossey-Bass.

Kuh, G. D., Ikenberry, S. O., Jankowski, N. A., Cain, T. R., Ewell, P. T., Hutchings, P., & Kinzie, J. (2015). *Using evidence of student learning to improve higher education*. Jossey-Bass.

Linkon, S. L. (2005). How can assessment work for us? *Academe*, *91*(4), 28–32.

Shephard, K., Rogers, T., & Bogt, E. (2020, February 27). Impacts of engaging in research into teaching and learning on academics' conceptions of their development as teachers and on the roles of academic developers. *International Journal for Academic Development*. Advance online publication. https://doi.org/10.1080/1360144X.2020.1731814

Walvoord, B. E. (2010). *Assessment clear and simple: A practical guide for institutions, departments, and general education* (2nd ed.). Jossey-Bass.

Western Association of Schools and Colleges Senior College and University Commission (WSCUC). (2011). *Acceptance letter of the CSUMB interim report*. https://csumb.edu/academicaffairs/wscuc-accreditation-2011.https://edit.csumb.edu/sites/default/files/images/st-block-37-1415911690664-raw-wasc_eer_report_-_notice_july_2011-1.pdf

PART FOUR

INSTITUTIONAL EFFECTIVENESS AND ASSESSMENT

17

A STRUCTURED PROTOCOL FOR DEMONSTRATING INSTITUTIONAL EFFECTIVENESS

Eric D. Stamps

Suskie (2015) states that *institutional effectiveness* "refers to the effectiveness of an entire college, as opposed to specific programs, services or initiatives" (p. 52). However, data from across the entire spectrum of programs, services, and initiatives collectively make the argument for institutional effectiveness. The California School of Podiatric Medicine (CSPM) at Samuel Merritt University, a 4-year podiatric medical school, has created a structured protocol for curricular assessment and strategic planning that incorporates programmatic accreditation requirements, university learning outcomes, and program learning outcomes to demonstrate institutional effectiveness. The school has created a culture that utilizes data from multiple levels across the institution and ties outcomes to its mission, vision, and values. It demonstrates what Ross and Cooley refer to as "the use of data in decision-making and higher educational professionals who think and strategize about data and their use across the institution, school, or program" (Hundley & Kahn, 2019, p. 200).

This chapter outlines the collaborative process the school has used to develop, refine, and implement this assessment system. The process starts with a quinquennial refinement of the college's mission, vision, and values statement that informs the strategic goals. Measurable tactics are then developed and linked to the program learning outcomes, which are in turn linked to the university's institutional learning outcomes. Outcome measures are then added to an assessment plan, which is organized by data collection year and month. An assessment action plan is used to track detailed results of the measured data, including actions that were taken—all of which leads back to the strategic plan. The system has helped guide and document ongoing improvements and curricular change and has helped to demonstrate curricular effectiveness.

The CSPM is one of nine schools of podiatric medicine in the United States that prepares students to enter podiatric residency. The school, which is a college within Samuel Merritt University, is accredited by the Council on Podiatric Medical Education, a programmatic accrediting body under the U.S. Department of Education.

Goal of Assessment

A principal goal of assessment at the CSPM at Samuel Merritt University is to demonstrate institutional effectiveness, measured primarily by how well our institution meets the objectives stated in our mission, vision, and values (MVV) statement. The CSPM MVV statement, which is updated about every 5 years, and which is considered important enough that it is read aloud at the start of every monthly faculty meeting, was last updated during a day long session at a CSPM faculty retreat. During this retreat, every faculty member contributed to the MVV, which was based partially upon the preceding MVV and partially on a general consensus of what needed to be added.

An MVV update occurred in 2020 and was completed using a structured approach. First, a group of seven key members of the faculty and administration met to review the current MVV statement, focusing on updating the statement to keep pace with both changes in podiatric education and changes in the mission, vision, and values of the university. Several probing questions were considered.

1. What changes have occurred over the past half-decade?
2. What are our institutional strengths and have those been captured in the document?
3. Have we objectively been able to meet and assess our MVV as determined by our assessment action plan, or has the MVV been simply words on paper?
4. Does the current MVV correlate well with our program's current strategic plan?
5. Is it aligned with the university's learning outcomes and our own program learning outcomes?

6. Are there new aspects of our mission that should be added to the MVV statement?
7. Are we being strategic in our approach—that is, can we better use our MVV to distinguish ourselves from our competition?

After this self-study process was complete and a new MVV draft was developed, the document was presented for feedback to the institutional stakeholders: faculty, staff, current students, alumni, and the university administration. After feedback was received, the comments were reviewed by the original seven-person committee and a final MVV statement was drafted, rereviewed by the CSPM executive committee, and distributed to CSPM stakeholders. The current CSPM MVV as adopted October 2016 is shown in Table 17.1.

TABLE 17.1
MVV 2016

CSPM Mission Statement	The CSPM provides education and instills the professional values for podiatric medical students to be effective healthcare practitioners and leaders in the podiatric medication profession.
CSPM Vision Statement	The CSPM commits to creating and sustaining an environment that promulgates an education that is intellectually, socially, and personally transformative.
CSPM Values Statement	The CSPM shall: 1. Promote excellence and innovation in education 2. Advocate and maintain an environment of dignity, compassion, and respect 3. Promote collaborative, interprofessional healthcare delivery 4. Provide podiatric care and treatment to the underserved 5. Encourage and support scholarly activity and research 6. Foster the principles of lifelong learning and self-reflection

Strategies to Support Achievement of the Goals

In 2016, after the current MVV was published, work began on an update of the institutional strategic plan (Figure 17.1), with the goal of verifying that CSPM was meeting its mission, vision, and values, and therefore helping to demonstrate its institutional effectiveness. A small strategic planning committee was created from the CSPM executive committee, consisting of the dean and three associate deans. From the start, it was clear to the group that it would be easier to demonstrate attainment of the CSPM values than achievement of the mission or vision. The mission and vision were complex concepts that were at least partially aspirational and more difficult to measure directly. Fortunately, this was not an obstacle, as the values statements directly reflected the mission and vision and were more readily assessed. The strategic plan update was then started by designating each of the six vision statements as a strategic goal. For example, the vision statement "The California School of Podiatric Medicine shall promote excellence and innovation in education" was selected as strategy I. For each strategic goal the small working group then brainstormed to identify current and potential tactics that are currently being implemented or could be implemented to help achieve the strategic goal. For strategy I, eight tactical approaches were identified: (a) implement curricular changes; (b) develop and assess clinical simulation in the curriculum; (c) ensure the presence of cultural awareness, professionalism, and ethics in the curriculum; (d) establish benchmarks for assessing student learning competencies and track achievement of outcomes; (e) attract, enroll, and retrain the highest quality students; (f) recruit, develop, mentor, and retain faculty

Figure 17.1. Portion of the CSPM strategic plan.

CALIFORNIA SCHOOL OF PODIATRIC MEDICINE 2017-2022 STRATEGIC PLAN – 1/9/18 – V 1.1				
Strategy I: Promote excellence and innovation in education				
Tactics	Outcome Measures	Actual Outcomes	PLO's	Responsibility

A. Implement curricular changes
  1. Align course content
  2. Disperse course schedules evenly
    a. Stagger final exams
  3. Allocate APMLE Part I study time
    a. Provide test taking consultant for APMLE Part I
  4. Monitor subject specific performance on APMLE Part I
	☐ Improved student satisfaction
	  • Focus groups
	  • Surveys
	  • Course evaluations
	☐ Performance on APMLE Part I
			1. a-e
			2a.
				✓ Dean
				✓ Director of Curriculum Development

B. Develop and assess clinical simulation in the curriculum
  1. Assess 2nd year Simulation Center rotation
  2. Assess 3rd year Medicine
	☐ APMLE Part II medicine pass rates
	☐ APMLE Part II surgery pass rates
	☐ Improved student clinical
			1. b-c
			2. a-g
			3. a, f, g
			4. a-f
			5. a-b
				✓ Dean
				✓ Director of Curriculum Development

members; (g) faculty will incorporate best teaching practices and state of the art learning methodology; and (h) review and restructure as appropriate the CSPM assessment plan.

For each of the major tactics, subtactics were identified, with the requirement that these subtactics would be relatively small, concrete, and do able. For strategy I, tactic A (Implement curricular changes), four subtactics were identified: (a) align course content, (b) disperse course schedules evenly, (c) allocate board exam study time, and (d) monitor subject specific performance on the part I board exam. The working group then identified outcome measures that would help reflect level of achievement for each tactic. Outcome measures for tactic A included improved performance on the part I national board exam and improved student satisfaction as determined from student focus groups, student surveys, and student evaluations of courses and faculty. These outcome measures were then updated on the CSPM assessment plan and the CSPM assessment action plan, documents that are used in concert with the strategic plan.

The actual outcomes for some of the outcome measures were also included in the strategic plan as the CSPM strategic plan is considered a living document, one that is regularly reviewed and updated at faculty meetings and at biannual faculty retreats. For example, the document lists board exam first-time pass rate results and a notation that curricular changes 1, 2, and 3, as noted, were implemented.

To help demonstrate that our tactics are also supporting our program learning outcomes (PLOs), each major tactic was linked to the most appropriate PLOs, providing additional evidence that we are working to demonstrate institutional effectiveness. This linkage also connects the CSPM curriculum to recommended competencies generated by the podiatric programmatic accreditation organization, the Council on Podiatric Medical Education (CPME). These CPME recommended competencies (CPME, 2019) served as the basis for the CSPM PLOs.

Putting this all together, the CSPM PLO 1 (Figure 17.2), "Be knowledgeable in the preclinical sciences and use this knowledge as a foundation for learning outcomes 2 through 9," was derived from the CPME competency 1: "Demonstrate knowledge of the preclinical sciences which provide the foundations of podiatric clinical training, residency training, and practice." In turn, CSPM PLO 1 was linked to strategy I, tactics A, B, and D and was also mapped to the university's institutional learning outcomes (ILOs) via a commercially available mapping application. The ILO map, in graphic form, then facilitates assessment of instructional gaps and confirmation of instructional coverage. For example, a new university ILO, released in 2019, "engage in self-care practices for personal health and wellness," is not well

Figure 17.2. Portion of the CSPM program learning outcomes.

Program Learning Outcome	Assessment Measures and Goals

1. Be knowledgeable in the preclinical sciences and use this knowledge as a foundation for learning outcomes two through nine.
   a. Describe and explain the bodies of knowledge concerning normal human anatomy, physiology, biochemistry, and the structure and function of the human body.
   b. Describe and explain the causes of disease and the consequences of altered structure or function of the human body and its organ systems.
   c. Describe and explain pharmacological principles and interventions.
   d. Describe and explain the role of microbes, parasites and the diseases that they cause.
   e. Describe and explain the structure and function of the immune system.
	Annual Anatomy, Biochemistry, Histology, Immunology, Microbiology, Pathology, Pharmacology, Physiology course pass rates > 90%.
	
	Annual APMLE Biochemistry, General Anatomy, Lower Extremity Anatomy, Microbiology/Immunology, Pathology, Pharmacology, Physiology section pass rates > 90% for first time takers.

Program Learning Outcome	Assessment Measures and Goals

2. Formulate successful patient management strategies based upon sound, applicable diagnostic and assessment skills.
   a. Apply knowledge of the preclinical sciences in clinical decision-making and patient care
   b. Perform and interpret a history and physical examination.
   c. Identify and interpret common clinical, laboratory, imaging, gait and other studies used to diagnose pathologies.
   d. Describe, recognize and explain the pathologic manifestations of common conditions of the lower extremity.
   e. Formulate appropriate differential diagnoses and plans of management.
   f. Select and administer, under supervision, appropriate medical and surgical treatments.
   g. Recognize patients with life threatening emergencies and institute initial therapy.
	Annual Biomechanics, Dermatology, General Medicine, Intro to Clinical Medicine, Jurisprudence, Podiatric Medicine, Podiatric Surgery, Public Health, Radiology, Pediatrics course pass rate > 90%.
	
	Annual APMLE Community Health/Jurisprudence/Research, Medical Imaging, Medicine, Orthopedics/Biomechanics/Sports Medicine, Surgery/Anesthesia section pass rates > 90% for first time test takers.
	
	AACPM DPM Competency Survey results of "adequate" or "more than adequate."
	
	CSPM 3rd year OSCE results with 100% pass rate.

supported by the current CSPM PLOs and will need to be addressed in the updated CSPM MVV statement, strategic plan, assessment action plan, and ultimately in the CSPM curriculum.

Assessments Used to Determine Progress Toward Goals

The CSPM assessment plan (Table 17.2) currently includes 26 different data points, lists the data collection year and month, the responsible office for the data collection, and most significantly, how the data are used. The data points align with the strategic plan, the assessment action plan, and are included in the CSPM PLOs as assessment measures and goals. The assessment plan, which was created via a collaborative effort of the CSPM executive committee, was organized by collection year and month. During year 1, for instance, the only assessment data that are collected are the results of a learning style inventory instrument (Kolb & Kolb, 2013) that is given to all incoming students at orientation. According to the assessment plan, those results are used to assign students to a faculty mentor with a similar learning style, with the expectation that this strategy will ultimately help students improve their learning. Of the 26 data points collected, an item with a high potential for impact are the results of the part I podiatric national board exam, The American Podiatric Medical Licensing Exam Part I. This is a comprehensive exam given at the start of the third year of the program, after the students have completed their preclinical sciences coursework. The results, if positive, help confirm attainment of PLO 1, help confirm that

TABLE 17.2
Excerpt From 2018–2019 CSPM Assessment Plan

Data Collected	Collection Year	Collection Month	Person Responsible for Data Collection	How Data Are Used
Learning Style Inventory	1	August	Assoc. Dean for Educational Affairs	Assign incoming student to faculty mentor with similar learning style
2nd Year Research Symposium	2	January	Assoc. Dean for Educational Affairs	A 100% participate rate helps demonstrate attainment of PLO#4
AMPLE Part I	3	July, Nov	Assoc. Dean for Administrative Affairs, Assoc. Dean of Admissions	Help confirm attainment of PLO#1 ....
Clinical Course Pass Rate	3	Jan, June	Assoc. Dean for Administrative Affairs	Help confirm attainment of PLO #2 ....
3rd Year Biomechanics Rotation Research Participation	3	June	Assoc. Dean for Educational Affairs	A 100% participate rate helps demonstrate attainment of PLO#4
3rd Year OSCE	3	April	Dean	Help confirm attainment of PLOs 2, 3, and 9, use student scores to determine 40% of their clinical ranking ...

our students have at least minimal competency in the preclinical science subject areas and, by examining admissions benchmarks, help identify potential markers of student success or failure (i.e., the biology section score on the Medical College Admissions Test). The annual report of a residency director's survey is an example of data collected that generally has lower impact. This subjective report, with a historically lower response rate, asks residency directors to rate their current 1st-year residents in six areas (interpersonal skill, communication skills, patient care, practice knowledge, professionalism, and systems-based learning). The results are considered less specific indicators of overall program effectiveness, especially as the survey is given early in the residency program, before the residency directors get to know the residents well. However, the survey is given early enough to capture an incoming impression of each resident, before the resident's knowledge base and attitudes have been influenced by their residency experiences.

Use of the Findings

Each of the 26 data points listed in the assessment plan are examined, but only seven have resulted in change. Those changes are listed and discussed in the CSPM assessment action plan (Table 17.3). The results of the part I national board exam have had a substantial impact on our program. In 2009, for example, a lower than anticipated first-time pass rate on the exam not only triggered a full in-house program review by the university, but also triggered several years of curricular "experimentation," resulting in course sequence reshuffling, modifications in course hours, and increased course oversight by the dean. The long-term results were mixed, with higher first-time board exam pass rates, but with worse student satisfaction with the schedule changes.

More recent changes based on American Podiatric Medical Licensing Exam results, and on feedback from student focus groups, had a positive impact. In 2017, the first-time national licensing exam pass rate was below our benchmark of 90%. As a quick fix, one that could show immediate results, students were given more time off prior to the exam. This action was taken as a result of an informal focus group that found that many students complete their most intense studying during the week immediately prior to the exam. Students were also given access to a commercially available question data bank, and an exam specialist was hired to help coach students. The results of the July 2018 exam met our benchmark of 90% and beat the national average among the schools of podiatric medicine. The same changes were carried over for the July

TABLE 17.3
Excerpt From the CSPM Assessment Action Plan

Data Collected	Results	Action Taken
Learning Style Inventory	2018 results did not correlate with performance on the AMPLE Part I Exam, indicating no particular learning style is associated with better or worse APMLE results.	
APMLE Part I	June 2017 results: 81% first time taker pass rate. All subject areas scores below national average. July 2018 results: 90% first time taker pass rate—exceeding national average by 1%.	Based on 2017 poor results: (a) students excused from clinical obligations for the week preceding the APMLE Part I exam; (b) purchased online board exam preparation test questions for students; (c) hired test-taking expert to provide strategy sessions for students. Based on 2018 results: same strategies as employed for 2018.
Clinical Course Pass Rate	Not used in 2018.	None
3rd Year OSCE	100% pass rate for class of 2019.	None
4th Year Student Exit Survey	For 2018, confirm that specific faulty member's courses were not well received.	Faculty member removed from lecture courses and individual's contract reduced to part time.
APMLE Part II	Jan. 2018: first time pass rate 88%. All subject areas scores below the national average.	The pass rate was below our benchmark of 90%, the same actions were taken as noted for APMLE Part I Exam.

2019 administration of the exam. Unfortunately, the 2019 results were 11 percentage points below our benchmark—resulting in another round of introspective thought and brainstorming at a faculty curricular review in December 2019. The following reasons were presented as potential contributors to ongoing difficulty with this exam: 2nd-year classes limited to 3 days per week, students have to balance classes with clinical rotations, CSPM has a high retention rate (about 89%; among the colleges of podiatric medicine the lowest retention rate is 69%), a diverse student body with many first-generation students, and all students who complete the 2nd-year curriculum are eligible to take the board exam; CSPM does not require passage of a shelf exam prior to the American Podiatric Medical Licensing Exam. To attempt to improve the CSPM first-time board exam pass rate, a new policy was implemented, a policy that was based on the finding that the majority of students who fail the board exam have a year cumulative GPA of less than 3.0. Therefore, any 1st-year student who receives a grade of C or lower on any examination or quiz is referred to the associate dean for educational affairs for a one-on-one discussion. Are there clear contributors to poor performance? One standout is that the majority of poorly performing students are first-generation college graduates. This fact led us to create a first-generation support group starting with the class of 2024.

In addition to American Podiatric Medical Licensing Exam Part I pass rates, several other assessment data have contributed to changes in our program. Fourth-year exit surveys, completed by every graduating senior, were used as evidence to reduce one faculty member's teaching contract. Student focus groups, conducted by an associate dean, informed a number of curricular changes, including revision of the 2nd-year course schedule and restoration of final exam weeks. Data from student focus groups and exit surveys offered outcome measures that were embedded in our strategic plan and were used to validate tactics that promoted two strategies: promotion of excellence and innovation in education, and advocating and maintaining an environment of dignity, compassion, and respect.

By continually referencing and updating our strategic, assessment, and assessment action plans, the assessment and improvement process at CSPM helps ensure that we remain anchored to our mission, vision, and values. Our process also helps demonstrate that we are meeting the learning outcomes of our program and the university, thereby demonstrating institutional effectiveness. As this chapter has illustrated, assessment, like evolution, is seldom linear. We have good years and better years. Hopefully by following our plans, we will make each year a little better than its predecessor.

References

Council on Podiatric Medical Education. (2019, October). *CPME 120, standards and requirements for accrediting colleges of podiatric medicine.* https://www.cpme.org/colleges/content.cfm?ItemNumber=2445&navItemNumber=2241

Hundley, S. P., & Kahn, S. (Eds.). (2019). *Trends in assessment: Ideas, opportunities, and issues for higher education.* Stylus.

Kolb, A. Y., & Kolb, D. A. (2013). *The Kolb learning style inventory: Version 4.0, a comprehensive guide to the theory, psychometrics, research on validity and educational applications.* Experience Based Learning Systems, Inc. www.learningfromexperience.com

Suskie, L. (2015). *Five dimensions of quality: A common sense guide to accreditation and accountability.* Jossey-Bass.

18

TRANSFORMING FROM WITHIN

Strategic Planning as a Tool for Institutional Reflection, Direction, and Transformation

R. Ray D. Somera and Marlena Montague

When the chair of our visiting team announced during our 2018 exit accreditation interview that the team had *zero* recommendations for compliance and *zero* recommendations for improvement for our institution, Guam Community College, an audible gasp in the entire multipurpose auditorium was immediate and palpable. Though it was music to everyone's ears, it took a while for this announcement to sink in. Then a few seconds later, in a long and sustained applause, the entire hall erupted in wild jubilation. How we arrived at this point and why we received this commendation, through well-grounded assessment processes deeply entrenched at the college, is the subject of this chapter. We will link this success to the use of our strategic planning process as a tool to mobilize and harness human capital to invest in a collective undertaking that has led to the transformation of the institution through a "students first, mission always" value system. We will share how the institution's grounding in island culture tapped and capitalized on cultural strengths and foundations, such as the cultural significance of the *latte stone*, an iconic symbol of the resiliency of the CHamoru people, the indigenous inhabitants of Guam.

Assessment Goal: Strategic Planning as a Thoughtful and Intentional Activity

For the past 43 years, the Guam Community College (GCC) has served our island as the premiere institution for workforce training and development, responding to the critical workforce needs of the economy. Because of its strategic location, Guam is considered the American gateway to Asia and the Pacific Rim. As such, Asian investors have access to U.S. investment and related banking, financial, legal, and dispute resolution services. As a U.S. territory, Guam also provides accessibility for students in the region to U.S. accredited educational institutions, such as GCC. As the only community college on an island of 159,538 people (U.S. Census Bureau, 2010), the core of GCC's mission is to provide the "highest quality, student-centered, education and job training for Micronesia" (Guam Community College, n.d., para. 1).

At GCC, the mission statement serves as the cornerstone in the institutional planning process. Not only does it articulate the college's primary purpose for existence and sets the tone for the organization, this statement also communicates, to internal and external audiences, the college's essential aims (e.g., student learning, and the focus of its effort to aid in the cultural, economic and intellectual development of its service area). The ultimate reason why mission statements are developed is to provide, in writing, not only the *raison d'etre* of the institution but to engage stakeholders in fulfilling it.

Maintaining a systematic and consistent process, three strategic planning cycles have unfolded at the college encompassing the years 2009–2014, 2014–2020, and the most recent, 2020–2026. The process is iterative, with the most recent strategic plan building upon the prior years. The resulting strategic plan document has become the most concrete artifact with which all assessment activities at the college—at the course, program, administrative, student services unit, and institutional levels—are grounded, implemented, and deemed useful and meaningful. The systematic assessment of the entire strategic planning process itself has shaped the practice of planning as a thoughtful and intentional activity at the college. This strategy is the overarching assessment goal in all three cycles of planning that have occurred at GCC. How have we been able to achieve this through more than a decade of systematic strategic planning at the college? The planning processes GCC employed can be described as follows:

- GCC's annual planning cycle integrates priorities and key initiatives articulated in the college's institutional strategic master plan, which essentially integrates the individual plans developed by various departments and units.
- The physical master plan serves to address the expected growth of campus facilities, classrooms, and parking due to enrollment estimates and environmental factors.
- The strategic resource plan sets forth a framework for the board of trustees and the college administration to examine future implications

of major financial decisions. The annual budget is partially based on each department's need, which is justified through using a data-driven dedicated planning process (3DP). The 3DP framework links every aspect of the institution's operations and services to assessment, based on which all decisions and actions are made. This particular plan bridges strategic planning, budgeting, and planning for institutional growth needs with program review, assessment, and the self-study process. The college's business office reviews and incorporates requests into the college's annual budget request. The board of trustees reviews and approves the final budget. The purpose of the strategic resource plan is to identify baseline data, evaluate, and establish financial and other resource priorities that the board of trustees and the college administration should plan for and address.

- The distance education strategic plan guides the college in its distance education efforts. The impact of rapid change in educational technologies and increased need for technological support from the college require continual assessment. The plan takes into consideration the various factors that impact distance education, such as academic planning and technology services that enable the promotion of growth, effectiveness, and efficiency of robust implementation. The distance education plan allows the college to carefully determine resources needed to provide access to students.
- The comprehensive professional development plan covers the professional development needs of all the important sectors of the college, from faculty to staff to administrators. A section is also devoted to the professional development of adjunct faculty. This plan provides a distinct focus in which professional development is implemented with the central goals of improving instructional practices and increasing the delivery of services to our students. Institutional priorities for professional development consist of organizational and academic priorities.
- The GCC marketing plan outlines the college's marketing goals in order to elevate GCC to new levels of engagement with regard to career and technical education and workforce development, on local, regional, national, and international levels. The various components of the marketing plan are designed to highlight and promote GCC programs, technology, facilities, and most importantly, student/graduate successes.
- The comprehensive assessment of instructional programs, student services, administrative units, and the board of trustees provides the direction for systematic and consistent evaluation of all programs,

units, and departments of the college on a regularly scheduled cycle. Two assessment deadlines occur each year: one in March and another in October. It is this plan, in existence since 2001, which has made assessment almost like a "second skin" to all GCC constituents through the years. The gradual transition from manual to electronic processes (i.e., the early adoption of electronic data management software that has remained to this day) has surely contributed greatly to this institutional mindset.

Activities/Strategies to Support Achievement of Assessment Goal

At GCC, the employees primarily responsible for delivering education and job training are the faculty, both instructional and noninstructional. The administration and faculty recognize this, and thus the faculty evaluation rubric was derived and developed to reflect all the institutional strategic master plan goals. The college's full-time faculty, adjunct faculty, administrators, and staff are evaluated at stated intervals through a systematic formal written process. All evaluation processes are designed to encourage improvement by giving faculty, staff, and administrators meaningful feedback on the established criteria of the positions they hold. The faculty evaluation process is tied to the institutional strategic master plan goals to ensure institutional effectiveness and improvement. Additionally, the evaluation rubric that is used offers examples of the types of tasks and activities that the college recognizes as necessary in its drive toward maintaining and increasing effectiveness, thus encouraging improvement in specific ways.

All instructional faculty, according to faculty job specifications in the board–union agreement, are tasked with participating in the institutional assessment process and utilizing the results to improve teaching and learning. College employees directly involved in the instructional process use Nuventive's Improve assessment management system for the analysis and evaluation of actual assessment results to determine if the desired student learning outcomes are being met. The assessment system also shows budgetary implications for the maintenance or improvement of teaching and learning. Faculty identify one or more student learning outcomes (SLOs) for a particular course, and then follow the established assessment cycle schedule, which includes uploading evidence to gauge whether or not the SLO is being met. After SLO results have been entered and student work has been uploaded, the faculty member must record how the results will be used for improvement. According to GCC's vice president for academic affairs:

We can monitor annual progress of individual programs or services through the stages of planning, data collection, reporting, and implementation of results. We are thus able to document incremental improvements that programs or units have put into practice over time, and most importantly, the impact of these improvements in sustaining student learning and achievement at the college. (Somera, 2005, p. 2)

As part of the evaluation, faculty include a narrative for each institutional strategic master plan goal in which they can describe ways that they have used the results of the students' assessment of learning outcomes to improve teaching and learning. Quality of teaching is assured by requiring a prescribed evaluation process administered at regular intervals and in a formal written process. The criteria related to classroom teaching are clearly delineated and emphasized in the documentation that accompanies the evaluation process. The college evaluates its faculty by using classroom observation and key indicators grouped in the goals of the institutional strategic master plan. The key indicators or elements in the evaluation process include the effectiveness of instructional delivery, content expertise, course management, institutional assessment, professional development/scholarly activity/creative endeavors, enrollment management, and institutional involvement. Additionally, part of the performance expectation is the ability of the instructor to demonstrate superior knowledge of current teaching methodologies and apply them in ways that stimulate independent learning in the students. This process involves creativity in building the lesson and utilizing previous lessons to heighten students' learning of the material in a well-organized manner. Student learning outcomes play a huge part in the college's institutional planning, resource allocation, and decision-making processes.

GCC maintains its physical resources to enhance and support student learning programs and services. Physical resource planning is integrated with institutional planning. The planning process for GCC's physical resources in support of its programs and services has evolved from an informal to a formal process. The collaborative informal process includes brainstorming sessions to assess need and sustainability. An announcement for capital improvement projects is posted online as well as at the department chairpersons' meeting to give faculty and other personnel an opportunity to provide feedback in addition to the regular budgetary process to submit projects. Capital improvement projects are compiled and presented to the resources, planning, and facilities committee, which gives priority to critical projects addressing the health or safety of those who learn and work at GCC. The priority list is then forwarded to the college governing council for consideration. Approved projects are presented to the president and the board for funding consideration. Funding for additional facilities to meet future workforce development needs are also relentlessly pursued from federal and local government sources. GCC continues to cultivate its partnerships with industry leaders and seeks funding through joint ventures or cooperative arrangements. These funding avenues are necessary in order to complete the myriad projects needed to enable the college to accommodate the anticipated needs of the community and the dynamic workforce requirements of the island.

Based on the results of the assessment, projects are proposed and submitted to fulfill the needs of the instructional programs. Examples of the college's response to results of the assessment and planning processes are the conceptualization, design, and construction of the Anthony A. Leon Guerrero Allied Health Building that houses GCC's practical nursing and medical assisting programs, and the inclusion of science laboratory classroom within the building. Guided by these plans, construction and maintenance of capital projects, such as the Learning Resource Center, the Student Center, the Foundation Building, and the renovation of Buildings 100 and 200, further supports GCC's students, programs, and mission.

The physical master plan allows the college to monitor student population and program expansion, and to make facility adjustments where needed. Having experienced a nearly 20% surge in student population since the implementation of the first institutional strategic master plan, GCC had, with its latest plan (2014–2020), established initiatives to further upgrade the physical campus and plan for additional growth. When the economy spikes, a corresponding decrease in student enrollment is typically seen. Therefore, with the 2020–2026 institutional strategic master plan, the college is addressing a slow but steady decline in student enrollment through the adoption of various programs, such as boot camps and preapprenticeship programs, to continue to address the needs of the community and industry partners in line with the GCC mission.

Resources are allocated according to guidelines for prioritization. Each department or unit's assessment of financial needs is one basis for budgeting. Additionally, the list of institutional priorities and stipulations in the master plan serves as a guide for the channeling of funds. All departments' budget requests are justified utilizing the performance budgeting process. GCC's financial planning involves stakeholders at all levels. Budget input is made at the department level and reviewed by the department's respective department chair. Once compiled, the college's overall budget request is reviewed by the resource, planning, and facilities committee and then the college governing council for comments and recommendation. Faculty, staff, students, and administrators have representation on both the resource, planning, and facilities committee and the college governing council. The board of trustees serves as the last and final review and approval in the college's annual budget process and has oversight in determination of the college's financial needs. Quarterly and annual financial reports are posted on the GCC website under "Public Reports," and the college undergoes an annual audit by an independent auditor. Allocation of resources is guided by the institutional priorities list, the master plan, and an established protocol to determine prioritization of funding among the different departments and units. Management and the board of trustees hold monthly meetings to discuss the college's financial position. Based on the status of the financial position, instructional expenditures, health, and safety issues are given priority to ensure minimal class disruptions. Other expenditures are then addressed in order of need. A thorough scrutiny of the proposed expenditure for capital improvement projects is among the effective practices that safeguard institutional security with regard to monetary resources.

Financial planning and management of resources are consistent with GCC's annual planning cycle that is guided by the strategic resource plan, the institutional strategic master plan, program and course assessment plans, and program reviews. As part of the annual fiscal planning process, GCC reviews its institutional mission and department goals. Each fiscal year, all departments must indicate: (a) between three to five goals and objectives, (b) performance indicators, and (c) proposed outcomes for each of these goals. For departments with multiple degree programs, the three requirements must be linked to each individual program. The goals, objectives, performance indicators, and proposed outcomes are used to assess departmental budget requests for the current fiscal year and in the future. GCC has documented guidelines for budget preparation that are clearly linked to both short-and long-range plans. Current and future budget requests must be justified. Growth budget is accepted with the approval of the deans and the vice president for finance and administration and is required to be linked to the assessments documented in the assessment management system.

One of the most important components of GCC's financial planning is program review. Assessment ties in directly with growth budget requests. In accordance with prudent financial management, GCC's management team reviews and discusses local and national economic conditions that may impact the financial standing of the local government. These initiatives of the management team are essential because the college's budget appropriation is affected by developments in the island's economy. With the reviews and discussions, the college is proactive in terms of foreseeing economic scenarios and adjusting according to financial imperatives. In these efforts to be fiscally responsible and stable, GCC is determined to deliver quality education and training in order to fulfill its vision and mission.

The office of the president encourages innovation of student-focused success through the president's Innovative Ideas Program. This program supports the master plan goal 1: retention and completion by encouraging college personnel to develop strategies that address developmental education and skills gaps, completion challenges, as well as pathways to improve college readiness, and increase completion and success rates of students with developmental education issues. Additionally, the office of the vice president for academic affairs developed the Small Assessment Grant Award, which supports the master plan goal 2: conducive learning environment; goal 3: improvement and accountability; and goal 4: visibility and engagement. The Small Assessment Grant Award provides funding support for departments and faculty to develop and improve course assessment, enhance student learning outcomes, and serves as an incentive to those willing to engage in small research projects. Examples of these awards include the dual enrollment accelerated learning program and the dual credit articulated program of study for secondary students. The dual enrollment program agreement with public and private schools on Guam allows eligible high school juniors and seniors to simultaneously earn college credit for math and English courses. The dual credit program allows students completing GCC trades and technical courses in the public high schools to earn college credit. College credits awarded range from six to 15 credits across various career and technical education programs, thus streamlining the postsecondary process and reducing college completion time. The development of these programs supports the college's 2014–2020 institutional strategic master plan goals of strengthening and improving student success and course improvement through visibility and engagement. Since the inception of the dual credit articulated program of study, there has been a steady increase of high school graduates enrolling in college courses, and this information is disseminated to stakeholders through the Small Assessment Grant Awards reports and the college's fact books.

Assessments Utilized

The college has used a variety of assessment tools such as the Student Ratings of Instruction Survey, the President's Performance Appraisal Survey, the Institutional Effectiveness Survey, Strategic Planning Survey, the Board of Trustees and Foundation Board of Governors Survey, and other similar surveys to gather and report statistics related to key components of the institution and provide analysis and meaningful recommendations for data-driven improvement. This information is supplemented by qualitative data gathered through student focus groups, town hall meetings, key informant interviews, and document review, as well as breakout session reports presented during college assemblies that are conducted every semester.

Since the creation of the Office of Assessment, Institutional Effectiveness, and Research in 2004, it has published an annual institutional assessment report, better known as AIAR. These reports are published online at the GCC website, with hard copies made available at the AIER office. These documents are produced by AIER to develop and sustain assessment momentum on campus through capacity-building efforts that empower college constituents to use data as evidence for accountability and improvement. These annually reports from the AIER office have grown more substantive and complex through the years. The data reported have demonstrated how assessment has become an integral part of the college's daily activities and have provided crucial evidence of the impact of assessment on learning outcomes, institutional reflection, planning, and decision-making processes.

Under her leadership and direction, the president guides the college community through the comprehensive strategic planning process in setting institutional goals and priorities linked to data-driven evidence. The president is responsible for the financial and overall management of local and federal resources to ensure that all funds are managed with the highest level of accountability, including accountability of financial resources in accordance with federal requirements as directed by Board of Trustees Policy 200. Since the beginning of her tenure, the president's strong background in finance and accounting has served as an advantage to GCC. An example is seen in the active pursuit of local and federal funding sources to meet the college's needs, including various federal grants to allow for the construction and refurbishment of the college campus environment, which is vital to student learning and success. The efforts are evident in the awarding of millions in dollars of federal grants and contracts from the United States Department of the Interior, United States Department of Education, Federal Emergency Management Agency, and low-interest loans from the United States Department of Agriculture. The president's critical responsibility is to uphold and safeguard the quality of the institution for student-centered success by selecting personnel who meet professional, educational, industry, and administrative standards. Furthermore, in alignment with the comprehensive professional development plan and Board Policy 400, the president supports and ensures the availability of funding for the administration of the professional development review committee activities for employee professional development and personnel training. In addition, the president has integrated professional development training sessions for employees as part of the agenda during annual college assemblies. The president emphasizes the importance of how our data-driven planning process directly ties in assessment to planning, decision-making, as well as human, and financial resource needs of the college.

The president uses various avenues to communicate college effectiveness to the community, students, staff, faculty, and administrators. The president conducts a 2-day "Meet the President" event with students every semester to communicate the college's goals, discuss the college's sustainability, campus improvements, current issues, and other significant activities to improve GCC's institutional effectiveness. Following her presentation, the president welcomes the students to ask questions or raise their concerns. The steady increase in the number of event attendees verifies it has become a popular avenue for students to communicate directly with the president.

The president communicates institutional values, goals, and college updates to staff, faculty, and administrators at yearly convocations and college assemblies. At these assemblies, the president discusses college enrollment; provides financial updates, planning, and campus developments; and provides various training sessions for employees' professional development. In addition, the president communicates through, and participates in, the governance process as set forth under the participatory governance structure. The president communicates to external stakeholders via statements titled "President's Message" in various college documents such as the introduction in the institutional strategic master plan, annual reports, and college catalogs. These avenues allow leadership to communicate the achievement of master plan goals and college successes.

The president regularly communicates to the board, at its monthly meetings, the college's financial status, capital improvement projects, changes to local and federal rules and regulations, operational procedure changes, and policy updates. In line with the mission, the president's assessment plan includes collaborative efforts to measure progress toward achieving the institutional strategic master plan goals. The president, through designation from the board of trustees, is responsible for the overall management of the operations and finances of the college. She oversees the college's finances and operations through effective leadership and guidance in institutional planning, documentation and updates of processes, collection of data, and decision-making processes in alignment with GCC's mission. She maintains leadership by making sure the campus facilities are maintained, and that improvements are aligned with strategic plans, such as the physical master plan and the institutional strategic master plan. GCC continues to be a role model for the community in adherence to statutes, regulations, and policies. The president has gained the trust of grantees for multiple federal grants and

GCC compliance is exemplified in the maintenance of 18 consecutive years of designation as a "low risk" auditee, based on the most recent financial audit (GCC, 2019, pp. 28–29).

Use of Findings

According to Astin et al. (2001),

> In considering the nature and extent of change that is typically needed to transform the most basic dimensions of institutional functioning, it becomes apparent that the institution's capacity for self-assessment can be of key importance in planning, initiating, sustaining, and evaluating transformation efforts. (p. 60)

This has been the most important lesson learned and insight gained in shaping, improving, and strengthening our institution through the ways we have utilized our strategic planning process as a guide to evaluate our mission and how we have remained steadfast in its accomplishment.

One tangible result of the assessment of our strategic planning process is the realization of "revisioning" our college, and positioning it for innovation, in the same manner advocated by Sydow and Alfred (2013). Hence, the transformation initiative at the college was born, with the primary aim of discovering areas of underperformance and therefore opportunities for improvement. The evidence for this initiative stemmed from a critical analysis of our strategic planning process as a participatory governance activity. Based on quantitative and qualitative data gathered mostly through college assemblies each semester, we realized that we needed a collective reflection of our strengths and weaknesses as an institution, and documentation of what specific strategies we can pursue to turn these into opportunities for institutional effectiveness. Beginning in fall 2015, the transformation initiative was introduced to the campus community with a Breakfast of Champions, the first cohort of employees who voluntarily accepted the transformation vision of GCC, which indicated Guam Community College is engaged in transformation to ensure 100% student-centered success. Thereafter, two cohorts of faculty, administrators, and staff completed the 40-hour Transformation Leadership Academy during which participants were challenged to develop a "transformation mindset" and to develop critical skills for leading transformational change. The transformation initiative was an effort to engage faculty, staff, and administrators in guiding GCC's organizational change process leading toward institutional revitalization. The primary focus was on continually identifying areas of improvement and overcoming barriers to serving students as effectively as possible.

On June 15, 2018, GCC was awarded a full 7-year accreditation for the period 2019–2025—the longest period possible for a community college by the Accrediting Commission for Community and Junior Colleges, under the umbrella of the Western Association of Schools and Colleges. This award presented an ideal opportunity to align the strategic planning process with the newly awarded accreditation period. Hence, planning commenced for a new 7-year institutional strategic master plan. Consultant partners for GCC's ongoing transformational journey were engaged to facilitate the planning process using the transformation framework of cocreative participation of all stakeholders. This homegrown organic approach sought to harvest the contributions of leaders and managers, support staff, faculty, students, and industry partners in envisioning the way ahead for the entire institution.

Numerous meetings with stakeholder groups throughout the fall of 2018 and spring of 2019 yielded an abundance of ideas that were shaped into goals and objectives. This foundation was meant to guide the development of annual initiatives and activities that programs, departments, and units within the GCC community would plan and implement for the next 7 years. Planning meetings included extensive engagement by a core team comprising representatives from all the stakeholder groups. The core team met regularly to refine the feedback collected from the comprehensive discussions with the 2018 college assembly, industry partners forum, and with student leaders representing all the student-based organizations on campus. The feedback was then used to inform the way ahead.

The formal planning process was kicked-off on August 13, 2018, during the 2018 fall convocation: *Beyond Accreditation: Strategic Thinking for 2025*. Brainstorming sessions on goal formation followed on October 9 and October 30, 2018, with key leaders of the college. On November 6, 2018, during the 2018 fall college assembly with the theme *Envisioning GCC's Future by Design*, locally based consultants Souder and Betances conducted a critical part of the planning activity entitled *Imagining GCC in 2026: Planning Framework and Thematic Categories*. Small groups of administrators, faculty and staff engaged in intensive brainstorming related to developing objective statements for the following goals:

- Goal 1: Advancing Workforce Development and Training
- Goal 2: Fostering 100% Student-Centered Success
- Goal 3: Leveraging Transformational Engagement and Training
- Goal 4: Optimizing Resources
- Goal 5: Modernizing and Expanding Infrastructure and technology

The core team reconvened after the 2018 college assembly to organize and integrate the feedback received. The student focus groups held on December 14, 2018, and January 18, 2019, and the industry partners' forum on January 24, 2019, completed the brainstorming activities designed to maximize the gathering of input from stakeholders. The resulting final planning document reflects the voices and contributions of all who participated in the crucial process of strategic thinking and planning for our college.

Synthesis

In Guam, *latte stones* are considered iconic. In ancient CHamoru history, they served as the foundations of houses. According to Farrell (2011), latte stones are composed of two parts. There are vertical pillars (*haligi*) placed about 6 feet apart and put in two parallel rows. Each pillar supported a cupstone (*tasa*) which was in the shape of a hemisphere. Ancient CHamorus built their houses on top of these two-part latte stones.

We have always considered our strategic planning process an integral part of our institutional culture. At GCC, our practice of looking inward and evaluating which aspects of institutional culture and identity are currently guiding our assessment practices served as a powerful tool for identifying strategies for institutional effectiveness, directing decision-making, priority-setting, and practices for the transformation of our college from within. Indeed, as Keup et al. (2001) have stated, "in many instances, culture unconsciously serves as a trigger for change on campuses" (p. 47). At our institution, our strategic plans, in their various iterations through the years, have served as our latte stones that have become the firmest foundation of our entire assessment initiative at the college.

As we gear up for the next accreditation team's visit in 2025, we are hopeful that our strong and firm foundation in strategic planning that has led to our institutional transformation will further strengthen our tenacity and resolve to continuously address the unique workforce needs of our island territory.

References

Astin, A. W., Lindholm, J. A., Walker, A. A., & Keup, J. R. (2001). Facilitating transformative change efforts through the use of assessment. In A. W. Astin & H. S. Astin (Eds.), *Transforming institutions: Context and process* (pp. 59–81). Higher Education Research Institute, UCLA.

Farrell, D. A. (2011). *History of the Mariana Islands to partition*. (I. Propst, Ed.). Public School System, Commonwealth of the Northern Mariana Islands.

Guam Community College. (n.d.). *Mission*. https://guamcc.edu/mission

Guam Community College. (2019). *Focused on the Future: 2018-2019 Annual Report*. https://guamcc.edu/sites/default/files/annual_report_18-19_electronic.pdf

Keup, J. R., Astin, H. S., Lindholm, J. A., & Walker, A. A. (2001). Organizational culture and institutional transformation. In A. W. Astin & H. S. Astin (Eds.), *Transforming institutions: Context and process* (pp. 21–58). Higher Education Research Institute, UCLA.

Somera, R. R. D. (2005). *Guam Community College depends on Trac Dat for a rich harvest of evidence for accountability and improvement*. http://ifs.guamcc.edu/adminftp/academics/services/aad/aier/2018iser/mailed/EVIDENCE%20FOR%20ISER/Standard%20III/296_tracdatcasestudy.pdf

Sydow, D., & Alfred, R. (2013). *Re-visioning community colleges: Positioning for innovation*. Rowman & Littlefield.

U.S. Census Bureau. (2010). *Census of demographic characteristics: Guam demographic profile*. https://www.census.gov/newsroom/releases/archives/2010_census/cb11-cn179.html

19

BEING SAGE ABOUT INSTITUTIONAL EFFECTIVENESS

Elisa Hertz

Guttman Community College defines *institutional effectiveness* as the integration of planning, assessment, and resource allocation in support of the college's mission and goals. The college's institutional effectiveness framework is known as the Systematic Approach for Guttman Effectiveness (SAGE). SAGE promotes a culture of planning and assessment by: (a) creating a foundation for a useful, user-friendly, uniform process for documenting plans, evidence, resource needs, and ideas for improvements, (b) linking unit-level information with institutional-level priorities to study collective progress toward the college's mission and goals, and (c) engaging participants in collaborative and interactive professional development.

An evaluation team representing the Middle States Commission on Higher Education recognized the value of SAGE. The team stated:

> The college is commended for the development and use of SAGE to guide planning and assessment. . . . Through the use of SAGE, the college is able to effectively document the linkages between planning and established goals and standards, current and planned activities, sufficiency of resources, assessments, and reflection to support evidence-based decision-making, and problem solving resulting in continuous improvement. (Stout et al., 2017, p. 8)

Goal of the Assessment

The purpose of SAGE is to answer the question "How well are we collectively meeting our goals?" This question can be clarified as follows:

- "How well" refers to the quality, efficiency, cost effectiveness, and/or impact of annual practices related to specific activities, operations, services, learning opportunities, student learning outcomes, and/or policy initiatives.
- "Collectively" refers to participation by all college units, including academic programs, administrative departments, student support offices, and some committees.
- "Our goals" refer to unit-level goals, divisional goals, and institutional-level goals in support of the college mission.

These points reinforce that the purpose of SAGE and institutional effectiveness is about people and progress, not perfection. Planning and assessment are not about being perfect. They are not about a perfect template or software package. They are not about 100% participation. They are not about meeting objectives 100% of the time. They are about getting started, engaging people in the process, and making progress. The SAGE template has evolved through different versions. SAGE participants have different skill levels. Units' SAGE profiles show different levels of quality and completion. Over time, we adapt. Over time, we advance. Over time, we progress.

Strategies to Support Achievement of the Goal

Guttman's Center for College Effectiveness uses three primary strategies to sustain a SAGE culture of planning and assessment, as summarized in Table 19.1. The center leads work related to institutional effectiveness, strategic planning, institutional research, data dashboards, and college-wide surveys. The center's staff has ranged from one to three people.

Strategy 1: Create a Useful, User-Friendly, Uniform Process for Documenting Plans, Evidence, Resource Needs, and Ideas for Improvements

SAGE, like most institutional effectiveness and assessment frameworks, relies on a standard template and an annual reporting calendar. Supplementing these methods with a set of SAGE mini-guides with concise explanations and concrete examples increases participants' levels of understanding about the process, increases the quality of units' SAGE submissions, and minimizes the amount of individual support that a small office needs to provide.

TABLE 19.1
Strategies to Advance Institutional Effectiveness Initiatives

Strategies	Methods
1. Create a useful, user-friendly, uniform process for documenting plans, evidence, resource needs, and ideas for improvements.	a. Develop template b. Set integrated schedule c. Share examples
2. Link unit-level information with institutional level priorities to study collective progress toward the college's mission and goals.	a. Streamline with alignment b. Synthesize emergent themes c. Collaborate with business office
3. Engage participants in collaborative and interactive professional development.	a. Be creative b. Show appreciation c. Learn from feedback

Develop Template

The SAGE profile is a uniform template completed annually by each unit. To ensure it is useful and user-friendly, it has evolved over time based on feedback from participants. It started as a four-page Word template, then was streamlined to a one-page Word template, and is now in a homegrown electronic format. There are three parts of the SAGE profile: planning, inquiry, and insight.

For the planning part, each unit identifies big picture goals, describes specific practices to achieve the goals, and aligns practices to institutional priorities. For the inquiry part, each unit frames assessment questions about its practices, identifies target outcomes, selects data sources and assessment methods, and reports actual outcomes and target ratings. For the insight part, each unit documents reflections about accomplishments, challenges, resource needs, and ideas for improvements. Figure 19.1 shows the key elements of the profile with definitions for each item.

Set Integrated Schedule

The annual schedule takes into consideration the college's academic calendar and budget calendar. It reinforces participants' roles through the different stages of the SAGE completion cycle. The midyear review is the critical time when units (a) study progress toward current year practices and (b) start planning and budgeting for the next academic year. The annual cycle concludes with participants recording evidence-based reflections. By the next academic year, participants restart the cycle with new or refined practices. The integrated calendar emphasizes the cyclical connections among planning, assessment, and resources. Figure 19.2 shows the annual SAGE cycle.

Figure 19.1. Elements of the SAGE profile.

Planning
Goal #
Big picture outcome that unit strives to achieve in support of the college mission.
Practice #1
Specific and meaningful details about activities, operations, services, learning tt opportunities/outcomes, or policy initiative to advance big picture goals. Practices are not tasks on a to-do list. They are substantial enough to assess.
Alignments
Strong, obvious, direct link(s) between specific unit practice and other college priorities, such as strategic plan goals, divisional goals, accreditation standards, and/or student learning outcomes.
Inquiry
Assessment Question #1
What a unit wants to learn about a practice's effectiveness (i.e., quality, efficiency, cost effectiveness, completion, and/or impact). Multiple assessment questions may be associated with a practice. Avoid yes/no questions.
Target outcome #1
Ideal answer to the assessment question and idea level of performance a unit strives to achieve. Multiple target outcomes may be associated with an assessment question.
Data Sources/Assessment Methods
Approach(es) used to answer the assessment question and study progress toward the target outcome (i.e., quantitative and/or qualitative data sources, direct or indirect assessment methods)
Actual outcome
Real answer to assessment question.
Target Rating
Indicator of how close the actual outcome is to the original target outcome. *Did Not Meet Expectations	Partially Met Expectations	Met Expectations	Exceeded Expectations*
Insight
Accomplishments
Evidence-based reflection about what went well with the practice.
Challenges
Evidence-based reflection about what issues arose with the practice.
Ideas for improvement
Plan to enhance the practice.
Resource needs
Budget, supplies, staff, technology, or space needed for the practice.
Overall practice performance rating
Indicator that summarizes performance across all targets and reflections. *Not Effective	Somewhat Effective	Effective	Very Effective*
Improved Practice for Next Year's Profile
Refined description of practice or new practice for the next year.

Share Examples

To sustain quality and consistency across different units' SAGE profiles, the assistant dean of institutional effectiveness and strategic planning created a set of mini-guides as a practical reference for participants of all experience levels. It uses nontechnical language to describe each element and provide examples. Each page features one SAGE element, an explanation, and examples. The guide is used during professional development activities and is

Figure 19.2 Annual SAGE cycle.

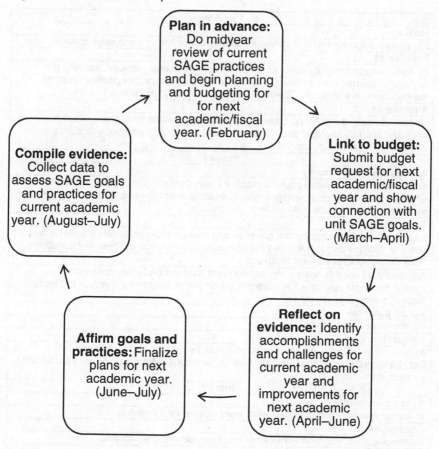

distributed for participants' independent use. Figure 19.3 shows an example from the mini-guide for developing goals, specific to the SAGE definition.

Strategy 2. Link Unit-Level Information With Institutional-Level Priorities to Study Collective Progress Toward the College's Mission and Goals

By aligning unit SAGE practices to institutional priorities, the same information is used to study strengths and challenges at both the unit level and the college level. This streamlined approach maximizes efficiency and minimizes burdens placed on participants for assessment, planning, and budgeting. The annual *Emergent Themes Report* summarizes college-level progress by synthesizing existing information from unit-level SAGE profiles.

Figure 19.3. Example from SAGE mini-guide.

SAGE Mini-Guide to Developing Goals

Background
- ✓ Goals represent big picture outcomes that your area strives to achieve in support of the college mission.
- ✓ Goals tend to carry over from year to year.
- ✓ Goals may focus on student learning, student support, operational activities, employee culture, and/or policy.
- ✓ Goals are broader than "practices," which are specific activities performed in a given year.

Examples
- Integrate career exploration and professional competencies into the curriculum.
- Support college operations and decision-making by preparing accurate and timely institutional data.
- Sustain strong employee retention.
- Promote employee growth with professional development.
- Promote students' academic growth in 1st-year courses.
- Ensure students meet program learning outcomes.
- Promote students' professional growth.
- Enhance students' leadership skills.
- Ensure fiscal responsibility across the college.
- Ensure college facilities are well maintained.

Streamline With Alignment

SAGE profiles streamline assessment and data collection efforts by aligning unit-level practices with institutional priorities. In this bottom-up approach, participants first set their unit-level SAGE practices. Then, they align their unit practices to other college priorities. Having participants initially focus on their units and the work most. Familiar to them creates a sense of ownership. Then, when a unit practice is aligned with a strategic plan goal, that same information can be used by the unit and in relation to the strategic plan to assess progress.

The value of the alignments is the creation of a series of standard reports, such as "alignment strength" with the number of practices linked to each strategic plan goal, "alignment detail" with a list of practices linked to each strategic plan goal, and "effectiveness summary" with the percentage of effective or very effective rated practices linked to each strategic plan goal. These standard reports are also available for practices aligned to divisional goals or accreditation standards. In the electronic SAGE system, the report creation is automated; prior to the availability of the electronic version, these reports were created manually. The alignments allow units' SAGE profiles to be used for both studying progress toward units' goals and studying collective progress toward the college's mission and goals.

Synthesize Emergent Themes

At the conclusion of the annual SAGE cycle, information from unit SAGE profiles is synthesized into themes and supplemented with feedback from college surveys and findings from data reports. The *Emergent Themes Report* is an annual snapshot that uses existing information to represent "the voice of the college," and identify collective strengths and challenges related to strategic plan goals. The report promotes transparency by summarizing prior year's performance and acting as a foundation for setting priorities for next academic year's plans and budgets. Figure 19.4 illustrates the relationship between the *Emergent Themes Report* and other aspects of the institutional effectiveness process.

Collaborate With Business Office

Since SAGE is an integrated process, it involves collaboration. The budget director and the assistant dean of institutional effectiveness and strategic planning partner to ensure there are intentional links among planning, assessment, and resources. The SAGE profile has a section to document resource needs for each practice, and the business office requires a rationale about how funding supports specific goals. The administrators in budgeting and institutional effectiveness copresent at an annual workshop to communicate the importance of using assessment findings for planning and budgeting.

Strategy 3. Engage Participants in Collaborative and Interactive Professional Development

People work in higher education for many different reasons—to teach, to advise students, to recruit applicants, to manage registration records, to

Figure 19.4. Role of emergent themes.

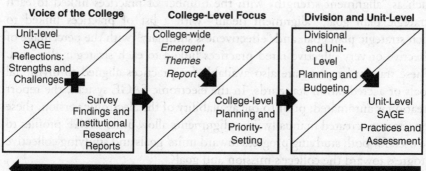

oversee facilities, or to administer budgets. Many colleagues of the assistant dean of institutional effectiveness have primary responsibilities not related to assessment. However, this type of work has become everyone's responsibility. Therefore, it is that assistant dean's role to create a community of practice by making the SAGE process engaging, showing appreciation, and being receptive to feedback.

Be Creative
SAGE depends on participants dedicating time and energy to complete the annual profile and to attend professional development sessions. Commitment to the process is increased by acknowledging that participants do not need to be assessment experts and by designing interesting professional development sessions to support their work. Examples of creative workshop strategies include the following:

Interactive questions. To encourage active learning, survey software is used to create pre/posttests about a workshop topic. In this anonymous forum, participants feel more comfortable answering questions. For example, in a workshop about writing assessment questions, participants electronically select which questions they think are well written. After the initial submissions, pretest results are shown. Then, a brief presentation relates the relevant information. Afterward, participants answer the same questions again, so they can apply what they just learned. Finally, the posttest results are shown so changes can be seen. This electronic method not only engages participants, it provides useful data about how well the workshop meets its learning objectives.

Peer reviews. To foster collaboration, the assistant dean of institutional effectiveness developed a series of rubrics to assess the quality of SAGE profiles. During workshops, participants use the rubric to self-review their SAGE profile. Then, a colleague uses the rubric to peer-review the same SAGE profile. Finally, they compare ratings and discuss what was well done and what needs improvement. The peer review partnerships expand opportunities for participants to get and give feedback and to become more familiar with the expectations outlined in the rubrics.

Speed data-ing. To focus on "closing the loop," participants go on 10-minute "dates" to explain a challenge in their SAGE profile, obtain advice from their date, and brainstorm a plan for improvement. When the buzzer rings, partners switch, and repeat the steps. This method infuses the workshop with energy, as participants move around. It works best with participants who typically do not work together and can offer different perspectives.

SAGE makeovers. Participants are asked to be SAGE makeover contestants to provide peer examples. In advance of the workshop, SAGE profiles are reviewed and elements are refined. Prepared before-and-after slides are presented by participants at the workshop as model examples. This approach reinforces peer-to-peer learning and that participants do not need to be assessment experts to do quality work.

Show Appreciation
Participants' contributions deserve recognition. To show their work is valued, certificates are awarded upon completion of SAGE fundamentals and SAGE advanced workshops. Ongoing participants are awarded customized licenses with ID card photos and reminders about the stages of SAGE or key deadlines. After a few years, participants continue to display their certificates and licenses, like "License to SAGE," "SAGE Jedi," and "SAGE Wizard," by their desks. These are low-cost and well-received ways to recognize participants.

Learn From Feedback
After each SAGE professional development session, the assistant dean of institutional effectiveness collects feedback from participants to assess the workshop's effectiveness. An electronic form or a paper quarter-sheet for "instant input" is completed in the last 5 minutes of the session. Participants answer three questions:

1. One thing I learned.
2. One thing I'd suggest or like to learn more about.
3. My overall impression was . . . (with a 5-point scale from very negative to very positive).

In fact, the idea for mini-guides came from positive instant input about a workshop handout. Other instant input recognized the strength of the SAGE process. One participant stated, "It dawned on me how purposeful it feels to do assessment/planning with colleagues led by peers." Another participant expressed, "The structure of SAGE is organized *and* open enough to support the process it's designed to. Feel that we are effective brainstormers and assessors during our SAGE sessions."

Assessments Used to Determine Progress Toward Goal: What Assessment Methods Contribute to Institutional Effectiveness Initiatives?

SAGE contributes to assessment at the unit level and institutional level. The institutional-level assessment builds on the unit-level assessments. Since SAGE units include academic programs, administrative departments, student support offices, and some committees, multiple assessment methods are used. In the inquiry part of SAGE, participants identify assessment and questions, target outcomes, data sources/assessment methods, and actual outcomes for each practice.

The foundation of the assessment section is a well-written assessment question that focuses on a range of quality, rather than yes/no answers. For example:

- Learning outcomes: To what extent do students meet or exceed the rubric expectations?
- Participation: How strong is attendance at the activity/workshop/event?
- Quality: How satisfied are participants with the service/activity/workshop/event?
- Operations: How cost effective is the service/activity/workshop/event?
- Trends: To what extent have results changed over time?

Participants' assessment methods vary depending on their defined questions. For example:

- Units that engage in teaching and learning focus on direct assessment of student work by reviewing assignments with rubrics.
- Units that host events focus on assessing levels of participation with ID card swipes and satisfaction with surveys.
- Units that provide operational services focus on assessing efficiency by studying number of individuals served, cost per individual, and time to completion.

Then, at the end of the cycle, units compare their target outcome and actual outcome to assign a rating about the extent to which they met expectations.

At the institutional level, the *Emergent Themes Report* synthesizes information from all unit SAGE profiles into a high-level summary of strengths and challenges that assesses collective progress toward the college's mission and goals. The annual *Emergent Themes Report* is a summative assessment for each year and a formative assessment toward achieving multiyear strategic plan goals. Figure 19.5 shows an excerpt from the *Emergent Themes Report*.

Use of the Findings

Findings documented through SAGE answer the question, "How are we collectively meeting our goals?" Findings are used in three ways.

1. At the unit level, participants summarize their findings as accomplishments, challenges, resource needs, and areas for improvement on an annual basis. Based on these findings, participants select an overall effectiveness rating for their practice. Then, they complete the final step of the SAGE profile by recording an "improved practice for next year's plan," which "closes the loop" between the current year's findings and an identified improvement for the future.
2. At the institutional level, the *Emergent Themes Report* presents an annual summary of patterns that emerge across units' SAGE findings. These collective strengths and challenges are shared with the college community and used as the basis for annual priority setting and improvements. First, senior staff and the strategic planning and budget committee review the *Emergent Themes Report* to set priorities. Then, the findings are presented at an all-college meeting or a college assessment day, where faculty and staff work in thematic breakout groups to identify what we are already doing to address challenges and what we could do in the future. Then, divisions and units consider which action items to implement in their following year's plans and budgets.
3. For long-term planning, a review of multiple *Emergent Themes Reports* shows progress over time. It shows which strengths persisted, which challenges were overcome, and which issues remained. The collection of reports shows the college's commitment to its mission and goals for the strategic plan's lifespan. It also provides information for the development of the next strategic plan.

Figure 19.5. *Emergent Themes Report* excerpt.

EMERGENT THEMES FOR GUTTMAN PLANNING

STRATEGIC PLAN GOAL 1. IMPROVE THE EDUCATIONAL MODEL
GCC will deliver, assess, improve, and plan to scale its integrative educational model to serve all students with equity—especially those traditionally underserved in higher education—by engaging them through curricular, cocurricular, and extracurricular opportunities to learn, serve, and grow academically and socially.

Overall Strengths	Overall Challenges
✓ Students appreciate support from ✓ Students feel prepared to . . . ✓ Alumni feel prepared to . . .	⊗ Overall student satisfaction shows . . . ⊗ Continuing students feel. . . ⊗ Employees are uncertain about. . .

Conclusion

The top 10 ways for an institution to be SAGE:

1. Focus on progress and people, not perfection.
2. Create a structure with templates and timelines.
3. Provide support with concrete examples, nontechnical language, and creative presentations.
4. Align existing work with institutional priorities.
5. Use unit-level work to learn about institutional-level progress.
6. Form partnerships between institutional effectiveness and business officers.
7. Acknowledge that participants do not need to be assessment experts.
8. Recognize participants' contributions.
9. Use feedback to improve the process.
10. Be patient. Be persistent. Be positive.

Reference

Stout, K., Cruise, D., Railey, C., Anderson, W., Rosero, N., & Casablanca, M. (2017). *Report to the faculty, administration, and student[s] of The Stella and Charles Guttman Community College by a visiting team representing the Middle States Commission on Higher Education* [Unpublished internal report].

20

DO WE HAVE IT? DO WE DO IT? DOES IT WORK?

A Three-Question Framework for Addressing Accreditation Standards and Ensuring Institutional Effectiveness

Dawn L. Hayward, Nancy Ritze, and Rebecca Gullan

As part of the self-study process, the Middle States Commission on Higher Education (MSCHE) expects that colleges and universities demonstrate compliance with each standard for accreditation through a systematic assessment of institutional effectiveness. Applying a simple framework of three questions—"Do we have it?"; "Do we do it?"; "Does it work?"—can provide a powerful and meaningful approach for this otherwise complex task. This chapter describes how utilizing these three questions can help faculty and staff demonstrate compliance with the standards and identify opportunities for improvement, using examples from a 4-year private master's medium university (Gwynedd Mercy University) and a 2-year large public college (Bronx Community College of the City University of New York [CUNY]).

The Three Questions

As part of the 8-year cycle of review for reaffirmation of accreditation, the MSCHE requires the participant universities and colleges to prepare a self-study report that includes a comprehensive and systematic assessment of the overall effectiveness of the institution as related to each of the standards. In addition to identifying areas for targeted improvements and innovation, the central focus of the self-study process is reaffirmation of accreditation. This approval is necessary for institutions to qualify for Title IV funding, without which the majority of students would be unable to finance their education. Self-studies are complex and high-stakes events. Therefore, the process has the potential to overwhelm faculty and staff as they examine every level of the institution, identifying what works well—and what does not—in their search for both accountability and continuous improvement. To help simplify the effort, this chapter describes a three-question framework intended to provide a straightforward line of inquiry for conducting a comprehensive and informative self-study.

The framework suggests that institutions answer the three questions for every standard. Responses to the questions help identify the required supporting evidence and detect critical gaps in policies/plans and processes/procedures, as well as the overall effectiveness of their implementation.

1. *Do we have it?* This first question leads the institution toward the identification of the policies and plans necessary for demonstrating compliance with each standard.
2. *Do we do it?* Once policies and plans are inventoried, answering this second question leads the institution to an audit of the processes and procedures meant to ensure that policies and plans are being implemented.
3. *Does it work?* To answer the third question, institutions reflect on key assessment findings in order to determine whether or not the policies/plans and processes/procedures have been effective in achieving the desired goals of the institution; if they have been implemented with appropriate levels of fidelity and integrity; and whether they have been received as intended.

When gathering evidence for electronic evidence rooms and uploading files to support claims of compliance with accreditation requirements, the tendency is to consider policies/plans and processes/procedures as one conflated whole: focusing on what we have and what we do as if the two were the same. Often, assessments of the plans, policies, and practices have failed to account for the perceptions of the participants (students, employees, and faculty) as to whether all were implemented as intended. However, a self-study process where the institution examines the answers to each question separately can help identify which part(s) don't work, enabling differentiation between the content of policies and plans (what is being done) from processes and procedures (delivery mechanisms). By using a separated, threefold inquiry method, institutions can more readily identify and isolate the individual component that is not working, the precise part that could benefit from revision. Using this method, participants can determine if the appropriate plans are in place or if the necessary policies exist, and whether or not they are clearly expressed or broadly understood. They can identify if the institution has a process and procedure for implementing the plans and policies, and if a person, or committee of persons, has been specifically tasked with this charge. They can conclude if the implementation of the plan/process is operational, including if there are concerns with one component, but not another, with both, or with neither. For example, if policies exist for ensuring inclusivity and diversity across the campus, is there a mechanism for ensuring that the policy has been put into play as intended? Is there a committee charged with the oversight of the implementation for this policy? What assessment evidence provides information on the overall effectiveness of the committee? Finally, what assessment evidence helps the institution ascertain if the policy led to the desired results?

The three-question framework, which opens all of these aspects to both scrutiny and action, is modeled in this chapter using actual examples from two distinctly different institutions, both of which recently completed successful self-study reports and were identified by MSCHE as exemplars of best practices. Gwynedd Mercy University is a private, religiously affiliated, 4-year, nonprofit institution, located in a large suburb 20 miles from Philadelphia, with an undergraduate enrollment of approximately 2,200 students and a graduate enrollment of approximately 800 students. The university's primary academic programs include professional programs in nursing and health professions, biology, education, business, criminal justice, computer science, and psychology. Bronx Community College of CUNY is a large, 2-year institution located in Bronx, New York, with an undergraduate enrollment of approximately 10,000 students.

Goal of the Assessment

While the primary purpose of any accreditation self-study report is to verify that the institution meets standards, the self-study process also supports additional, critically important goals in its assessment of institutional effectiveness including (a) reflecting on the institution's greatest strengths, (b) identifying its most difficult challenges, and (c) planning for improvement.

Activities and Strategies to Support Achievement of the Goal

The initial step in assessing institutional effectiveness is to identify the existing evidence for both plans and policies as well as process and procedures. By asking the first question, "Do we have it?," faculty and staff can begin their wide-ranging inventory of plans and policies. In fact, attempting to respond to the first question leads the members through a kind of scavenger hunt:

- Does the institution have plans that support each standard? What are they? Where are they housed?
- Does the institution have policies that support each standard? What are they and where are they located?

Attempts at answering the second question, "Do we do it?," also involve some skills in sleuthing:

- Which committees or individual(s) has/have been specifically tasked with ensuring the implementation and oversight of the plans/policies?
- Where is the evidence of the competent practice of these committees or individuals?
- Where are the committees' by-laws?
- Is there evidence of effective practice within meeting minutes?

Finally, the last step is for members to ask the most compelling question of all, "Does it work?" Responding to this question requires members of the self-study team to analyze the effectiveness of the institution's plans, policies, and practices, including careful consideration of the perceptions of participants (as reflected in responses to surveys and focus groups) as well as of key findings culled from outcomes data. Through this assessment, institutions can better determine if a plan or policy was ineffective due to poor design, to poor implementation, or to some combination. If the plans are determined to be insufficient, incomplete, or out-of-date, such as a strategic enrollment management plan that does not address the regional changes in student demographics, the response to "does it work?" could include an articulation of next steps, such as: "The plan needs to be updated or revised to reflect changing enrollment patterns." If the policies are determined to have been inconsistently applied, such as an inconsistent process for reviewing applications for students who do not meet the university's admissions criteria, the response to "does it work?" could lead to an identified next step, such as: "The general admissions committee needs to revise its process and procedures to more fully address the student retention data directly related to this policy." In this way, institutions examine the integrity of plans/policies to ensure they have been accurately and effectively conceived, while simultaneously determining the fidelity of their implementation.

As part of a larger system for integrity monitoring, institutions amending the final question from "does it work" to "does it work for *everyone?*" will develop an ability to assess not only whether the plan, policy, or practice was successful, but whether every participant experienced all components as intended (Lakin Gullan et al., 2009; Perepletchikova & Kazdin, 2005). Data collected from perception-indicators provide meaningful sources of information that help institutions pinpoint areas needing improvements and modifications. For example, even if aggregated outcomes at the institution level indicate positive findings, such as professional licensure first-time pass rates that are consistently above national or state averages, the disaggregated results may reveal inequitable differences, such as pass rates of students enrolled in online or accelerated programs that are consistently below standards. Consider, as an additional example, an institution's plans, policies, and practices for tenure and promotion. Even though appropriate plans and policies may exist, and even though evidence exists that the practice and implementation of those plans/policies have been supported through the work of a fully functioning tenure and promotion committee, survey results from female faculty of color may provide compelling evidence that the participants are not experiencing the process as intended. In other words, even if the response to the question of "does it work?" is "yes," it is entirely possible that the full answer—and key finding—may be much more complicated: "Yes, for many *but not for all.*"

Assessments Used to Determine Progress Toward Goal

The three-question framework can help institutions identify where to improve practice and lead to the identification of key findings or areas where members need to know more or do more. That information may lead to the articulation of next steps which are crucial to the institutions' efforts for innovation and continuous improvement.

In each of the following sections, examples from actual findings of Gwynedd Mercy University and Bronx Community College of CUNY are provided in order to demonstrate how answering three simple questions can help institutions precisely identify where action is needed and what type it should be.

Standard I: Mission and Goals—Bronx Community College of CUNY

MSCHE Standard I states, "the institution's mission defines its purpose within the context of higher education, the students it serves, and what it intends to accomplish. The institution's stated goals are clearly linked to its mission and specify how the institution fulfills its mission" (MSCHE, 2015, p. 4).

Do We Have It?
As part of a process related to answering the question "do we have it?" faculty and staff responsible for preparing the self-study at Bronx Community College of CUNY inventoried the existing policies and plans related to its mission and goals, a necessary practice to demonstrate compliance with the standard. The research on policies and plans demonstrated that the college's mission and goals had been widely publicized; understood and embraced across the campus; and used to drive budgeting, planning, and decision-making. The college clearly documented the purposeful alignment of goals, with the department, college, and university goals aligned not only with each other, but with MSCHE accreditation expectations as well. In addition, the recently completed Academic Master Plan provided comprehensive analysis and evidence to inform future directions for academic programming at the college. *Answer: Yes.*

Do We Do It?
Complying with MSCHE standards entails providing evidence that practices, process, and procedures have, in fact, activated the aligned goals, plans, and policies. For this requirement, the college provided documentation of the process and procedures adhered to by members of its committees/councils (e.g., president's cabinet, college senate and senate committees, deans and chairpersons committee, academic assessment committee, and administrative council). Evidence compiled and examined also included the existence of copies of meeting minutes and relevant annual reports (e.g., annual departmental and college assessment and planning reports).

The evidence from these reports and the bylaws/charters of the committees documented the process through which policies and plans are translated into the actions of the institution. For Bronx Community College of CUNY, several of these actions have served as particular points of pride. One of the key findings of the review process was to note that the college's CUNY ASAP (Accelerated Study in Associate Programs) program has become a nationwide example of best practices to improve student success and leveraged by the college community as a catalyst for institutional redesign. *Answer: Yes.*

Does It Work?
To determine the effectiveness of its policies, practices, processes, and procedures, the college assessed two categories of evidence: perception indicators (collected through surveys and focus groups) and quantitative trend data.

Results of the campus mission/goals survey, faculty/staff satisfaction survey data, student satisfaction survey data, focus group summaries, and analysis of key performance metrics helped the college assess if the attempts at innovation and continual improvement had been successful.

One positive finding identified in the self-study was that the 3-year graduation rate had almost tripled since the last self-study. One challenge identified in the self-study was that although the campus community clearly embraces the mission, vision, and goals of the college, their statements could be more succinctly phrased. Also, it was noted that the college was ready to begin work on a new strategic plan. As a result, the self-study report recommended as "next steps" that the upcoming strategic planning process should assure that all of the recommendations from the self-study and the academic master plan are used to inform the new plan and to rework the language of the mission and vision to provide clearer and more succinct messaging. *Answer: Yes.*

Standard II: Ethics and Integrity—Gwynedd Mercy University

MSCHE Standard II states,

> ethics and integrity are central, indispensable, and defining hallmarks of effective higher education institutions. In all activities, whether internal or external, an institution must be faithful to its mission, honor its contracts and commitments, adhere to its policies, and represent itself truthfully. (MSCHE, 2015, p. 5)

Do We Have It?

In preparing an answer to the question, "do we have it?" the faculty and staff at Gwynedd Mercy University inventoried the extensive plans and policies related to the standard for ethics and integrity. For example, the institution has maintained comprehensive policy manuals, revised and updated annually, that include appropriate policies supporting academic freedom, ensuring nondiscrimination, and regulating conflicts of interest. In addition, the university could provide evidence of policies and plans written to ensure institutional compliance with state and federal regulations. Through its self-study review process, the institution confirmed that multiple policies and plans were in place. *Answer: Yes.*

Do We Do It?

Members preparing the self-study report were able to readily catalog evidence documenting its processes and procedures demonstrating the university's ethical practices. Faculty/staff uncovered ample evidence of ethical practice in the work of its assigned committees (e.g., mission and values committee, tenure and promotion committee, deans council, staff council, executive council, faculty committee, university-wide compliance oversight committee) and through evidence of the articulated process and procedures designed to ensure ethical practices (e.g., student code of conduct process, board of trustees orientation, residence life contracts, conflict of interest process). Evidence of programming provided the institution with additional opportunities to affirm its integrity (e.g. "Conversations That Matter" programming, etc.) and confirm the institution's commitment to ethical practice. *Answer: Yes.*

Does It Work?
The assessment results examined by the university in order to answer the third question, "does it work?," revealed an area of potential concern. Although there was convincing evidence that the policies and practices exist and that these policies, plans, and practices "work," the research question for the self-study includes an important corollary: does it work *for all* ? Have these policies, plans, and practices been received as intended by all populations within the institutional community? Preliminary results of perception indicators, collected through surveys such as the Higher Education Research Institute (HERI) Diverse Learning Environment survey and the National Survey of Student Engagement (NSSE), provided some limited, emerging evidence that the college climate was not being perceived as uniformly inclusive. These recently obtained survey data results, considered together with quantitative data such as retention and graduation rates, were noted by the members of the self-study team as key findings. Although members were able to demonstrate that the institution's written policy directly supported non-discriminatory, inclusive practices, they also determined that there was no mechanism for implementation. These identified findings, the need for a plan and a need for a process, led directly to articulating next steps for continuous improvement. These steps included advancing the effectiveness of the institution through developing a targeted, strategic plan initiative for inclusive excellence and creating a new position for diversity coordinator. *Answer: Yes, but more investment in innovative processes is needed.*

Standard III: Design and Delivery of the Student Learning Experience—Gwynedd Mercy University

MSCHE Standard III states,

> an institution provides students with learning experiences that are characterized by rigor and coherence at all program, certificate, and degree levels, regardless of instructional modality. All learning experiences, regardless of modality, program pace/schedule, level, and setting are consistent with higher education expectations. (MSCHE, 2015, p. 6)

Do We Have It?
In answer to the question "do we have it?," the self-study determined that the institution offers academic programs at the undergraduate and graduate level that have been designed to provide students with a rigorous and coherent academic experience appropriate to the standards of higher education. The self-study also indicated that the institution has maintained a roster of core faculty, full time or part time, qualified to provide students with a consistent and meaningful academic experience. As an institution providing a growing number of graduate-level and online courses, the university had also taken steps to increase full-time faculty and other supports to ensure student needs were met across level and modality of learning. *Answer: Yes.*

Do We Do It?
The university has had numerous procedures and practices in place to ensure that the institution has continually provided students a strong educational experience. For example, programs and coursework have been regularly monitored through an education review committee and related processes. Faculty development have been supported through a faculty development committee and monitored through annual faculty development plan and activity reports completed by all full-time faculty. High-impact practices are imbedded in programs, with opportunities for experiential learning, common experiences, and opportunities to participate in research with faculty. *Answer: Yes.*

Does It Work?
Data such as student retention rates and postgraduate success, program-level student-learning assessment results, and faculty scholarship indicated that the institution was effective in the design and delivery of the student learning experience. The results from perception indicators such as the NSSE also supported the university's conclusions that the students were satisfied, overall, with the design and delivery of their learning experience.

One area where the assessment data suggested that the university was not meeting expectation was the implementation of high-impact practices. Specifically, data from the 2018 NSSE report indicated that graduates of the institution reported engaging in high-impact practices at a lower rate than similarly sized institutions. Looking back at the first question ("do we have it?"), faculty and staff reported that many programs provided, and often required, students with opportunities to engage in high-impact practices, such as internships. This discrepancy between policies/plans and student perception indicators suggested that the deficit may be in the second question, "do we do it?" To understand and address this deficit, the university included a focus on high-impact practices in the strategic plan. As part of this process, a team of faculty and staff attended intensive training, conducted a university-wide inventory of high-impact practices, and worked to identify factors that may affect student participation and experience in high-impact practices. The team also explored opportunities to develop faculty and staff understanding of the quality components of high-impact practices and to directly support student reflection on these experiences, such as through the use of ePortfolios. *Answer: Yes, mostly.*

Standard IV: Support for the Student Experience—Gwynedd Mercy University

MSCHE Standard IV states,

> across all educational experiences, settings, levels, and instructional modalities, the institution recruits and admits students whose interests, abilities, experiences, and goals are congruent with its mission and educational offerings. The institution commits to student retention, persistence, completion, and success through a coherent and effective support system sustained by qualified professionals, which enhances the quality of the learning environment, contributes to the educational experience, and fosters student success. (MSCHE, 2015, p. 8)

Do We Have It?
As a university that serves students with diverse social, economic, and educational needs, it is critical that the institution provides and effectively implements support services to meet the needs of students as they progress through three levels of experience: at the point of entry, during their time of enrollment, and after graduation. The self-study found that there were a number of policies and plans at all three levels addressing the question of "do we have it?" For example, there were policies in place to support the successful entry of students in their 1st year as well as transfer students. Committees and programs at the institution were also dedicated to providing students with a supportive cocurricular experience, such as the Office of Student Activities, Residence Life, and Athletics. At the point of graduation, there were also supports in place (e.g., lifetime access to career development for all graduates.) *Answer: Yes.*

Do We Do It?
In answer to the question of "do we do it?" the self-study identified evidence of practice and processes at all three levels—at the time of the students' entry (input), during their years attending the institution (environment), and at the time at graduation and beyond (output)—to ensure that

these policies were successfully implemented. For example, the strategic enrollment management team guided the decisions on admitting the "best fit" students. Members serving on the general admissions committee reviewed student applications in order to ensure adequate supports were in place for incoming 1st-year students. A retention committee provided evidence of ongoing monitoring and support for student retention initiatives. Career services actively tracked employment and placement rates. *Answer: Yes.*

Does It Work?
Assessment of student perception through surveys of student satisfaction, as well as the number of students who used support services at the point of entry through the postgraduate years, provided evidence that the institution achieved desired results ("does it work?") in a number of areas. Although outcome data largely demonstrated success in providing student support from orientation through graduation, assessment also indicated an opportunity to develop practices, processes, and procedures to more effectively inform and support students during the application and admissions process (i.e., "do we do it?"). For example, although the institution provided information on cost on the university website as well as other financial aid resources, examination of the financial aid process identified the need to educate students more about the cost of their education. This was particularly important in light of the large percentage of first-generation college students, for whom navigating the financial aid process and cost can be overwhelming. A retention committee task force was formed to identify how to address this and other needs for new and prospective students. This effort resulted in the implementation of the Griffin K.E.Y.S. (Kickstart and Envision Your Success), a preorientation program to help students and families navigate the application process, including the development of a financial plan in addition to an academic plan. These events also included time for students/families to meet with representatives from a wide range of programs across campus. These events came to be offered regularly throughout the year. *Answer: Yes, making progress.*

Standard V: Educational Effectiveness Assessment—Gwynedd Mercy University

MSCHE Standard V states, "Assessment of student learning and achievement demonstrates that the institution's students have accomplished educational goals consistent with their program of study, degree level, the institution's mission, and appropriate expectations for institutions of higher education" (MSCHE, 2015, p. 9).

Do We Have It?

In order to demonstrate compliance for the standard for educational effectiveness assessment, the university provided evidence that it had policies and plans supporting assessment processes for student learning and achievement at all levels: program, degree, mission, and institutional. The inventory included the institutional assessment policy, plan, and schedule for every component of the university—academic and cocurricular programs, service units (e.g., registrar, library, financial aid), mission, and institution-level divisions. After gathering and examining the evidence for this standard, the members were able to affirm that the university had the policies and plans in place to meet this standard. *Answer: Yes.*

Do We Do It?

Through its review process, the university concluded that the institution had the appropriate policies and plans in place. Members confirmed that the faculty were properly charged with the assessment of student learning, and that cocurricular staff members assessed student learning with outcomes appropriately aligned with the mission of the institution. The university was able to identify the active engagement of multiple, interrelated assessment committees, including program assessment committees; budget/resource advisor committee; general education committee; mission and values committee; and the institutional outcomes assessment committee. The assessment reports provided by these committees included the institution-wide assessment summary report and program assessment plans and reports. In addition, multiple professional programs participate in program-accreditation efforts with external professional accreditation reviews and self-study reports. *Answer: Yes.*

Does It Work?

Members writing the self-study report noted the positive results from faculty/staff surveys regarding their perceptions of the assessment process. They also examined the positive quantitative data attesting to the effectiveness of the institution's assessment efforts, including the total number of programs assessed per year, the percentage of assessment reports (for institution, program service units) that meet/exceed internal standards, the percentage of programs with identified next steps connected with the budget resource allocation processes, and the number of professionally accredited programs with approved/reaffirmed status. These positive findings notwithstanding, during the drafting of the self-study report it became clear that the question of "does it work?" was, at the institutional level, "not as intended." Although annual report templates had been designed to deliver assessment results and key findings necessary to inform budget requests and strategic planning initiatives, the self-study process identified that submitted reports did not provide sufficient data. As a direct result of this key finding, the institution created the "Quality Council," an institutional effectiveness assessment committee comprising representatives from executive council, deans council, staff council, faculty council, and an invited student representative. This newly formed institution-level assessment committee has been charged with analyzing assessment reports to increase accountability for using assessment data to inform planning, budgeting, and practice across the university, and to provide a more holistic understanding of internal and external data sets to better inform strategic planning. This effort to increase the connections among constituents with assessment findings, statistical data reports, and strategic planning and budgeting is helping the institution better support the whole of the student learning experience. *Answer: Yes, almost.*

Standard VI: Planning, Resources, and Institutional Improvement—Bronx Community College of CUNY

MSCHE Standard VI states that "the institution's planning processes, resources, and structures are aligned with each other and are sufficient to fulfill its mission and goals, to continuously assess and improve its programs and services, and to respond effectively to opportunities and challenges" (MSCHE, 2015, p. 10).

Do We Have It?

For Bronx Community College of CUNY, the self-study process identified existing policies and plans that provided compelling evidence for this question. Examples include a strategic plan with goals aligned with the MSCHE standards and to those of the university and performance management program; an operating budget planning cycle aligned with college planning and budgeting calendar and processes, 5-year capital and technology plans, and a college governance plan. The institution's further analysis demonstrated that the college is financially stable and has adequate resources to support its operations, educational purpose, and programs.

Several challenges were highlighted in the self-study, which included an enrollment decline impacting the college's budget allocation and facilities challenges resulting from the aging infrastructure of the buildings as well as the landmark status of several of the campus buildings. *Answer: Yes.*

Do We Do It?

As evidence of the college's practices, process, and procedures that were identified to provide assurances of meeting the standard for planning, resources, and institutional improvement, members inventoried the capital investments made over the past decade in support of the strategic plan (including construction of a state-of-the-art classroom and library building, onsite early childhood center, the campus quad, and infrastructure/programmatic upgrades). An annual report documents investments and outcomes relating to the college's strategic plan and goals including completion of the Academic Master Plan (AMP) expected to inform academic programming and investments over the next 5 years. *Answer: Yes.*

Does It Work?
The college analyzed perception indicators (e.g., results from the annual faculty, staff, and student survey), as well as key quantitative data (e.g., university and college performance metrics, external and internal audit results, key performance indicator administrative reports, and budget reports to the college senate). While the self-study demonstrated that the college "has it" and "does it," the institution identified that significant effort would be required to assure that it is "working." As a result, the self-study report recommended the development of a comprehensive enrollment plan designed to maintain/increase enrollment in support of both student success (retention) and corresponding fiscal health and converting the detailed assessments of infrastructure systems and annual reviews of life cycle duration of facilities infrastructure systems into actionable items.

With respect to the college's ability to continue assuring that what is done also works, concerns were expressed about the extent to which the budget would support both the core functions and strategic directions of the institution. In response to these concerns, the self-study report also recommended accountability measures, including clear and transparent budget and administrative reports and annual evaluations to include assessments of communication, consultation, timeliness, transparency, collaboration, and effectiveness. All of these recommendations were embedded in the college's draft strategic plan for 2020–2025. *Answer: Yes, in many areas but not all.*

Standard VII: Governance, Leadership, and Administration— Bronx Community College of CUNY

MSCHE Standard VII states,

> the institution is governed and administered in a manner that allows it to realize its stated mission and goals in a way that effectively benefits the institution, its students, and the other constituencies it serves. Even when supported by or affiliated with governmental, corporate, religious, educational system, or other unaccredited organizations, the institution has education as its primary purpose, and it operates as an academic institution with appropriate autonomy. (MSCHE, 2015, p. 11)

Do We Have It?

For the faculty and staff preparing the self-study for Bronx Community College of CUNY, finding the answer to the question "do we have it?" entailed demonstrating that the institution had appropriate policies and plans in place. Inventories included policies such as the college's written manual of general policy and conflict of interest policies. The college also provided evidence of plans such as the college governance plan and organizational charts and in the policies that comprised the college's various committees, including college senate, faculty council, president's cabinet, college personnel, and budget committee. *Answer: Yes.*

Do We Do It?

Members identified extensive evidence of active practice including annual/periodic executive evaluations, annual surveys, monthly reports, systems of checks and balances, and documentation of reappointment, tenure, promotion, and leave decisions. In addition, procedures were made evident in documents such as the university bylaws. The self-study demonstrated that shared governance is exercised effectively by the college's senate and that the college's strategic plan provided strong direction for the college.

One challenge identified in the self-study was the lack of formal orientation programs for campus leadership positions such as members of governance bodies, senate committees, department chairpersons, and campus executives. The recommendation to develop clear learning outcomes and orientation programs for campus leadership is underway. This effort is expected to improve the quality of evaluations, the efficacy of the checks and balances, and the effectiveness of the shared governance processes. *Answer: Yes, mostly.*

Does It Work?

Faculty and staff investigated the evidence that the institution's assessment processes led to innovation and continual improvement. The evidence identified positive trends from perception indicators, with results culled from annual faculty, staff, and student surveys, and documentation of annual/periodic progress reports on strategic plan goals and metrics. The college senate and senate subcommittees (curriculum, faculty council, student government, space and facilities) provided monthly reports that delivered additional evidence that processes were working.

By analyzing the patterns of key findings from these assessment activities, the college not only developed a holistic sense of what was working and what was not, members could determine whether the evidence from the assessments were being used for the purposes of innovation and continual improvement. *Answer: Yes.*

Use of the Assessment Findings

Asking three simple questions as part of an overall self-study strategy can help institutions articulate key findings, identify next steps, improve plans and processes if needed, and target efforts for improvement. In addition, these questions can help ensure that institutions maintain their overall integrity. The framework model presented here can alter the paradigm of the entire self-study process. Instead of focusing only on content—"what we have"— members of the institutions train their attention on the implementation: watching and listening for evidence that both the having and the doing, are, in fact, positively impacting those for whom each institution's mission has striven to affect in the first place: students and their learning.

We have proposed in this chapter a new kind of monitoring system— one that supplies a practical way to identify gaps and name the challenges, while also remaining respectful of those it was designed to support. Three questions can shift the entire focus of the assessment of practice. Three questions can lead to a deeper understanding of the integrity of the whole of an institution's endeavors by paying close attention to the participants' engagement with its processes and the effectiveness of its efforts.

References

Lakin Gullan, R., Feinbert, B., Freedman, M., Jawad, A., & Leff, S. (2009). Using participatory action research to design an intervention integrity system in the urban schools. *School Mental Health*, *1*, 118–130. https://doi.org/10.1007/s12310-009-9006-9

Middle States Commission on Higher Education. (2015). *Standards for accreditation and requirements of affiliation.* https://www.msche.org/standards/

Perepletchikova, F., & Kazdin, A. E. (2005). Treatment integrity and therapeutic change: Issues and research recommendations. *Clinical Psychology: Science and Practice*, *12*(4), 365–383. https://doi.org/10.1093/clipsy.bpi045

EDITOR AND CONTRIBUTOR BIOGRAPHIES

Jane Marie Souza, PhD, serves as the associate provost for academic administration/chief assessment officer and accreditation liaison officer at the University of Rochester. She served as the 2019–2020 president of the Association for the Assessment of Learning in Higher Education and previously served as editor for the organization's publication, *Intersection*. Souza has served on accreditation teams for the New England Commission on Higher Education, Middle States Commission on Higher Education, Accreditation Council for Pharmacy Education, and Council on Podiatric Medical Education, where she was a member of the council 2016–2019. She has been involved with assessment in education since the 1990s, when her class was designated a "Lighthouse" site in the state of Massachusetts for her work with curricular alignment and assessment. While working with pharmacy education 2011–2015, she was elected chair of the Assessment Special Interest Group of the American Association of Colleges of Pharmacy and recognized with an Excellence in Assessment award. Souza served as an assessment consultant for institutions across the country, offering workshops on the use of technology in the classroom, mapping curricular outcomes, and meeting accreditation standards through effective assessment. She has presented at conferences including the Association for Institutional Research, Middle States Commission on Higher Education, Association for the Assessment of Learning in Higher Education, Drexel Assessment Conference (keynote), Assessment Institute in Indianapolis (section keynote), Texas A&M, and Association for Medical Education in Europe. Souza holds a PhD in higher education administration from the University of Nebraska, an MEd in curriculum development from Curry College, and BA in English from the University of Massachusetts.

Tara A. Rose, PhD, is the director of assessment at Louisiana State University. Working collaboratively with faculty, staff, and administrators, she leads academic quality efforts at the course, program, and university levels that reflect current trends and best practices in higher education. Rose has 20 years of experience in assessment and outcomes analyses. She began her career with a nonprofit organization and has also spent time at the state level working for the Kentucky Legislative Research Commission and the Kentucky Council on Postsecondary Education. She previously served as the director of assessment at the University of Kentucky and has also taught at Eastern Kentucky University in the Department of Homeland Security. Since 2010, she has participated as a board member on the Association for the Assessment of Learning in Higher Education (AALHE), previously holding the position of president in AY 2015–2016. In 2019, Rose was appointed as senior fellow with the Association of American Colleges and Universities (AAC&U). She holds a PhD in public policy and administration and an MPA (both from Walden University), an MS in criminal justice, and a BS in corrections and juvenile services (both from Eastern Kentucky University).

Contributor Biographies

Scott Carnz, EdD, has worked in higher education for nearly 25 years. He teaches courses in various design disciplines, as well as in leadership and management. Carnz holds a BA from The Evergreen State College, in which he studied intersections of art and science, completing a thesis on the geometry of Gothic cathedrals in France. His MA in whole systems design is from Antioch University, focusing on design theory and cybernetics and the role of epistemology in experiential design. Carnz earned a PhD in education with an emphasis in leadership from Argosy University. He serves as a peer evaluator for the Northwest Commission on Colleges and Universities. He also has worked as an organizational training and development consultant, working with organizations to design, implement, and assess training and development programs that support the organization's strategic goals and assist in creating a culture of learning.

Sarah Cercone Heavey, PhD, MPH, is a clinical assistant professor in the Department of Community Health and Health Behavior (CHHB) at the University at Buffalo. She serves as the program director for the MPH programs in the Department of CHHB, including launching the online individualized concentration of the MPH and further growing the department's traditional concentrations and multi-award programs. Under her leadership, these MPH concentrations have more than tripled in size, expanded online course offerings, and worked to place students in a variety of field placements across the United States. Heavey sits on the university's CEPH Steering Committee and the MPH Coordinating Committee. She also teaches both online and in person in the MPH program, including courses on health behavior and program planning and evaluation. For her research, Heavey focuses on public health implications of mental illness and substance use, specifically opioid overdose and suicide.

Keryn Chalmers is dean of Swinburne Business School in the Faculty of Business and Law at Swinburne University. Her education and research interests are in financial accounting. As an executive of the International Association of Accounting Education and Research, she sits as an official observer on the International Panel for Accountancy Education. Chalmers is a former Australian president of the Accounting and Finance Association of Australia and New Zealand (AFAANZ), a former Victorian Divisional Council member of CPA Australia, and member of the CPA Australia national education accreditation board, special considerations committee, and examination policy advisory committee. She has coauthored accounting textbooks prescribed by various Australian universities.

Sonya Christian, PhD, has had a 3-decade career in higher education. She began with a faculty position in the Math Department at Bakersfield College in 1991, where she became a dean before moving to Lane Community College in Eugene, Oregon, to become the associate vice president for instruction in 2003. She remained in Eugene for 12 years, eventually becoming the chief academic officer at Lane. In that time, Christian led extensive work on the state Degree Qualifications Profile, which brought $789,000 to the college to improve learning outcomes. In 2013, Christian became the 10th president in the history of Bakersfield College. Christian currently serves as the chair and commissioner on the Accrediting Commission for Community and Junior Colleges (ACCJC). Christian earned her BS degree from University of Kerala in Kerala, India; an MS in applied mathematics from University of Southern California; and her PhD from University of California, Los Angeles.

Jay Cohen is an associate professor and director of online learning and teaching at Charles Sturt University. In this role Cohen provides leadership in online subject design and development and online teaching, as well as the associated workflows and management processes enabling large-scale rollouts. His education and research interests are in online learning, learning analytics, learning innovation, and higher education assessment. He has also developed his research in the scholarship of teaching and learning, with recent publications relating to online assessment, learning design, and online learning innovation. He is the vice president of the newly formed Open and Distance Learning Association of Australia (ODLAA).

Patricia A. Coward earned her PhD in English literature and composition at Bowling Green State University. She served as professor of English at Frostburg State University in Maryland for 15 years, where she developed an interest in faculty development and assessment of student learning. She was appointed the director of the Center for Teaching Excellence at Canisius College in Buffalo, New York, in 2005, where she consulted with faculty and programs in topics regarding assessment of student learning. During that time, she conducted a number of workshops and conference sessions on topics related to the scholarship of teaching and learning and assessment. In addition, she was a member of nine Middle States review teams and cochaired the Canisius College self-study in 2015. Coward continues to work in assessment as the coordinator of assessment and instruction in the Andrew L. Bouwhuis, SJ Library at Canisius College.

Dana S. Dunn, PhD, is a professor, chair of psychology, and the director of academic assessment at Moravian College. He earned his PhD in experimental social psychology from the University of Virginia and his BA in psychology from Carnegie Mellon University. A fellow of the American Psychological Association (APA) and the Association for Psychological Science (APS), he is past president of APA Division 22 (Rehabilitation Psychology) and of APA Division 2 (the Society for the Teaching of Psychology), and former president of the Eastern Psychological Association (EPA). Dunn was the 2013 recipient of the Charles L. Brewer Award for Distinguished Teaching from the American Psychological Foundation. He is the author or editor of over 30 books, as well as over 170 articles, chapters, and book reviews. He is editor-in-chief of the *Oxford Bibliographies: Psychology* and the incoming editor of the APA journal *Scholarship of Teaching and Learning in Psychology*.

David D. Dworak, PhD, is the deputy provost for the U.S. Army War College in Carlisle, Pennsylvania. He has a background in strategic planning, academic assessment, and military history. His academic credentials include a PhD and MPhil in history from the Maxwell School of Syracuse University, an MSS in strategic studies from the U.S. Army War College, an MS in logistics management from the Florida Institute of Technology, and a BA in political science from the University of Texas at Arlington. Dworak is a certified Demonstrated Master Logistician.

Lara M. Evans, PhD, is a scholar, curator, and enrolled member of the Cherokee Nation. She earned her PhD in art history at the University of New Mexico in 2005. Evans joined the Institute of American Indian Art (IAIA) in Santa Fe, New Mexico, in 2012 after 8 years as faculty at The Evergreen State

College in Olympia, Washington. Since 2015, she has also been program director for the IAIA Artist-in-Residence Program, which brings 12–14 artists to campus each year for residency sessions. Evans became associate dean of academics in 2018. She has maintained an active curatorial practice at the IAIA Museum of Contemporary Native Art. Recent publications include the essay "Edna Massey and Native Modernism" in *Action / Abstraction Redefined* (IAIA, 2018), and "Setting the Photographs Aside: Native American Photography Since 1990" in *Native Art Now! Developments in Contemporary Native American Art Since 1992* (Eiteljorg Museum, 2017).

Jessica Greene, PhD, associate vice provost for assessment and accreditation at Boston College, has responsibilities that include providing the institution's senior leaders with studies and analytics that support and inform the development of university policy, the assessment of academic and cocurricular progress, and the evaluation of operational and strategic outcomes. Greene has spent her entire career in the institutional effectiveness arena, first working in market research in the private sector and then transitioning to educational research via her first position at Boston College in 1997 as a data manager. She earned her BA in economics from the College of the Holy Cross, her MA in communication research from the University of Southern California, and her PhD in educational research, measurement, and evaluation from Boston College.

Rebecca Gullan, PhD, is a professor of psychology at Gwynedd Mercy University. Gullan's research focuses on mentorship and identity development in adolescence and emerging adulthood. Gullan received her BA in psychology from Cornell University and her MA and PhD in clinical psychology from Bowling Green State University.

Jana Hanson, PhD, has served South Dakota State University as the director of institutional assessment since 2015. Prior to this appointment, she was a research analyst in the Department of Institutional Effectiveness at Kirkwood Community College. She holds an MA in psychology from Boston University and a PhD in higher education and student affairs from the University of Iowa. As the director, Hanson provides creative and innovative leadership fostering a culture of assessment, institutional effectiveness, and continuous quality improvement as integrated, understood, and practiced in ways consistent with the university mission, values, and vision. In 2019, Hanson received the Champion Award from Campus Labs. Hanson's publications have focused on college outcomes and assessment research. She has published in numerous academic journals, such as *Journal of College*

Student Development, *The Journal of Higher Education*, and *Teaching in Higher Education*.

Brian Harlan, PhD, is currently the associate provost for integrated learning at California Institute of the Arts. He has served as a volunteer collaborator with University of the People on strategic planning, assessment, and accreditation since 2011. Harlan has functioned as the accreditation liaison officer for WASC Senior College and University Commission, as well as the lead for national, specialized accreditation, and is currently active within WSCUC as an evaluator and committee member. Other administrative posts include assistant dean for academic assessment and planning at Occidental College, and director of assessment and access services for the University of Southern California library system. Harlan earned his PhD at the University of Southern California, and his MA at the University of California, Los Angeles.

Dawn L. Hayward, PhD, serves as assistant vice president for assessment and compliance at Gwynedd Mercy University. Hayward supports the assessment processes for the university and serves as regulatory compliance administrator. With a PhD in English literature from the University of Kansas, she seeks to tell compelling data stories that transform institutional practice.

Mary Kay Helling, PhD, vice provost, and professor emerita, served at South Dakota State University for 38 years in a variety of roles including director of the Division of Economics and Management, interim dean of the Graduate School and University College, and most recently as vice provost for academic affairs. Areas of responsibility included student success programs and initiatives focusing on developmental advising, the exploratory studies program, and numerous other programs. Helling also led efforts to enhance the general education curriculum, institutional program reviews, and partnering with institutions in and out of state to build pathways to pursue higher education for students. She led the institutional accreditation efforts including the 10-year reaccreditation process. Helling also facilitated a university culture committed to the assessment of student learning and improvement of academic programs. She earned her PhD at Purdue University, partially funded by a Bush Leadership Fellowship.

Elisa Hertz is the director of the Center for College Effectiveness at Guttman Community College of the City University of New York (CUNY). Prior to joining Guttman, Hertz was the director of assessment and accreditation at CUNY's Hunter College School of Education, and earlier worked as coordinator of academic program review and institutional research analyst at New

York University. Hertz holds an MA in speech and interpersonal communication from New York University and an MS in applied social research from Hunter College, CUNY.

Gregory G. Homish, PhD, is professor and chair of the Department of Community Health and Health Behavior (CHHB) at the University at Buffalo. Prior to becoming chair, he served as the program director for the CHHB concentration of the MPH and founding director of the individualized concentration of the MPH. Under his leadership, the individualized concentration was expanded to offer the program in a fully online format. Homish was also involved in the creation and expansion of a number of multi-award programs with the MPH including collaborations with programs in social work, pharmacy, urban planning, physical therapy, and management. In terms of research, Homish's work focuses on social and environmental influences on changes in substance use and mental health over time. His research has been supported by NIH, CDC, New York State, the VA Health Care System, and private, nonprofit foundations.

Burton Howell is the executive director of Intersections and the Center for Ignatian Spirituality at Boston College. These two offices invite faculty and staff to discuss vocation, discernment, mission, student formation, the Ignatian spiritual tradition, and Jesuit education. Intersections and the Center for Ignatian Spirituality, under the direction of the division of University Mission and Ministry, sponsor seminars, retreats, lunches, immersion trips, and pilgrimages. Prior to his current positions, Howell worked in the Boston College Office of Residential Life. Howell received a BA in history from Whitman College and an EdM in higher education from the Harvard Graduate School of Education.

Sondos Islam, PhD, is the chair of the Department of Urban Public Health and director of the MPH Program in Urban Health Disparities in the College of Science and Health at Charles R. Drew University of Medicine and Science. Islam has a BS and MS in microbiology and immunology from the University of Washington, an MPH in epidemiology and biostatistics, and a PhD in preventive medicine/health behavior research from the University of Southern California. Her expertise is in curriculum development, assessment, and evaluation of public health programs. She brings to her classes a hands-on application of her expertise in strategic planning and evaluation, research methodology, community needs assessments, and cultural competency in planning public health programs targeting ethnically and racially diverse populations. Her research interests include investigating the sociocultural factors influencing the health behavior of ethnically diverse adolescents, and the planning, implementation, and evaluation of public health programs.

Ryan Jopp, PhD, has coordinated a range of undergraduate, postgraduate, and online units at various institutions, across the fields of management, tourism, and marketing. In 2012 he successfully completed his PhD and has several publications in top-rated journals and has presented his findings at international conferences. In his role as academic director (education quality and assurance) at Swinburne University he is responsible for ensuring quality and consistency of course delivery. He has also developed his research in the scholarship of teaching and learning, with recent publications relating to authentic learning and assessment choice.

Katherine A. Kelley, PhD, is currently associate dean for assessment and strategic initiatives and professor of clinical pharmacy at the Ohio State University, College of Pharmacy. In her current capacity, she leads the Office of Educational Innovation and Scholarship, whose strategic areas of focus include program development, assessment, and helping faculty disseminate scholarly work related to their teaching. Kelley received her BA in chemistry from Miami University, MS in pharmaceutical sciences from the University of Cincinnati, and MS in pharmaceutical administration and PhD in higher education administration from the Ohio State University. She teaches in the PharmD program as part of a team delivering cocurricular content instruction and another team for program-level assessment. Her areas of research interest include educational assessment, program evaluation, student learning, and pharmacy education.

Kimberly A. Krytus, MSW, MPH, CPH, is assistant dean and director of graduate public health programs at the University at Buffalo School of Public Health and Health Professions. Prior to this, Krytus was the MPH program coordinator for the school. She is also a founding member of the university's Interprofessional Education Leadership Team, which launched an interprofessional education and collaborative practice initiative that trains over 800 graduate students in health and related professional programs each semester. Krytus leads the school's Council on Education for Public Health (CEPH) Steering Committee and the MPH Coordinating Committee, which coordinates components of the program across seven different concentrations. She is a member of the Association of Schools of Public Health (ASPPH) Accreditation and Credentialing Advisory Committee and the ASPPH Academic Affairs Section and has served as an item writer and reviewer for the Certified in Public Health (CPH) exam.

Jeffrey R. Lindauer, PhD, is the interim assistant vice president for academic affairs and associate professor of kinesiology at Canisius College. In addition, he serves as Middle States accreditation liaison officer and assists college administration, faculty, and staff in assessment and accreditation policies and procedures. He previously served as kinesiology department chair and dean of the School of Education and Human Services at Canisius and as a kinesiology faculty member and program director at the University of Wisconsin-Eau Claire.

Sandra Luxton, PhD, is a successful researcher, educator, and leader with a strong focus on relationship management. She is widely published and has over 20 years' experience as an academic at Monash University, University of South Australia, QUT, and Swinburne University and has been recognized for her teaching excellence. She has significant experience in online education and is committed to flexible learning and student mobility. Before moving into her current role as dean, Luxton held many leadership roles and has successfully supervised a number of research students. Having worked in industry for 10 years prior to entering academia, including time as a research consultant in private industry, Luxton brings a commercial sensitivity to her work. She maintains strong links to industry, and a commitment to bridging the relationship between practitioners and academia.

Mary Mara, MLIS, has worked in higher education for nearly 17 years. Her experience includes development of the City University of Seattle's integrated information literacy instruction program, directing library and learning resource center services, assessment of the impact of library resources and services on student achievement, directing the Center for Curriculum and Instruction, and leading the implementation of the university's curriculum development system and program assessment plan. Mara teaches adult learning theory and research at the graduate level and serves as a peer evaluator for the Northwest Commission on Colleges and Universities.

Marianne McCollum, PhD, professor emerita, served as assistant dean for assessment and academic affairs at Regis University School of Pharmacy for 11 years. She earned her BS in pharmacy and her PhD in pharmaceutical outcomes research from the University of Colorado Health Sciences Center. She held a faculty position with the CU School of Pharmacy until 2009, when she joined the Regis School of Pharmacy as a member of the founding faculty. During her time at Regis, McCollum was involved extensively in accreditation activities both as an assistant dean supporting the development of the school and also as a site team member working with other pharmacy programs. She continues work in the areas of scholarship of teaching and learning, accreditation activities with the Accreditation Council for Pharmacy Education and as a consultant in the areas of assessment and accreditation.

Melissa S. Medina, EdD, earned her BS in experimental psychology and EdD in educational psychology from Rutgers University in New Jersey. She joined the faculty at the University of Oklahoma College of Pharmacy in 2000 and is a presidential professor and the associate dean for assessment and evaluation. Medina also serves as the director of Preparing Future Faculty for the University of Oklahoma Graduate College. She has won 12 teaching awards, including the Regent's Award for Superior Teaching. Medina is very involved in the American Association of Colleges of Pharmacy (AACP) and served as the 2013 chair for the Center for the Advancement of Pharmacy Education Outcomes Committee. She received the 2018 AACP Chalmers Educator of the Year Award and the 2016 AACP Distinguished Teaching Scholar Award. She also serves as an associate editor for the *American Journal of Pharmaceutical Education*.

Kristina A. Meinking, PhD, earned her doctorate in Classics from the University of Southern California. She serves as associate professor of classical languages and assistant director for assessment of Elon University's core curriculum, where she works with faculty and colleagues across campus to enhance, encourage, and evaluate assessment tools and practices. Before moving into this assessment role, she served for 2 years as an assistant director of Elon's Center for the Advancement of Teaching and Learning. Here, among other responsibilities, she developed communities of practice on the scholarship of teaching and learning as well as fostered faculty professional development opportunities around teaching and mentoring. In addition to her disciplinary research, Meinking's scholarly work is located in the scholarship of teaching and learning with an emphasis on critical pedagogy, students-as-partners, and cocreation in teaching and learning.

Marlena O.P. Montague, MS, is assistant director for the Office of Assessment, Institutional Effectiveness and Research at Guam Community College (GCC). She holds an MS in computer information systems from the University of Phoenix and a BS in business administration, management information systems from California State University Long Beach. As the college's data gatekeeper, she has spearheaded the implementation of practices that sustain systematic and regularized assessment of all programs and curriculum in continuous and alternating cycles. As an Employee of the Year awardee under the governor of Guam's government-wide recognition program, she was recognized for her work in GCC assessment, technology, negotiations, faculty job specifications and evaluation, professional development, and accreditation committees. She has also joined two accreditation visit teams to ACCJC institutions. She has over 15 years of experience in automation and integration of business processes and services in higher education, including the complex management of assessment data and reporting.

Bill Moseley, PhD, is in the 23rd year of his higher education career at Bakersfield College. During this time, he has invested 16 years as a computer science faculty member and 4 years as the dean of academic technology. Moseley has also spent over 15 years teaching in Pepperdine University's Graduate School of Education and Psychology and has done extensive work in pioneering innovative teaching and learning methods using technology and online platforms. Moseley spends his free time programming and working on projects with his seven kids. Moseley completed his MA in educational technology from Pepperdine University and a PhD in educational leadership at the University of Nebraska-Lincoln.

Shawn Moustafa, EdD, is the vice provost for academic affairs at the University of the People. Moustafa has 20 years of experience working in higher education and is also an active instructor of business at various universities including Washington State University, where he teaches in the Executive MBA program. He holds an EdD from the University of Southern California, specializing in higher education administration.

Leigh M. Onimus, JD, is associate dean at the Stillman School of Business, Seton Hall University. She has served in this position since 2012 and prior to that served as assistant dean. She oversees the school's undergraduate assessment process and has shared responsibility for the school's MBA assessment process. She has implemented a comprehensive redesign of the MBA assessment process focused on the implementation of course-embedded assessments, standardized rubrics, and increasing faculty engagement. Onimus has presented at the AACSB Assessment Conferences and has provided guidance to schools on matters related to outcomes assessment. She was certified in 2019 as an "Expert Scorer" in critical thinking through AAC&U's Value Institute. She sits on Seton Hall's assessment steering committee and served in a leadership capacity on the university's Middle States Accreditation Committee. She earned her BS and MBA from Seton Hall and her JD at Seton Hall School of Law.

Heather F. Perfetti, EdD, JD, is an experienced high-level executive with a demonstrated and diverse history of working in complex educational environments. Perfetti became president of the Middle States Commission on Higher Education on July 1, 2020, having previously served as vice president liaison, vice president for legal affairs and chief of staff, senior vice president, and president-elect. Over the course of her career, she has made an impact in numerous areas of higher education, including academic and student affairs, faculty affairs, legal and regulatory affairs, strategic planning, policy development, and innovative, organizational change management. Perfetti earned her EdD with specialization in higher education leadership from Northcentral University (CA), a JD degree from the University of Mississippi School of Law, the MS degree in criminal justice from Troy University (AL), and a BA in English from Frostburg State University (MD).

Amy Portwood, MA, has worked in higher education for more than 15 years in a variety of roles, including teaching U.S. diplomatic and cultural history at Rutgers University for more than 5 years, recruiting international students to study in the United States, managing an online information center, and leading enrollment and advising and campus operations teams. In addition, Portwood has designed and implemented customer relations management (CRM) systems as well as built, validated, and rendered institutional data for operational and strategic planning purposes via an integrated data warehouse. She currently serves as the director of data analytics at City University of Seattle. She holds a BA from Whitman College and an MA in history from Rutgers, The State University of New Jersey.

Nancy Ritze, PhD, is the dean for research, planning, and assessment at Bronx Community College. Ritze oversees all institutional effectiveness functions, including the development, coordination, facilitation, assessment, and reporting activities related to the college's strategic and operational planning and assessment efforts and outcomes. She earned a PhD in sociology from Fordham University.

Michael Sacco, PhD, is the executive director of the Center for Student Formation and Office of First Year Experience at Boston College. Sacco has held positions within the areas of both student affairs and university mission and ministry at Boston College and the University of Notre Dame. He began his career at BC in 1995 and considers himself fortunate to have accompanied many students through their formative years on the Heights. His work allows him to spend significant time with students and his insights have been developed through contacts made on retreats, international service trips, and various mentoring programs. Sacco holds a BA in communications from John Carroll University, an MS in college student personnel administration from Indiana University, and an EdD in higher education management from the University of Georgia.

Kevin Sackreiter, EdD, serves as the director of the Center for the Enhancement of Teaching and Learning at South Dakota State University. In this role Sackreiter provides university-wide leadership for teaching and learning-focused professional development efforts for all university faculty and graduate teaching assistants. These efforts include (but are not limited to) facilitating workshops/seminars, consultations, observations of teaching, certification programs, and advocating for the scholarship of teaching and learning. He brings to the current project expertise in teaching and learning pedagogy, teaching-based research (the scholarship of teaching and learning), faculty mentoring, and graduate teaching assistant professional development. Previously Sackreiter served as assistant professor of speech communication and director of forensics at Northern State University. He holds an MS in communication studies from South Dakota State University and an EdD in educational administration from the University of South Dakota.

Dan Shapiro, PhD, is the interim associate vice president for academic programs and dean of university college and graduate studies at California State University, Monterey Bay (CSUMB). He is on leave from his regular appointment as the director of the Center for Teaching Learning and Assessment. He is a graduate of the WSCUC Assessment Leadership Academy (ALA) and coordinates the ALA mentoring program. Prior to that he was professor of environmental studies, also at CSUMB. He has a BS in biology from the University of California, Los Angeles, and a PhD in ecology and evolutionary biology from Cornell University.

Roxie Smith, PhD, is the vice provost for academic development at University of the People. She brings considerable experience in higher education administration to her volunteer role with UoPeople, having previously served at Columbia University as vice provost and before that as associate vice president for arts and sciences. Prior to her time at Columbia, she was at Northwestern University, where she served as an associate provost and before that as associate dean for academic affairs in the School of Education and Social Policy. She received her PhD from the University of North Carolina, Chapel Hill.

R. Ray D. Somera, PhD, is the vice president for academic affairs at Guam Community College since October 2007. Prior to this appointment, he was associate dean and assessment director, developing and implementing a comprehensive outcomes assessment program at the college that utilized TracDat as an assessment data management tool. He capitalized on his training as an anthropologist (MA and PhD in anthropology, Michigan State University) to focus on issues of building a culture of evidence, sustainability of assessment, faculty buy-in and engagement, as well as the assessment of the nonacademic areas that support student learning. He has completed two accreditation visit cycles since he became vice president and accreditation liaison officer (ALO). At the most recent team visit in March 2018, GCC received zero recommendations for compliance and zero recommendations. He has joined six visiting teams to other ACCJC institutions, in both California and Hawaii.

Eric D. Stamps, DPM, received his degree with honors from the California College of Podiatric Medicine in 1993. He completed a podiatric surgical residency at Kaiser Foundation Hospital in Hayward, California, and began an academic career in podiatry in 1996 at the California School of Podiatric Medicine at Samuel Merritt University in Oakland, California, where he has been dean since 2018. Stamps is board certified by the American Board of Podiatric Medicine. His interest in accreditation began in 2014 when he was appointed to the Accreditation Committee of the Council on Podiatric Medical Education, the programmatic accrediting body for podiatric medical education. His outside interests include his family, fitness, golf, hiking, travel, and, during the SARS-CoV-2 pandemic, finally learning to play chess.

Joyce A. Strawser, PhD, is dean of the Stillman School of Business at Seton Hall University, a position she has held since March 2012. Strawser joined the Seton Hall faculty in 1995 and has taught courses in many of the subfields of accounting, at both the undergraduate and graduate levels. As a faculty member, she earned awards for her excellence in teaching and service to students. Strawser has provided advice to business schools seeking to develop learning outcomes assessment programs and has made numerous conference presentations on business program outcomes assessment and business school accreditation. Strawser is currently a member of the Association to Advance Collegiate Schools of Business's (AACSB) Initial Accreditation Committee (IAC) and Board of Directors. She is one of 16 business school deans across the world to serve on the AACSB's Business Accreditation Task Force (BATF), which was charged with reimagining business school accreditation.

Burgunda V. Sweet, PharmD, FASHP, is assistant dean for curriculum and assessment and clinical professor at the University of Michigan College of Pharmacy. She earned her PharmD degree at the University of the Pacific

College of Pharmacy and completed 2 years of postgraduate training in clinical pharmacy practice. Sweet is responsible for ensuring compliance with accreditation standards and providing continuous review of the pharmacy curriculum and student outcomes. She serves on the executive committee for the U-M Center for Interprofessional Education (IPE) and cochairs the IPE Curriculum Committee. Sweet teaches courses related to interpreting and applying clinical data in practice and collaborates with others to integrate IPE offerings within the PharmD program. In addition to her academic role, Sweet continues to practice as a clinical specialist in the field of medication use policy. She has authored numerous articles and book sections in her areas of specialty.

Porter Swentzell, PhD, is from Santa Clara Pueblo, New Mexico, where he grew up participating in traditional life in his community and developed an interest in language and cultural preservation. He is associate academic dean, chair, and associate professor of Indigenous Liberal Studies at the Institute of American Indian Arts, a regent for Northern New Mexico College, and serves on several nonprofit boards. Porter holds a PhD in justice studies from Arizona State University, an MA in interdisciplinary studies with concentrations in history and political science from Western New Mexico University, and a BA in integrated studies with an emphasis in Pueblo Indian studies from Northern New Mexico College. He lives at Santa Clara Pueblo along with his wife and three children.

Carol Traupman-Carr, PhD, is the vice provost and professor of music at Moravian College. In her administrative capacity, her primary responsibilities are new program development, accreditation, and assessment. She serves as the institution's accreditation liaison officer and has participated in a variety of accreditation reviews for the Middle States Commission on Higher Education. She was a member of the 2015–2016 cohort of the Senior Leadership Academy, run by AALI and the Council of Independent Colleges. She is the founder and president of Alpha Alpha Alpha, a national honor society for first-generation college students. Traupman-Carr holds a PhD and MA in musicology from Cornell University and a BA in social studies and BMus in music from Moravian College.

Stephen Wall is an enrolled member of the White Earth Nation. He was born in Roswell, New Mexico, and was raised on and near the Mescalero Apache Indian Reservation in southern New Mexico. After graduating high school, he attended Fort Lewis College in Durango, Colorado. Upon completing his BA in anthropology at Fort Lewis, Wall attended law school at the University of New Mexico, graduating in 1975. He has served in tribal communities as a community organizer and health administrator. He was the prosecutor and judge in the Mescalero Apache Tribal Court for 12 years. In May of 2006, Wall was appointed department chair for the Indigenous Liberal Studies Program at the Institute of American Indian Arts (IAIA) in Santa Fe, New Mexico, a position he held for 12 years. In 2019 he was voted faculty emeritus in Indigenous Liberal Studies by the IAIA Board of Trustees.

Debra Wetcher-Hendricks, PhD, is a member and former chair of sociology and anthropology and served as the director of academic assessment until 2018 at Moravian College. Publications include the textbook *Analyzing Quantitative Data: An Introduction for Social Researchers* (John Wiley & Sons, 2011), as well as articles that focus upon theoretical statistical processes and that apply statistical analysis to topics of interest. Her contributions to the Lehigh Valley Research Consortium, as a founding and executive board member of the organization, have included authoring multiple articles for and coediting the annual *State of the Lehigh Valley* publication. Various editions of *Marquis Who's Who in America*, *Who's Who Among American Women*, and *Who's Who in the World* have noted Wetcher-Hendricks' accomplishments and she received the 2013 Lindback Award for Distinguished Teaching. Wetcher-Hendricks holds a PhD in applied social research from Lehigh University.

INDEX

academic evaluation report (U.S. Army War College), 129–132
Academic Program Board (Canisius College), 37
Accelerated Study in Associate Program (Bronx Community College of CUNY), 271
accountability, 93, 184
accreditation: accreditors within, xiv; annual assessment within, 70–72; assessment requirements within, 53; within California State University, Monterey Bay (CSUMB), 198; within Council on Education for Public Health (CEPH), 140; within Guam Community College (GCC), 251; within Higher Education Institutions (HEIs), xii; institutions and, xii; leveraging within, 198; of Middle State Commissions of Higher Education (MSCHE), 266–268; peer reviewers within, xii
Accreditation for Pharmacy Education (ACPE), xiv, 182, 183–184
Accrediting Commission for Community and Junior Colleges (ACCJC), xiv
Accrediting Commission for Schools Western Association of Schools and Colleges Senior College (WASC), xiv
administration, 28, 90–91, 279–280
advisory boards, work of (UoPeople), 118

advocacy, cocurricular activities within, 188
Alfred, R., 250
alignment, streamlining of (SAGE), 259
alumni, engagement of, 117–118, 153, 157
American Association of Colleges and Universities (AAC&U), 19, 201, 202–203
American Association of Colleges of Pharmacy (AACP), 187
American Podiatric Medical Licensing Exam, 234–235, 236, 238
annual assessment, 70–72, 75–76
Anthony A. Leon Guerrero Allied Health Building (GCC), 245
Arendt, A., 97, 107
assessment: annual process of, 70–72, 75–76; assessing of, 46–49; assessment-task choice regime, 98–103; badging innovation within, 6–7; cafeteria assessment and grading, 97–98; community for, 60–61; culture of, 27–28; data disaggregation and, 8; defined, xiii; direct evidence as, 18; evaluation *versus*, 71; flexibility within, 96–97, 98; framework for, 53–54; indigenous methodologies within, 52–53; learners' choice within, 97, 101–103; measurability of, 55–56; objectivity of, 55–56; peer, 112–113; pressures within, 53; progress determination within, 11–12, 34–35; scaling of, 5;

299

software varieties within, 39; student feedback of, 8; subjectivity of, 55–56; technology within, 5; tools and techniques within, 5–6; value of, 12. *See also* data, assessment; *specific institutions*
Assessment, Institutional Effectiveness, and Research (AIAR) report (GCC), 248
Assessment 1.0, 198
Assessment 2.0, 198, 206
Assessment Academy (HLC), 57, 82–83
Assessment Academy (SDSU), 85, 87–91, 94
assessment leader, 60–61
Assessment Leadership Academy (ALA) of WSCUC, 208
assessment management software (AMS), 89
assessors, role of (Stillman), 153–159
assignment grading, students and, 112
associate vice president for academic planning and institutional effectiveness (AVP-APIE) (CSUMB), 204–205
Association of Schools and Programs of Public Health (ASPPH), 167
Association of Schools of Public Health (ASPH), 167
Association of the Assessment of Learning in Higher Education (AALHE), xii–xiii
Association to Advance Collegiate Schools of Business (AACSB), xiv
Astin, A. W., 250
authenticity, self-confidence within, 23

badges, 3, 6–7, 9–11
Bakersfield College: academic badges within, 3, 6–7, 9, 10–12; assessment strategy development within, 4–5; assessment tools and techniques within, 5–6; badging measurement within, 11–12; governance structure within, 6; ILOs within, 6; overview of, 3–4; PLOs within, 6; professional development badging within, 10–11; Program Pathways Mapper, 5, 9; SLOs within, 3, 4, 6, 9; statistics of, 5–6
Bass, Randy, 181
Blackboard, 40–41, 48
Bloom, Benjamin, 23, 172
Borrego, S. E., 16
Boston College: assessment findings usage within, 21–23; assessment goals within, 14–18; cocurriculum within, 16, 21–22; formative education goals within, 14; Halftime, 15, 18, 20–21, 22–23; high impact practices within, 17; student formation assessment within, 15–18
Boud, D., 111
Breakfast of Champions (GCC), 250
Bronx Community College of CUNY, 268, 270–272, 278–280
business faculty, engagement of (Stillman), 159–162
buy-in, 57, 223

cafeteria assessment and grading, 97–98
California School of Podiatric Medicine (CSPM): American Podiatric Medical Licensing Exam, 234–235, 236, 238; assessment findings usage within, 236–238; assessment goals within, 230–236; assessment plan within, 234–237; collaborative process within, 229–230; curricular assessment within, 229; data collection within, 234–236; ILOs of, 233–234; MVV statement within, 230–231; PLOs within, 233–234; strategic plan within, 232–234; survey use within, 236, 238

INDEX   301

California State University, Monterey Bay (CSUMB): accreditation leveraging within, 198; Assessment Leadership Academy (ALA) of WSCUC and, 208; AVP-APIE within, 204–205; CC coordinator within, 202; core competencies within, 201; CT coordinator within, 201–202; faculty learning community descriptions within, 207; faculty role within, 201, 206; IL coordinator within, 202; ILOs within, 197; overview of, 199–201; professional development within, 199; program review within, 204–206; rubric use within, 201, 202–203, 205–206; Social and Behavioral Sciences (SBS) program within, 208–209; success within, 208–209; ULOs within, 201–204, 206–208; VALUE rubric use within, 201, 202–203; WSCUC and, 200

Canisius College: Academic Program Board, 37; administrative structures within, 28; assessment goals of, 27–28; assessment review process of, 34; College of Arts and Science, 27–28, 31–33, 34–37, 35–37; faculty role within, 28–29, 33–34; goal strategies within, 28–34; Outcomes Assessment Advisory Committee, 29–30, 31–33; overview of, 27; Wehle School of Business, 28

career exploration, cocurricular activities within, 188

Carnegie Classification, xix

Carnegie Foundation, 8–9

Carnegie Unit, 8–9

Center for College Effectiveness (Guttman Community College), 255–262

Center for Engaged Learning (CEL) (Elon University), 217, 218

Center for Research on Global Engagement (CRGE) (Elon University), 217–218

Center for the Advancement of Teaching and Learning (CATL) (Elon University), 214–219

Certified in Public Health (CPH) credential, 167–168

Charles R. Drew University of Medicine and Science (CDU), 139, 141–145. *See also* Master of Public Health (MPH) in Urban Health Disparities (CDU)

choice complexity, 99

City University of Seattle (CityU): assessing the assessment within, 46–49; Blackboard use within, 40–41, 48; common definition findings within, 43; Core Management Reporting (CMR) team, 42–43; curriculum management system within, 46; Data Governance Committee, 43; data integrity within, 41–43; data visualization within, 44–45, 48–49; faculty assessment role within, 41; learning outcome assessment management systems of, 39, 40–41; outcome assessment practices of, 46–48; overview of, 39; PDG challenges within, 41; PeopleSoft use by, 41; Power BI use within, 44–45, 48; program health cards, 48; secondary rubric use within, 41, 47

closing the loop: defined, 54, 60; honoring within, 62; overview of, 63–65; process of (Morovian College), 74, 76, 79; within SAGE, 261, 264

cocurriculum: alignment within, 187; within Boston College,

16, 21–22; curricular activities and, 182; defined, 183; domain activities of, 188–189; high impact practices (HIPs) within, 181–182; importance of, 182; learning-intensive activities within, 181–182; mapping of, 192–193; within PharmD, 182–191; within SDSU, 83–84, 87
Cohen, R., 95, 98
collaboration, 92, 113, 163–164, 209, 260
colleagues, engagement of (Stillman), 163–164
College Assessment Committee (CAC) (Morovian College), 71
College of Arts and Science (Canisius College), 27–28, 31–33, 34–37
College Senior Survey (CSS), 19–20
Committee on the Assessment of Student Learning (CASL), 71
communication, 92–93, 101, 106, 249
community, 60–61, 66, 113
competency-based education, 166–167
Cook, A., 97
core competency coordinator (CC coordinator), 202
Core Management Reporting (CMR) team (CityU), 42–43
Core Theme dashboard, 44, 45, 48
Corporate Social Responsibility (CSR), 100
Council on Education for Public Health (CEPH), xiv, 140, 167, 169
Council on Linkages Between Academia and Public Health Practices, 167
Council on Podiatric Medical Education (CPME), xiv
course-embedded assessments (Stillman), 159–162
course evaluation report (U.S. Army War College), 125–129

course learning outcomes (CLOs), 124, 128–129
Creating Shared Value (CSV), 100
critical thinking coordinator (CT coordinator), 201–202
culture of assessment, 27–28
curriculum: alignment of, 5; cocurriculum and, 182; course design within (UoPeople), 113–114; management tools for, 40, 46; of MPH, 168–176; online courses as, 175–176; PharmD review of, 192; Program Pathways Mapper (Bakersfield College), 5; syllabus excerpt (CDU), 144
curriculum development system (CDS), 40
customer relationship management (CRM) system, 41

dashboards, 35–36, 44, 45, 48
data, assessment: analyzing process of, 5; CMR team within (CityU), 43; collection of (CSPM), 234–236; collection resistance of, 213; Data Governance Committee (CityU), 43; definition findings within, 43; disaggregation of, 8; gathering of (Morovian College), 75; granularity levels within, 9–10; integrity within, 41–43; quantitative, 65; validation of, 43; visualization of (CityU), 44–45, 48–49; warehouse for, 42
decision-making, data-driven, 41–42
Decolonizing Methodologies (Smith), 52
Degrees That Matter (Jankowski and Marshall), 8
direct evidence, 18
distance education, strategic plan for (GCC), 242
Distance Education Accrediting Commission (DEAC), xiv
Diverse Learning Environment (HERI) survey, 273

Doctor of Pharmacy (PharmD): academic training within, 182; ACPE requirements within, 182, 183–184; assessment findings usage within, 191–193; cocurricular activities within, 182–183; cocurricular goals within, 183–191; cocurriculum mapping within, 192–193; curriculum review within, 192; faculty role within, 187, 191–192; feedback within, 187, 192; reflection within, 192; requirements within, 182–183; self-reflection within, 187, 192
documentation, for assessments, 34–35
Does it work? question: Bronx Community College of CUNY and, 271–272, 279, 280; Gwynedd Mercy University and, 273, 274–275, 276, 277–278; overview of, 267; response process to, 269–270
Do we do it? question: Bronx Community College of CUNY and, 271, 278–279, 280; Gwynedd Mercy University and, 272–273, 274, 275–276, 277; overview of, 267; response process to, 269
Do we have it? question: Bronx Community College of CUNY and, 271, 278, 280; Gwynedd Mercy University and, 272, 274, 275, 277; overview of, 267; response process to, 268–269
Doyle, T., 91–92
Driscoll, A., 199
Dweck, C. S., 92

education, 9, 125
educational effectiveness, assessment of (Gwynedd Mercy University), 276–278

Elon University: Center for Engaged Learning (CEL), 217, 218; Center for Research on Global Engagement (CRGE), 217–218; Center for the Advancement of Teaching and Learning (CATL) within, 214–219; cultural shift within, 222; professional development within, 216–217; Project Interweave within, 214–215. *See also* scholarship of teaching and learning (SoTL)
Emergent Themes Report (Guttman Community College), 258–259, 260, 263, 264
employers, engagement of (Stillman), 158
engagement: of alumni (Stillman), 153, 157; of business faculty (Stillman), 159–162; of colleagues (Stillman), 163–164; of employers (Stillman), 158; interdepartmental (Stillman), 163–164; of learner, 96; SoTL and, 216–219; of stakeholders (Stillman), 152, 153–159
evaluation, assessment *versus*, 71
Evans, Lara M., 51
Ewell, P. T., 198
examinations, 4, 132–133, 175–176
external stakeholders, engagement of, 153–159
extracurricular activities, 183

faculty: academic evaluation report by, 129–132; Assessment 2.0 and, 198; assessment buy-in of, 223; assessment choice for, 105–106; assessment resistance by, 29; badge use by, 10; compliance mentality of, 213; data collection resistance by, 213; evaluation of, 244; incentives for, 223; learning communities for, 207; looking and talking assessment step and, 61; performance expectations of, 244;

PharmD role of, 187, 191–192; professional development badging for, 10–11; secondary rubric use by, 41, 47; SoTL and, 215–216, 219, 220, 221–224. *See also* professional development; specific institutions
Faculty Survey of Assessment Culture (SDSU), 85
Farrell, D. A., 252
feedback: assessment review process for, 34; from assessors (Stillman), 157; of cocurricular activities, 187; criteria for, 30; peer assessment and, 113; within PharmD, 192; reports for (Morovian College), 76; rubric for (Canisius College), 31–33; within SAGE, 262; student achievement, 48; at Swinburne Business School, 103–105; at U.S. Army War College, 133–134
Fernback, P., 110–111
finding the learning assessment step, 58, 61, 63
fitness/wellness, cocurricular activities within, 188
flexible assessment, 96–98, 99–101
formation, 14–15, 16–17, 23–24. *See also* student formation
formative practices, 17
formative program, 16
foundational public health competencies (FPHCs), 140, 143, 146–150, 169–176
foundational public health knowledge learning outcomes (FPHK-LOs), 140
Framing the Future Task Force (ASPPH), 167
Fuller, Matthew, 84–85

gamification, 7
gathering the community assessment step, 58, 60–61, 63

Gaumnitz, W., 8
giving life, 197
global relations, assessment approach within, 77
Google Drive, 175
governance, 6, 279–280
grading, 97–98, 112, 118
Griffin K.E.Y.S. (Kickstart and Envision Your Success), 276
growth mindset culture for assessment, 91–92
Guam Community College (GCC): accreditation process of, 240, 251; administration role within, 247, 248–250; Anthony A. Leon Guerrero Allied Health Building, 245; Assessment, Institutional Effectiveness, and Research (AIAR) of, 248; assessment findings usage within, 247–252; assessment goal within, 240–243; brainstorming within, 251; Breakfast of Champions within, 250; capital improvement projects within, 244–246; communication within, 249; distance education strategic plan within, 242; faculty role within, 243–245; financial planning within, 246; Innovative Ideas Program, 247; latte stone significance within, 252; marketing strategic plan within, 242; Nuventive Improve assessment management system, 243; overview of, 240–241; physical resource planning within, 244–246; SLOs within, 243; Small Assessment Grant Award, 247; strategic planning within, 240–243; 3DP framework within, 242; transformation mindset within, 250
Guided Pathways, 5
Guttman Community College, 254, 255–262, 263, 264. *See also*

INDEX 305

Systematic Approach for Guttman Effectiveness (SAGE) (Guttman Community College)
Gwynedd Mercy University: educational effectiveness assessment within, 276–278; ethics and integrity within, 272–273; faculty role within, 272–273; financial aid process within, 276; Griffin K.E.Y.S. (Kickstart and Envision Your Success) at, 276; overview of, 268; Quality Council within, 278; student experience support within, 275–276; student learning experience within, 273–275; survey use within, 273, 277

Halftime (Boston College), 15, 18, 20–21, 22–23
Hanewicz, C., 97, 105
Higher Education Institutions (HEIs), xii
Higher Education Research Institute (HERI), 273
Higher Learning Commission (HLC), xiv, 51, 53, 57, 82–83, 94
high impact practices (HIPs), 17, 181–182
Hispanic Serving Institution (HSI), CSUMB as, 199
holistic student learning, 19
honoring assessment step, 58, 59, 62–63, 66
humanities program, assessment approach within, 29
Hutchings, P. M., 220–221

Iceberg Illusion, 18–19
improving together assessment step, 58, 59, 63
incentives, for faculty engagement, 223
indigenous assessment model: assessment step within, 60–63; closing the loop within, 63–65; meta-assessment step within, 63–65; overview of, 57–65, 68; quantitative data within, 65; results of, 65–67; as values-based model, 65, 66
information literacy coordinator (IL coordinator), 202
innovation/entrepreneurship, cocurricular activities within, 188
Innovative Ideas Program (GCC), 247
Institute of American Indian Arts (IAIA): assessment goals within, 53–60; assessment questions within, 51–52; challenges within, 67; demographics of, 56, 68–69n1; faculty assessment role within, 55; Indigenous assessment committee within, 52–53; indigenous methodologies within, 52–53; measurability within, 55–56; objectivity within, 55–56; overview of, 67–68; subjectivity within, 55–56; values-based model of, 65, 66. *See also* indigenous assessment model
institutional effectiveness, 229, 254, 268–270
institutional learning outcomes (ILOs), 6, 124, 141–142, 143, 197, 233–234
Institutional Research (IR), 65
institutions. *See* Higher Education Institutions (HEIs); *specific institutions*
interdepartmental engagement (Stillman), 163–164
interdependent learning, 111

Jankowski, N., 8, 9
Jesuit universities, 14–15, 27
job postings, position descriptions within, 9
Jopp, R., 95, 98

Keeling, R. P., 16
Keup, J. R., 252
Kinzie, J., 199, 209
knowledge, community efforts within, 110–111
knowledge, skills, and abilities (KSAs) (U.S. Army War College), 128
Kolvenbach, Peter-Hans, 14–15
Kuh, G. D., 16, 17, 224
Kurz, L., 198, 206

latte stones, significance of, 252
Launch Experience (Stillman), 155–156, 157
leadership, 28, 90–91, 189, 279–280
learner engagement, 96, 97
learner performance (Swinburne Business School), 103
learner satisfaction, 96
learners' choice, 101–103, 105–106
learning, social component of, 110–111
learning goals and objectives (LGOs) (Canisius College), 29
learning outcomes, 23, 47. *See also* student learning outcomes (SLOs)
Liberal Education and America's Promise (LEAP) initiative (AAC&U), 19
Likert-type rating scale, 187, 191
looking and talking assessment step, 58, 59, 60, 61–62, 63, 67

Maki, Peggy, 200
marketing, strategic plan within (GCC), 242
Marshall, D., 8, 9
Master of Public Health (MPH): assessment findings usage within, 177; assessment process within, 177–178; competency attainment challenges within, 171–176; competency-based curriculum within, 168–176; comprehensive and complex competencies assessment within, 172–173; creative assessment within, 173–175; education changes within, 168; FPHCs within, 169–176; higher order educational objective assessment within, 172; knowledge areas within, 166–167; online course competency assessment within, 175–176; requirements for, 169; student attainment measurement within, 176; University of Buffalo and, 168–169
Master of Public Health (MPH) in Urban Health Disparities (CDU): assessment findings usage within, 145–151; assessment goals within, 141–145; course assessment strategies within, 151; faculty assessment role within, 142–143; learning outcomes within, 140; overview of, 139–140; urban health disparities competencies within, 140, 142
mathematics, assessment approach within, 77
MBA, assessment of (Stillman), 154–156, 161–162
meta-assessment, 59, 63–65
Metzler, E. T., 198, 206
microcredentials, 3, 7. *See also* badges
Middle State Commissions of Higher Education (MSCHE): accreditation process of, 266–268; quote of, 27; Standard III of, 273; Standard II of, 272; Standard I of, 270–271; Standard IV of, 275; Standard VII of, 279; Standard VI of, 278; Standard V of, 276; website of, xiv
mission, vision and values (MVV) statement (CSPM), 230–231
The Monster Show (IAIA), 57–58
Moodle, 120

INDEX   307

Morovian College: annual assessment report of, 75–76; assessment determination within, 74; assessment goals within, 72–78; assessment process within, 78; CAC within, 71; CASL within, 71; closing the loop within, 74, 76, 79; data gathering within, 75; departmental assessment approaches within, 77, 79; faculty assessment role within, 74, 78–79; feedback reports within, 76; overview of, 70; reflection within, 75; SLO assessment within, 73–74
motivation, badges and, 12
music, assessment approach within, 77
mutual learning, 111

National Board of Public Health Examiners (NBPHE), 167–168
National Institute for Learning Outcomes Assessment (NILOA), 87
National Survey of Student Engagement (NSSE), 19–20, 273
neuroscience, assessment approach within, 77
New England Commission of Higher Education (NECHE), xiv
Northern Virginia Community College, 54
Northwest Commission on Colleges and Universities (NWCCU), xiv
Nuventive Improve assessment management system (GCC), 243

objective research, standards for, 52
observational learning, 110–111
Ohio State University, 185, 190
Oklahoma University, 185, 190
online courses, competency assessment within, 175–176
Online Education Services (OES) (Swinburne Business School), 107n3

online modalities (Swinburne Business School), 95–96
open educational resources (OER) (UoPeople), 110
Outcomes and Assessment tool (Blackboard), 40
Outcomes Assessment Advisory Committee (Canisius College), 29–30, 31–33
outcomes-based education (OBE) institution (CSUMB), 199
Outcomes of Quality Initiative (SDSU), 89–90

patient card/health promotion, cocurricular activities within, 189
peer assessment, xii, 112–113, 115–116, 261
Peer Assessment Center (UoPeople), 120
peer learning, 111, 112–113
peer reviewers, xii
Pennsylvania Department of Education, 72
PeopleSoft, 41
PharmD (Doctor of Pharmacy): academic training within, 182; ACPE requirements within, 182, 183–184; assessment findings usage within, 191–193; cocurricular activities within, 182–183; cocurricular goals within, 183–191; cocurriculum mapping within, 192–193; curriculum review within, 192; faculty role within, 187, 191–192; feedback within, 187, 192; reflection within, 192; requirements within, 182–183; self-reflection within, 187, 192
Piaget, Jean, 111
Power BI, 44–45, 48
Pretorius, L., 98
proctoring, software for, 175–176
ProctorU, 175–176

professional development: badging within (Bakersfield College), 10–11; cocurricular activities within, 189; plan within (GCC), 242; role of (CSUMB), 199; within SAGE, 260–262; SoTL and, 216–217
program design guides (PDGs), 40, 41
program health cards (CityU), 48
program improvement plan (PIP) (CSUMB), 205
program learning outcomes (PLOs), 4, 5, 6, 124, 133, 233–234
Program Pathways Mapper (Bakersfield College), 5, 9, 10
Project Interweave (Elon University), 214–215
Propensity Score Matching (PSM), 20
psychology, assessment approach within, 77
public health, competency-based education within, 166–167

Quality Council (Gwynedd Mercy University), 278
quality initiative (QI) project (SDSU), 82–89
quantitative data, 65

Real-Time Student Assessment (Maki), 198–199
reflection, 21, 23, 75, 187, 192
Regis, cocurricular programs for PharmD within, 186, 190
repeating the cycle assessment step, 58
research, objective, standards for, 52
Respondus Monitor, 175–176
retention, 96, 238
Rideout, C., 97, 98, 107
Roscoe, D. D., 210
rubrics: benefits of, 57; feedback (CAS), 31–33; planning, 60; purpose of, 61; for scoring sessions, 162; secondary, 41, 47; student grading and, 112; use of (CAS), 35; use of (CSUMB), 201, 202–203, 205–206; use of (Stillman), 154; use of (U.S. Army War College), 133; VALUE, 201, 202–203

Samuel Merritt University, 229
San Diego Mesa College, 56
satisfaction, learner, factors within, 96
Scholar Program (Elon University), 217
scholarship of teaching and learning (SoTL): assessment and, 219–224; Elon University and, 214–219; faculty role within, 215–216, 219, 220, 221–224; overview of, 214; professional development within, 216–217
School of Health and Social Sciences (CityU), 48–49
scoring sessions, (Stillman), 162
secondary rubrics, 41, 47
selected assessment, 96–97
self-awareness, cocurricular activities within, 189
self-reflection, 21, 23, 75, 187, 192
self-study, 205, 266–270, 281. *See also* Does it work? question; Do we do it? question; Do we have it? question
Senior Service and Command and General Staff College Academic Evaluation Reports, 129, 133
sensory input, learning within, 111
service, cocurricular activities within, 189
SharePoint platform, 40
single point of truth, 42
Skidmore, S., 84–85
Sloman, S. A., 110–111
Small Assessment Grant Award (GCC), 247
SmartCatalog, 46
Smith, Linda Tuhiwai, 52
Social and Behavioral Sciences (SBS) (CSUMB), 208–209

social learning theory, research within, 111
software: assessment, 39; assessment management software (AMS), 89; for examinations, 175–176; Google Drive, 175; ProctorU, 175–176; Respondus Monitor, 175–176; SDSU use of, 86–87; WebEx, 175
sophomore/senior assessment panels (Stillman), 153–154
South Dakota State University (SDSU): accountability measures within, 93; administration support within, 90–91; Assessment Academy within, 85, 87–91, 94; assessment evaluation process within, 93; assessment growth mindset culture within, 91–92; assessment management software (AMS) use within, 89; assessment practices of, 83–86; assessment transparency within, 87; cocurricular assessment within, 83–84, 87; communication approach within, 92–93; expectation management within, 91; Faculty Survey of Assessment Culture within, 85; future processes of, 93–94; guiding values within, 90; limitations within, 81; online solutions within, 86–87; Outcomes of Quality Initiative within, 89–90; overview of, 81; quality initiative within, 82–89; showcase within, 93; steering committee within, 82; strategies and innovative approaches within, 90–93; Student Affairs Survey of Assessment Culture within, 85; surveys within, 83–86; team approach within, 92; Transparency Framework (NILOA) use within, 87

Southern Association of Colleges and Schools Commission on Colleges (SACSCOC), xiv
stakeholders, 37, 153–159
Stillman School of Business (Seton Hall University): assessors at, 153–159; Business Consulting class, 156; business faculty engagement within, 159–162; colleague engagement within, 163–164; course-embedded assessment within, 159–162; interdepartmental engagement within, 163–164; Launch Experience, 155–156, 157; MBA assessment within, 154–156; MBA Colloquium within, 161–162; overview of, 152–153; prerequisite assessment within, 159–161; rubric use within, 154; scoring sessions within, 162; sophomore/senior assessment panels at, 153–154; stakeholder engagement within, 153–159; subsequent course assessment within, 159–161; undergraduate assessment within, 153–154
strategic planning (GCC), 240–243
strategic thinking, evaluation of, 126
Student Affairs Survey of Assessment Culture (SDSU), 85
student choice, 96–97
student development, characteristics within, 16
student formation, 15–18. *See also* formation
student learning outcomes (SLOs): as add-on, 4–5; badges for, 10; of Bakersfield College, 3, 4, 6, 9; curriculum alignment and, 5; development of, 3; education and, 9; of Guam Community College, 243; of Morovian College, 73–74, 75. *See also* learning outcomes
students, peer assessment and, 112–113

Studiosity, 96
success, consideration of, 18
support, for faculty engagement, 223
surveys: alumni (UoPeople), 117–118; Diverse Learning Environment, 273; Gwynedd Mercy University and, 273, 277; National Survey of Student Engagement (NSSE), 273; use of (CSPM), 236, 238; use of (SAGE), 261; use of (SDSU), 83–86; use of (Swinburne Business School), 103–105; use of (UoPeople), 114–118
Suskie, L., 229
Swinburne Business School: assessment goals within, 96–98; assessment options within, 97; assessment selection regime within, 99–101; assessment-task choice regime within, 98–103; Bachelor of Business within, 98–99; communication within, 101; course selection within, 98–99; future assessment process within, 105–107; learners' choices within, 101–103; learners' outcomes within, 103–105; learning modalities within, 95; Online Education Services (OES) within, 107n3; survey use at, 103–105; Swinburne Online (SOL) within, 95–96, 98–99
Swinburne Online (SOL), 95–96, 98–99
Sydow, D., 250
syllabus, example of (CDU), 144
Systematic Approach for Guttman Effectiveness (SAGE) (Guttman Community College): alignment streamlining within, 259; annual cycle within, 258; appreciation demonstrations within, 262; assessment findings usage within, 263–264; assessment goal within, 254–263; assessment use within, 262–263; closing the loop within, 261, 264; collaboration within, 260; creative workshop strategies within, 261–262; documentation process within, 255–258; Emergent Themes Report within, 258–259, 260, 263, 264; example guide within, 257–258; feedback within, 262; integrated schedule within, 256; makeovers within, 261–262; overview of, 254; peer reviews within, 261; professional development process within, 260–262; profile within, 256, 257; purpose of, 254; success within, 265; survey use within, 261; template within, 256; unit-level practices and institutional priorities within, 258, 259

technology, within assessment, 5. *See also* software
3DP framework (GCC), 242
Tomkins, E., 8
Topping, K., 111
training, education *versus,* 125
transcript, information within, 8–9
transfer of learning, 18
Transparency Framework (NILOA), 87

undergraduate learning outcomes (ULOs) (CSUMB), 201–204, 206–208
University of Buffalo, 168–176, 177–178
University of Michigan, 186, 190
University of San Diego, 210
University of the People (UoPeople): advisory boards within, 118; assessment findings within, 119–120; assessment goals within, 110–113; assessment strategies

within, 113–114; course design within, 113–114; demographics of, 118–119; grading processes within, 118; overview of, 110; Peer Assessment Center within, 120; peer assessment within, 111–113; peer learning within, 111–113; student grading within, 112; survey use within, 114–118

U.S. Army War College: academic evaluation report within, 129–132; assessment goals within, 123–132; assessment insights within, 134–135; assessment problems within, 122; assessment progress by, 132–133; CLOs within, 124, 128–129; course evaluation report within, 125–129; data use within, 133–134; exam use within, 132–133; faculty assessment role within, 124, 133–134; feedback within, 133–134; ILOs within, 124; KSAs within, 128; overview of, 122–123; PLOs within, 124, 133; Senior Service and Command and General Staff College Academic Evaluation Reports, 129, 133

VALUE rubric (CSUMB), 201, 202–203
values-based model, indigenous assessment model as, 65, 66
vocational discernment, as learning outcome, 23
Vygotsky, L. S., 111

Wall, Stephen, 51
WASC (Accrediting Commission for Schools Western Association of Schools and Colleges Senior College), xiv
Watermark, 46
WebEx, 175
Wehle School of Business (Canisius College), 28
Western Association of Schools and Colleges Senior College and University Commission (WSCUC), 198, 200, 208
Wyman, K., 105–106

Zakrajsek, T., 91–92

Association for the Assessment of Learning in Higher Education

AALHE

PROMOTING ASSESSMENT FOR LEARNING

AALHE

Our mission is to develop and support a community of educators and inform assessment practices in higher education to foster and improve student learning and institutional quality.

History

The Association for the Assessment of Learning in Higher Education (AALHE) is an organization of practitioners interested in using effective assessment practice to document and improve student learning. As such, it serves the needs of those in higher education for whom assessment is a tool to help them understand learning and develop processes for improving it.

AALHE took shape in late 2009. Formed in part because no other organization had emerged to replace the range of resources and opportunities for interaction that the Assessment Forum of the American Association for Higher Education had offered until it closed in 2005, AALHE's Founding Board of Directors launched this organization with the intention of providing robust online resources and a wide range of both online and face-to-face interactive opportunities.

AALHE and its website constitute a wide range of resources for all who are interested in the improvement of learning, from assessment directors who organize and manage programs, to faculty and Student Affairs professionals who use assessment strategies to understand their students' learning, to graduate students and others who conduct research on the effectiveness of assessment processes and instruments, to institutional researchers who develop effective learning data systems. AALHE offers assessment practitioners a variety of ways to learn and share their thoughts about assessing and improving learning.

AALHE is an independently incorporated, member-funded, non-profit entity recognized by the Commonwealth of Kentucky. AALHE is a charitable organization recognized as tax-exempt under the Internal Revenue Service code 501(c)(3).